THE MOSAICS OF ROME

from the third to the fourteenth centuries

THE MOSAICS
OF ROME

from the third to the fourteenth centuries

WALTER OAKESHOTT

NEW YORK GRAPHIC SOCIETY LTD

GREENWICH, CONNECTICUT

LIBRARY OF CONGRESS CATALOG CARD NUMBER 67-25494
COPYRIGHT © 1967 WALTER OAKESHOTT
Printed in Switzerland and Great Britain
COLOUR AND MONOCHROME PLATES PRINTED IN SWITZERLAND BY
BUCHDRUCKEREI WINTERTHUR AG, WINTERTHUR
TEXT PRINTED IN GREAT BRITAIN BY THE CAMELOT PRESS LTD LONDON & SOUTHAMPTON
BOUND IN GERMANY BY KORNELIUS KASPERS DÜSSELDORF

CONTENTS

Arabic numerals in the margins refer to monochrome plates; Roman numerals, to colour plates

PREFACE

A STUDY OF THE SERIES OF MOSAICS which are the subject of this book gives rise, among a number of problems, to two that are to me of outstanding interest: the problem of their authenticity, and the problem of their independence of the Byzantine tradition. Are we justified in taking the mosaics, in their existing condition, as fairly representing the work of the artists who made them? Or are they, as a result of restoration, now no more than echoes of their originals? Are they to be regarded as a provincial offshoot of the Byzantine schools; or is their tradition to some extent independent, and, if so, to what extent?

The answers to these questions obviously have to be attempted largely in terms of style and of technique. This book is therefore not a contribution to art history in the proper sense of the term. Art history has its own discipline which differentiates it sharply from discussions of style—a matter in which opinions are so largely subjective. Art history involves the first-hand investigation of source material, as much as of the works of art themselves. I have inevitably had to approach near the border-line when discussing some of the problems that arise out of the book's main theme, such as the bearing which the mosaics have on the history of the Renaissance in Rome. But, throughout, I have had to be content, for the most part, with using sources at second-hand, in the work of those great practitioners whose main concern has been, or whose interests have extended to, mosaics: de Rossi, Wilpert, Matthiae, Demus and others. Thus the bibliography is not only an acknowledgment of debts, but also evidence of the limits of the use here of other authorities or of original sources. I cannot claim to have fully considered these mosaics in the enormous context to which they clearly belong: that of the arts as a whole in medieval Rome, or that of the religious ideas of which many of them are expressions. I have studied the mosaics themselves, compared them with one another (relying, as any student can now do, on the much wider photographic documentation available, which the great scholars of the past lacked), and have taken such opportunities as there have been of examining them minutely *in situ*.

These methods may sometimes produce answers more detailed and exact than have hitherto been obtainable. The façade mosaic of Sta Maria in Trastevere may be taken as an instance. The available photographs are good enough, and there is enough comparative material, for its history to be fairly clear, even if doubts persist about its subject. I suspect that we can approximately date, and even identify the artist of, the mosaic in the *confessione* of St Peter's, although the design has been drastically altered and although the mosaic itself has been entirely reset. There are adequate photographs, and enough has been retained of the style of the original for a judgment to be made. It now seems possible, moreover, to give some substance to an account of a revival of the art of mosaic in Rome by Byzantine craftsmen in the eleventh century. There are good photographs of the mosaic made in Grottaferrata, within a dozen miles of Rome, at that period; and the small mosaic in the chapel of S. Zenone in Sta Prassede (which seems to be related to it, and which is perhaps therefore the only strictly Roman eleventh-century example still surviving), though it is difficult to photograph satisfactorily, is set so low that close study is possible without ladder or scaffolding.

Sometimes—too often—the photographic resources at present generally accessible still allow nothing more than a preliminary judgment, involving much guess-work and no substantial conclusions. For the mosaics of Sta Maria Maggiore, the most important group in the series, we shall have to wait for the work, and the photographs, of Professor F. W. Deichmann. Is the nave series of the same date as the triumphal arch mosaic? Did Toriti incorporate actual classical material in his version of the mosaic of the apse, or only adapt its theme? I can only comment on the photographs that are already available (some of which, having been taken before the latest restoration, are valuable evidence for that reason, even if their quality is indifferent) and on those photographs in Dr Carlo Cecchelli's book that are recent, some of which are astonishing revelations of the qualities of the originals. But even Dr Cecchelli had to rely, for two panels, on reproductions published by Wilpert fifty years ago, which for present needs are quite inadequate. To reach firm conclusions on such a basis is, to my mind, not possible. Most of the mosaics discussed in this book fall between these extremes. There are often excellent photographs, but there are seldom all the photographs needed.

I record therefore my particular gratitude to those who have helped in this aspect of the book; first, to those who are in charge of photographic archives: Dr Hermine Speier, of the Archivio Fotografico delle Galerie e dei Musei Vaticane; Dr Carlo Bertelli, of the Gabinetto Fotografico Nazionale; the authorities of the Soprintendenza ai Monumenti del Lazio, who gave permission to re-photograph many of the fine photographs taken during restoration work carried out under their direction; to Dr H. Giess of the photographic archive attached to the Bibliotheca Hertziana; and to Dr Ernest Nash, of the Fototeca di Architettura e Topografia dell'Italia Antica. I would like to mention also the firms of Alinari and Anderson, whose representatives have met continual requests for new prints or enlargements with unfailing courtesy. And I owe a very special debt to Mr John Clark, whose firm of Scala in Florence took the colour photographs made for this book, and for whom no trouble seemed too much. As a result, at least the photographs in this book make a contribution to the study of the subject.

It may be permissible perhaps to choose for special mention a few at least of the personal debts incurred. Sir Mortimer Wheeler read an earlier draft and proposed a book of the present size and character. Without his encouragement I should certainly not have considered planning a book illustrated on this scale. I am grateful also to Professor Charles Mitchell of Bryn Mawr, and the Rev. Gervase Mathew of Oxford, both of whom reacted to earlier drafts with vigorous criticism which was of great value. Mr Michael Graham-Dixon and Mrs Pauline Baines of Messrs Thames and Hudson have worked on text, notes and illustrations with a thoroughness and understanding that has made their co-operation a most invigorating experience. My former secretary, Miss Phyllis Alcock, typed successive drafts in the early stages with exceptional patience and accuracy. Miss Anna Fazzari, M.B.E., Secretary of the British School in Rome, has made her name a byword with those who have the luck to have any connection with the School. I am in debt also to the kindness of librarians, especially those of the Ashmolean and Bodleian Libraries in Oxford and of the Bibliotheca Hertziana (with its fine collection of books and invaluable indexes, which it has been a privilege to use), the British School and the American Academy in Rome. Mr Martin Harrison helped me at very short notice with the proofs, and I am greatly indebted to him for this.

Lincoln College
Oxford

WALTER OAKESHOTT

I

THE TECHNIQUE OF
MEDIEVAL MOSAICS IN ROME

THE LITERARY AUTHORITIES: PLINY AND THEOPHILUS

There is no lack of indication from the mosaics themselves and from surviving records that many mosaics in Roman churches have undergone extensive restoration. Detailed accounts of some of these restorations, effected in the last century and a half, have been left by those who carried them out. During the first half of the nineteenth century, Vincenzo Camuccini restored both the Sta Costanza mosaics and those of Sta Pudenziana. He provided such information, and was the first to do so with the detail that a student would wish to have. In Sta Pudenziana he was concerned with a mosaic which had already been drastically repaired in plaster by Renaissance craftsmen; and indeed the most important mosaics in the series to be discussed have almost all been to some extent renewed, often in various periods, and some have suffered considerable alteration in the process. It is therefore necessary to discuss the techniques of the early artist in mosaic, since technical points can often provide a clue to the nature and extent of later alteration, as well as to the kind of effects at which from time to time the original artists were aiming.

The surface of mosaic is normally made up of numbers of small *tesserae*, or dice, often cut so that they are in shape a rough cube, though often (as a close examination of actual mosaics or of large-scale photographs will show) cut to different shapes and sizes. The Elder Pliny, writing in the first century AD, uses a Greek term, *lithostrota*, for mosaic paving: a word which implies natural materials, some kind of stone or marble. But in the passage in which he discusses the development of mosaic[1] he notes that the art which began to be practised in Rome 'in the time of Sulla', say 85 BC, had changed its character in two ways, one being the use of mosaics for ceilings as well as floors, and the other the use of what Pliny calls glass for mosaic. Unfortunately he gives no account, as he sometimes does in technical matters, of the way in which the glass, or glazed, *tesserae* were manufactured. By an argument, as it were *ex silentio*, that the new technique would have been used in a certain building if it had been available, he brings down the date of the adoption of glass as the material for mosaics in Rome to somewhere near the beginning of the Christian era.[2]

There is no doubt that when pictorial mosaics began to be made in classical times, the materials were at first, as Pliny's term implied, natural. Mosaics of the fourth to third century BC, found at Pella in Macedonia, are made of pebbles, outlines being sometimes emphasized in lead. The effect is produced by tone rather than richness of colour, and the subtle transitions from one tone to another are remarkable. Throughout the Roman imperial period natural materials, chiefly marbles, remained in use for mosaics or parts of them, and as a far larger number of floor mosaics have survived than of mosaics designed for ceilings or walls, a false impression may be given of the prevalence of natural materials. For by about the beginning of the Christian era, as Pliny indicates (but perhaps already in the second half of the second century BC), glass, sometimes clear but more often opaque, began to be used on occasion.

In a well known but comparatively late and comparatively rough example of a floor mosaic in the Terme Museum at Rome, representing chariots and charioteers of rival factions wearing their various colours, the materials are mixed, a clear coloured glass being used in this instance for some of the differently coloured tunics, to produce a striking contrast with the flat blacks and greys of the rest of the work. But for finer work on walls and ceilings glass seems to have been used with increasing frequency, often, as noted above, in conjunction with natural materials. And glass is probably the material of some mosaics described as being of marble. It might appear at first sight that all the fine mosaics, such as the series of which one famous example now in the Capitoline Museum at Rome copies a picture of doves by the Pergamene artist Sosus, were made entirely of marbles.[3] The surface has a high polish in the mosaics of this series, and, as with most mosaics, it is often difficult to tell for certain (except from a detached *tessera*) what is the character of the material, natural or artificial; and even for the detached *tessera*, chemical analysis may be needed. Some are certainly made of thin *tesserae* of coloured marbles. But other examples of mosaic with very small *tesserae*, in all of which the workmanship is specially fine, are differently constructed. Thus one surviving example has suffered damage which has opened up the surface and makes it possible to see the structure and bedding of the *tesserae*. They are in fact, in this mosaic, small rods of glass (rather than cubes) perhaps only $\frac{1}{8}$ inch in diameter but $\frac{1}{2}$ inch long or thereabouts, like those used in the manufacture of *millefiori* glass by being fused together. These small rods were bedded solidly in their mortar backing, and they do not seem to have any other binding element. The surface was finely ground and polished, as a result of which the interstices are virtually invisible, and the character of the material almost impossible, from the surface, to determine. As far as I am aware, no example in this technique occurs in the series to be discussed in this book. I mention it here for the sake of completeness.

Thus there is evidence of at least three different materials in use by the second century AD: natural stone (to which should be added, in some later mosaics at any rate, the occasional use of other natural materials such as mother-of-pearl); glass, generally opaque, cut into *tesserae*; and tiny glass rods, used when specially detailed modelling and specially delicate *chiaroscuro* were desired.

It is generally supposed that the term *opus vermiculatum*, which occurs already in a fragment of Lucilius dating from the second half of the second century BC, refers simply to the fineness of the 'worm-like' lines which can be drawn in mosaic when very small *tesserae* are used. The term is so interpreted, it would seem, in the important work by L'Orange and Nordhagen.[4] I am inclined to think that the term may have originally referred to the tiny worm-like rods of glass used in particularly fine work, as described above. The famous Alexander mosaic from Pompeii, in which the *tesserae* are often very small, but true *tesserae*, and much shallower than the rods of glass here under discussion, would not in fact be covered by this definition of *opus vermiculatum*, though it was given as an example of that technique by L'Orange and Nordhagen.[5] But their use of the term is almost standard now, though it was used in the eighteenth century (for example, in the inscription on the *Tribune of Benedict XIV*) simply as a synonym for mosaic, not to imply work of particular fineness. And the suggestion made above must be regarded, at best, as 'not proven'. The reference may always have been to the thin lines that could be achieved by the use of small units.

The ordinary *tessera* of opaque glass which is a common element in medieval mosaic seems to be referred to by the medieval authority on artistic technology whose work has survived under the name of Theophilus.[6] Unlike Pliny, Theophilus was a practical craftsman. But his main interest was in metal work, and he lived in Germany. These two facts may explain why his allusions to mosaic are not as informative as one might wish. He mentions that 'various colours in glass' were found 'in ancient classical buildings [*in antiquis aedificiis paganorum*], white, black, green, yellow, blue, red and purple', the glass being 'not translucent but opaque' and formed 'as it were into small squared stones'. He adds, obscurely, that 'from these are made enamels [*electra*] in gold, silver and copper'. The meaning may be that from this material, powdered, were made the enamel fillings used in metal settings.

In a later chapter he mentions that 'the Greeks [that is to say, the Byzantine Greeks] make pictures from a clear white glass', cutting it up with a hot iron into small squared pieces and covering them on one side with gold leaf over which they then work another layer of glass, reheating the pieces in the glass kiln. This statement also is not altogether precise. He seems to be discussing the Greek technique of making gold *tesserae*. But these are of course only one element in the pictures in which they occur. In *tesserae* manufactured as he describes, the gold leaf is sandwiched between the two layers, the upper layer so thin as to be almost a glaze rather than a layer of glass, and the gold leaf thus excellently protected by this thin layer.

An early ninth-century head from the chapel of S. Zenone in the church of Sta Prassede is $\quad$ v placed low enough for the *tesserae* to be examined in detail. The gold used in this mosaic was laid for the most part on a base of vivid green glass and gold leaf is sandwiched beween two layers, in the manner Theophilus describes. In another mosaic in this same chapel (a mosaic in an entirely different style, and to be dated much later), the glass used for the gold *tesserae* is red. In a valuable article[7] on the technique of the triumphal arch mosaics in Sta Maria Maggiore, G. Astorri pointed out that the glass used in the manufacture of the gold *tesserae* there was sometimes greenish, sometimes brown, yellow or red, sometimes colourless. This colourless glass was certainly often used, like that of the 'sandwich' portrait glasses, of which a number of third-century examples, or fragments, survive, and in which the portrait is engraved on the gold leaf and a second layer of colourless glass added to preserve it.[8] The way in which *tesserae* of gold were used will be discussed later.

Unfortunately, Theophilus gives no clue as to whether the *tesserae* in ordinary colours were always made simply of solid opaque glass (that is perhaps the implication), the material homogeneous throughout, or whether earthenware with a coloured glaze was sometimes used. He was familiar with the technique of glazing earthenware vessels; and for mosaics on a wall or apse, this might have been an economical and also a practical method of manufacture, the surface not being subject to heavy wear and tear. But I know of no certain evidence that glazed earthenware as opposed to glass was so used in antiquity or in medieval times.[9]

We are left with the impression that Theophilus had no first-hand knowledge of this particular craft. In the twelfth century (the period to which his work is assigned by its most recent editor, C. R. Dodwell) there were probably no mosaics made in western Europe north of the Alps, though the great decorative schemes in Sicilian churches belong to this period, and there were also several important mosaics made in Rome in the second and third quarters of the century. In any event, it seems likely, from the internal evidence of his work, that Theophilus never saw a mosaic actually being made. But from the fifth century onwards glass (a glass paste or enamel such as he evidently had in mind), made opaque by one or other of a number of different opacifiers, was probably the normal material used for Roman mosaics on the surface of a wall or apse. Exceptions are sometimes noticeable, as in the ninth-century apsidal mosaic in S. Marco, where a pale natural marble may have been used for many of the draperies. And a remarkable portrait-head surviving from the Triclinium of Leo III and now exhibited in the Vatican Museum, almost contemporary in date with, though notably different in style from, the Pope Paschal mosaics, seems to be made of stone materials throughout,[10] while, as we shall see, in certain Roman works of the seventh and early eighth centuries also, natural materials are used to represent the face or the hands. At this period, in particular, this practice is associated with Byzantine influence.

In the Pope Paschal mosaics of a few years later, to judge from the S. Zenone example already quoted, the ordinary material is undoubtedly coloured, clouded glass. But stones are used effectively by contrast, for jewels and buckles, as they had been in the Justinian mosaics in Ravenna (for example, the mother-of-pearl shown in Plate 13). One example is the chipped limestone buckle on the chest of the right-hand bust of the group of four in the chapel of S. Zenone. The crown and necklet on the saint whose bust is represented between that of Paschal's mother (with the square halo) and that of the Virgin may be of amethyst quartz. But to be certain whether some of the blue *tesserae* are of natural or artificial material is not feasible even with a magnifying glass. We can say confidently, however, that up to the ninth century, and perhaps beyond it in the later Middle Ages, allowance has to be made for the use of materials of mixed character,[11] natural and artificial, with glass, in Rome, normally predominating.

THE USE OF GOLD

In the use of gold, there is a notable difference between classical and medieval mosaics, and in this respect as in many others, the earliest Christian mosaics can be described as classical. Examples are occasionally found of classical mosaics in overall 'colour'. The series from Hadrian's villa, for example, which includes the Mosaic of the Doves mentioned above, is worked against a black background; but the normal background of a classical mosaic is a white, a buff, a neutral grey, or dun-colour. The typical medieval example, however (though some of the Paschalian mosaics in the early ninth century are, as we shall see, an exception), from the seventh to the fifteenth century has a background of gold. From the fifth century onwards, overall colour of some sort is an invariable rule for mosaics of a wall, apse or vault. Only on floors is the classical tradition of a neutral background for mosaic still followed as late as the thirteenth century.

The development is gradual. In the fourth-century mosaics of the Sta Costanza vault, gold is not used as background colour, the backgrounds being characteristically classical. Gold is used only to heighten details,[12] very sparingly but with charming effect, in the two corresponding sections, on each side of the arcade, which covered the immediate approach to the sarcophagus. These seem to symbolize Paradise, and the use of gold here may be linked with this symbolism. In the two mosaics of the small apses, which are explicitly Christian in theme and are sometimes thought to belong to a considerably later date, there is no gold used. Christ's halo in both these small mosaics is blue, and the general background is white, a powerful argument against a date later than the fourth century. In the niche[13] where the sarcophagus was once placed,

I Sta Costanza, mosaic in the vault (mid-fourth century). Paradise pattern.

there was a gold roundel of which traces remain, carrying the ☧ sign, the general background being white with black stars. Here again, like the 'Paradise' mosaics, this niche represented a climax in the decoration and the use of touches of gold seemed therefore appropriate. In the Sta Pudenziana mosaic (which is somewhat later, belonging to the last decades of the fourth century), gold is used more lavishly, but again only to heighten details, not to provide the background for the scheme as a whole. In the fragment representing St Paul, from the Vatican Grottoes, a fragment that goes back to the period soon after Constantine's death, the background is gold. But it is by no means clear that this was so in the original mosaic; this background is almost certainly a later alteration.

It is in the fifth century that the use of gold for background becomes more general, and this is to be seen in the earliest Sta Maria Maggiore mosaics. From the first, any extensive gold surface is varied by including in it *tesserae* of brown, black or dark blue, so that it should not overawe the surrounding work, and this practice can be seen in the mosaics both of the nave and of the triumphal arch in that church.

In the nave series, possibly the earlier of the two,[14] the method is unusual. For with only one or two possible exceptions (the mosaic of Pharaoh's daughter with the young Moses being perhaps[15] one), the gold is used for only a part of the background. It makes a splash of light, which does not compete with, or form part of, the sky, behind a single figure or a group, and so focuses attention on them. Or sometimes it forms a band at approximately waist-level right across the picture. This practice is found to some extent also in the mosaics of the triumphal arch, though there the general impression of a solid gold background (an impression that seems to be consciously avoided by the artists of the nave series) begins to develop. Here the gold is also extensively broken by the use of brown *tesserae*. Astorri pointed out[16] that the method of manufacture of the individual *tesserae* often damaged the gold leaf, with the result that the brash, slick surface of gold as it is in most modern mosaics was avoided. In the nave mosaic of the Quails in the Desert, it is not only the drawing of the three figures on the right of the design that proclaims the work of a restorer, but also the patch of unbroken gold behind the head of the figure on the right.

The mosaic of the vault of the chapel of S. Vittorio in Milan, contemporary with the earliest Sta Maria Maggiore mosaics, has a gold ground. The lovely vault of the chapel of St John Evangelist (probably fifth century) in the baptistry of St John Lateran is gold. The sixth-century mosaic of SS. Cosma e Damiano has a background of deep 'midnight' blue, which is magnificently effective with the lavish use of gold in the draperies; but the background of the lower band of mosaic, the traditional flock of sheep symbolizing the apostles, is gold. In the seventh-century mosaics of the chapel of St Venantius, and in Sta Agnese, there is a full gold background though in the latter the impression given is not as rich as usual, perhaps because the use of gold-leaf was less extravagant. Sometimes, however, this dull effect is deliberately secured by reversing the *tessera*: that is to say, by using it with the thicker glass film, normally used as the base, reversed so as to form the upper visible surface.

These gold backgrounds probably came increasingly to be associated with a *mise-en-scène* that was other-worldly, and had nothing to do with the mundane affairs of this life. The use of gold is what justifies the word 'metals' in inscriptions relating to some of these mosaics.[17]

Gold was used still more lavishly when the craft of mosaics was revived in Rome in the twelfth century; and in Toriti's two great apses of the thirteenth century its effect is superbly rich. In Pope Paschal's ninth-century mosaics, it had been used less often, though it is by no means unknown, as is sometimes suggested. It is replaced as a background at that date in a number of

III

X
IV

XI, XII, XIII

98, 87, XVI

14

II Sta Maria Maggiore, mosaic panel in the nave, No. 21 (early fifth century).
Above, the Ark about to cross the Jordan; below, Joshua sends out spies.

examples by broad horizontal bands of colour: dark and light greens and dark blues. The reason why gold was often avoided at this time may have been economic. It was certainly not technical, as can be seen from its full use in the chapel of S. Zenone. In twelfth-century Roman work, no large example comes to mind where the background was not gold.[18]

METHODS OF SETTING THE TESSERAE

Technical questions also arise in connection with the size and method of setting of the ordinary forms of the *tesserae*. The cubes of a medieval mosaic were bedded in mortar laid directly on to the material of the wall or vault. On the lower layer of the mortar a rough design (like the *sinopia* of a fresco) was sometimes sketched, though it was by no means necessarily followed precisely by the mosaicist later. In the example illustrated, found when the triumphal arch mosaics of Sta Maria Maggiore were restored, the surface of this lowest layer of mortar, carrying the first sketch, was later pitted with a pick in order to key into it a second layer. On this layer the design was sometimes elaborated in colour[19] before the mosaic *tesserae* were laid.[20] L'Orange and Nordhagen have a valuable diagram showing the method of fixing mosaic to the wall.[21] The lowest layer of coarse mortar was keyed into the wall under it by large nails with broad heads. Over this layer was one, or often two, of finer mortar, the uppermost layer being laid in sections for each day's work. On the triumphal arch of Sta Maria Maggiore the upper layer of mortar was coloured. According to Astorri, this was done so that if the mortar was seen anywhere in the interstices of the work, the total effect would not be prejudiced.

Occasionally (as perhaps in Plate 145) it is possible to trace the lines dividing one day's work from the next in the design as completed. On this top layer of mortar the design was sometimes 'frescoed' in much greater detail, in tones of grey or even colour. In the photograph of the mosaic of Christ in the character of Sun God, rediscovered in modern times under St Peter's, a large patch below the hole in the vault can be seen where the *tesserae* are missing. But their imprint is clear, as is also the frescoed design on the top level of mortar, which the mosaicist was following. This technique is by no means unique. Two examples can be found among the plates in the great work by J. Wilpert[22] in which this layer of mortar, with its coloured design, can be seen because *tesserae* are missing.[23] In one[24], two small patches of mortar can be seen, one on either side, in the border. Each has clearly been coloured. In the other[25] larger areas of the 'guide painting' can be seen. In the example below St Peter's just mentioned, the walls, as opposed to the vault above, have entirely lost their *tesserae*. But the designs are fortunately preserved thanks to the guide painting below. They show, incidentally, that the subjects were undoubtedly Christian. In all these examples, this surviving top layer of mortar, of course, has the marks of the *tesserae* once impressed into it. Whether coloured or not, this upper layer, from carrying the impression of the original *tesserae*, can give the restorer valuable information about the mosaic, even though all the surface material has gone. This is the probable explanation when we find that in the Sta Maria Maggiore Old Testament panels, the most recent restorers were able to sketch in more details than were obvious to Wilpert. He was working from the visible surface only. They stripped down the restorations, and could thus sometimes show features which were not apparent to him or to the artists who worked on his plates.

In Christian mosaics in Rome, the mosaic was still occasionally constructed on an independent bed away from the wall, so that it could be moved around in one piece. The technique can easily be recognized in earlier pagan mosaics, where the elaborate centre-pieces of designs, afterwards surrounded by patterns, were often made independently and were presumably so bought by the

16

customer in the workshop, the more commonplace pattern border being supplied later *in situ*.[26] The evidence of the nave mosaics in Sta Maria Maggiore has been used to suggest that these were actually made for a different church, and it is claimed of one of them that the scored lines on the back of its bed do not correspond with those on the surface of the wall to which it was eventually fixed. The evidence is controversial, and the conclusion that the mosaics come from elsewhere has been hotly contested.[27] There is no doubt, however, that the head of Christ (believed later to have appeared miraculously in the crown of the apse in St John Lateran when that was built by VIII the emperor Constantine) was independently bedded in this way, the base of the bed being a slab of Travertine marble.[28] When this mosaic was remade in the nineteenth century, this detail of its technique was followed, as can be seen in the plate. It is certain, then, that this technique was followed for some mosaics in the fourth and fifth centuries, whether or not there is a serious question of the Sta Maria Maggiore nave mosaics having been moved from elsewhere at an early date.

The Roman mosaicist of the classical period, in masterpieces like the Mosaic of the Doves from Hadrian's Villa, regarded it as desirable that the surfaces of all the constituent elements should be flush with one another in the same plane, as though 'ironed' after they had been laid. The spectator was thus hardly aware, in examples where the *tesserae* are set close together, of the joints between them, and thus the illusion of a continuous, as it were painted, surface could be created. Medieval mosaicists, by contrast, as early as the fifth century were conscious of the effects to be gained by setting the *tesserae* not in the same plane, but at different angles, so that light was reflected differently 12 from each one, and a scintillating quality of surface was achieved.

At this period (and indeed at most periods in medieval Roman work, except perhaps for short phases in the seventh and early eighth centuries which may be associated with particular artists brought up in the Byzantine tradition, and not with a fully-fledged local fashion) the medieval practice was to bed the base of the cube in mortar, but not to point up to the surface with mortar the interstices between one cube and another. This meant that the colour (and brilliant colour is of the essence of a medieval mosaic) had its full effect and was not toned down by lines of a neutral grey. The practice, sometimes adopted, of colouring the upper layer of mortar may have been partly designed to avoid this happening should the mortar here and there appear.[29] Some of the fragments from the oratory of John VII are a conspicuous exception since they were appar- 106 ently pointed up to the surface with uncoloured mortar. They follow in fact what seems to have been the early Byzantine practice (to judge by some of the sixth-century Salonika mosaics) and one is aware of the lines of mortar separating the *tesserae* on the exposed surface of the mosaic. Several of the other fragments of the mosaics in this series (made for an oratory in the old basilica of St Peter's, destroyed when the new building was built), the Byzantine character of which has often been remarked, show the mortar to a notable degree, particularly in the broken lines of the drawing.

But I have no doubt, either, that one form of restoration has sometimes been to brush a slurry of cement into the interstices of mosaics originally set 'dry', like a dry-stone wall without a pointed surface. An example of such a modern slurry can be seen on the left-hand lower half of Plate 111, the Christ from the *confessione* of St Peter's. Thus the technique originally used can be obscured. In the John VII group, the mosaic which reveals this happening most clearly was said, by those who saw to its preservation in 1631, to come from the ciborium of the oratory (Plate 110). There is a line of damage across the centre of the fragment. One cannot doubt that, above this, the head and shoulders of the Virgin and the head of the Child are nearer their original condition than the lower part. But they were set dry. The mortar between the individual *tesserae* is not visible and this part of the work still preserves some of its charm. But the lower part is a ruin, which has been consolidated by pointing up the surface with mortar, and it is probable that there were many pieces missing when this consolidation was done, so that the mortar is even more obvious than it would otherwise be. A fine example of the contrasting technique—that is to say, of setting dry—an incrustation on the surface rather than an inlay into it—is shown in Plate 12, a group of heads from Sta Maria Maggiore. The splendid heads of the Sta Pudenziana mosaic, on the other hand, are made with a flush surface: the *tesserae* are not pushing out of the surface but bedded into it.

42, 44

In the finest mosaics of antiquity, like the Doves mosaic, the *tesserae* (or in some instances the tiny glass rods) are set so close that the spectator is unaware of the lines between them. The coarser classical work that is so familiar was normally a floor covering, and this may partly explain why the *cloisons* of mortar were necessary to keep the *tesserae* in place. A single important fragment from a fourth-century mosaic, once in the old basilica of St Peter's, is an example of a fine late classical style in which, though no attempt is made to conceal the lines dividing each *tessera* from its neighbours, the *tesserae* are set so close that a knife blade could hardly be inserted between them. This style is known from a number of pagan examples outside Rome; for instance, from some of the finest details at Piazza Armerina in Sicily, from a group of mosaics found in Antioch, and also from some of the Imperial Palace mosaics in Istanbul.[30] The *tesserae* in these examples are not of the particularly small kind. They are sometimes chipped into narrow rectangles (to 'draw' the heavy line of the eyebrows or mouth) or into triangles, but each *tessera* is deliberately left large enough to make its own colour effect. Therefore, instead of blending in like a painted surface with transitions of colour that are shaded gradually from one tone to another, the artist deliberately juxtaposes different colours not in small dots but in sizeable areas. In this classical group, the surface is flat, with no attempt to tilt the *tesserae* individually into different planes. The results can be very effective, as in the fine head of a huntsman from Piazza Armenina. Here, as in some of the Old Testament series of mosaics in Sta Maria Maggiore, the technique of which has been to some extent anticipated by these works in Sicily and in the east, the effect of a momentary

III

11

10

III St Peter's, old basilica. St Paul, a surviving fragment apparently from the original Constantinian apsidal mosaic (mid-fourth century). Now in the Vatican Grottoes.

glance has been brilliantly given. This is because the craftsman had begun to concern himself not with line, but with light. We are already aware, here, that the real qualities of the medium are beginning to be exploited: qualities that it has in its own right, and which do not come from its being a good imitation of painting.

But while in the pagan late classical examples the surface is flat, by the time the triumphal arch mosaics of Sta Maria Maggiore were executed the tilting of the surface of each individual *tessera* to secure a glinting effect is common. In none of the few examples in Rome that it has been possible to study at eye-level have I seen gold *tesserae* set regularly oblique to the surface, as shown by L'Orange and Nordhagen in one diagram.[31] But Mr Martin Harrison (who was excavating in 1964–66 in Istanbul) told me that sections of mortar set in this way were found in St Polyeuktos.[32] To judge from photographs, this oblique setting was sometimes used in the mosaics of Hagia Sophia in Salonika, especially in setting the gold *tesserae* of a saint's halo.

Besides irregularities of surface effected by the method of setting the *tesserae* in the mortar bed, there are larger irregularities, which are also intentional and are due to the mortar not being laid with a plummet line but so as to give slightly undulating surfaces. Such unevenness of surface can readily be seen, for example, in the mosaics of the chapel of S. Zenone in Sta Prassede, and it adds variety to the impression. A recent critic has suggested that in Constantinople this or a somewhat analogous effect was calculated very precisely, the surface of the mosaic being, as it were, projected at a slight angle or on a curve, the angle or the curve planned to suit the spectator in a particular position below.[33] There seems no evidence in Roman mosaics to suggest that such a practice was followed in Rome. This is a different feature from the practice of adapting a design to the curve of a vault by developing certain distortions. The process described begins, as it were, at the other end. With an apsidal mosaic, the curve is an architectural *datum* which is necessarily accepted, and the artist, in Rome as elsewhere, adapts his design to it. The practice attributed to some of the mosaicists of Constantinople is the more sophisticated one in which the spectator's eye is taken as the focus, and what would be a plane, vertical surface is modified, in relation to the spectator's eye, into a curve. On the other hand, the small irregularities of surface in the gold background of the S. Clemente mosaic give the gold a splendid 'padded' quality. But these form an overall roughness, not an elaborately calculated curve. They are no doubt, however, deliberately used to avoid the hard, flat, metallic surface that the modern restorer often achieves.

The variety of surface in a ninth-century mosaic is at once plain when it is compared with work of classical antiquity, or of the thirteenth or fourteenth century. An analogous feature, not so easily described, is the disappearance in the western medieval work of the seventh, eighth and ninth centuries of the 'work lines' that are so often to be found in classical work, or in medieval 34, 10 mosaics done in the twelfth-century revival or after it. The surface of a classical mosaic often has an 'engine-turned' appearance, this being due to the methodical working of the craftsman and to the comparatively uniform sizes of the *tesserae* which he was employing. The effect varies from craftsman to craftsman. The technique of the ordinary craftsman stops far short of the engine-turned effect seen in one of our illustrations of a mosaic in Istanbul. But in the original sections of the Sta Maria Maggiore triumphal arch mosaic, for instance, or in those of the nave, there 7, 8 continually recur passages in which structural, or 'work lines', are apparent. The craftsman set the pieces in their places as though he were threading beads. Sometimes the lines are short, 8, 34 sometimes much longer. They may be straight, like those on the tunic of the bearer of the ark, or circular, like those in the background of the Sta Costanza vault. But the eye picks them up here and there over the surface.

IV Sta Maria Maggiore, mosaic panel in the nave, No. 11,
upper half (early fifth century). Hamar and his son Shechem approach Jacob.

The case is entirely different in the ninth-century work in Sta Prassede in the chapel of S. Zenone. 130, XIX Here every individual element seems to have been set independently of its neighbours. It is as if the craftsman were always thinking of the surface as a whole, and the next point of colour had to be v placed in relation to the whole effect, rather than to the last which had been set. In the twelfth-century revival, work lines reappear. We see them, for instance, in the fragmentary portraits of Innocent III and Ecclesia Romana from the old basilica of St Peter's, conveniently datable to 176, 177 within a few years (1198–1216); they already assume here a special character that will shortly be discussed further, in that the work lines have become part of the structure of the design. The regularity of work lines is generally maintained in the designs of the late thirteenth and early fourteenth centuries, though in some the artists seem now to be attempting, by the close juxtaposition of the *tesserae* with no mortar showing, to eliminate work lines altogether from the mosaic's appearance, in order that the subtlest transitions of light, shade and colour may be achieved without the eye being disturbed by these extraneous details. We are thus brought back at the end of the thirteenth century to the objective of some classical craftsmen: to make the mosaic in appearance as much like painting and as little like mosaic as possible.

One difference between Roman ninth-century and standard Byzantine technique is a contrast in degree rather than in kind. The smaller the individual unit, the more subtle the possibilities of modelling in it, as classical Roman mosaic artists had already discovered in their imitations of pictures. Byzantine mosaicists exploited this possibility specially when they were depicting the flesh of face or hands; and, to some extent at least in the earliest work (like the 'processions' in S. Vitale, Ravenna), and to a remarkable degree in that of the twelfth century, there is a contrast between the elaborately modelled face worked in tiny *tesserae*, the material for which is almost invariably stone, which chips easily, and a broader treatment of draperies, background, and so on. In the hands of a great artist this technique can (as with the head of St John Chrysostom at 19 Palermo) produce a superb result. To a greater or lesser extent this practice of using smaller units for the modelling of face and hands was followed in Rome from time to time. It is one sign of 79, 88 Byzantine influence, and appears strongly in the Veneto-Byzantine work done in the thirteenth century for the apse of S. Paolo fuori le Mura, or in Cavallini's work three-quarters of a century 20, 187–189 later. But in the ninth-century mosaics of Pope Paschal it hardly occurs, though, as we have seen, there is an important head worked in the reign of one of his predecessors in which the material seems to be stone, as it is, almost invariably, in mosaics that are certainly Byzantine.

Most noticeable in this mosaic portrait from Palermo, and in general in work of the twelfth-century revival in Rome or later, is the fact that the work lines, like brush-work in painting, are an integral feature of the portrait, the effectiveness of which depends, indeed, largely on this

V Sta Prassede, chapel of S. Zenone. A woman martyr, crowned (*c*. 820).

technical device. The technique is, as it were, some way between that of the painter and the stained-glass artist. The work lines are less delicate and flexible than brush-work, but they are more flexible, and considerably more delicate, than the lead lines in a stained-glass window. In painting, mosaic and stained glass, however, particular effects are achieved by those artists who make the work lines an essential feature of the design. In the portrait of St John Chrysostom, the structure of the face is brought out by the work lines of the mosaic. The same is true of the original heads surviving from the S. Paolo mosaic, and of that splendid fragment (of generally western character), the head of St Bernard originally made for St Peter's.

19, 20, 27

In the latter, the Byzantine technical device of very small *tesserae* was not adopted, though the craftsman deliberately used the work lines as part of his design, as a Byzantine artist would do, to suggest the structure of bone and flesh.

THE REPAIR, RESTORATION AND REPLACEMENT OF MOSAICS

The restorer's attitude towards his work has differed from period to period, and his patron's instructions no doubt differed also. Ideally, a mosaic should be regularly maintained so that replacements are on a small scale and the original form is preserved without recourse to new invention. In practice this has seldom happened (except, perhaps, in very early times), though it is now fortunately the policy adopted, so far as resources allow, for the conservation of all the great medieval Roman mosaics. From what has been said of the technical significance of the way *tesserae* were set, the importance of avoiding wholesale resetting, if the original character is to be preserved, will be appreciated. In many instances this has unfortunately been impossible to avoid, while in others perhaps it has not been avoided where possible. The new festoons of the triumphal arch in Sta Prassede, for example, were a disastrous error, partly because the smoothness of the work forms an inappropriate contrast with the original rough irregularities which can still be seen in so many of that church's noteworthy mosaics. Modern materials make themselves obvious, even where old techniques of setting *tesserae* have been to a greater or lesser extent followed. Patches of modern red force themselves on the attention here and there in the chapel of S. Zenone. But the work carried out in Rome in the 1960's shows a fine appreciation of these problems.

There are reasons, discussed in more detail later, for thinking that a number of the fourth- or fifth-century Old Testament panels in the nave of Sta Maria Maggiore were restored at a very early date.[34] The earliest fragment from the old basilica of St Peter's has, as is argued elsewhere, a gold background added later (though probably not much later), the mosaic thereby being made more splendid. And there are references to repairs or restoration of mosaics at various times in the following centuries, the context of these references generally being an account of the achievements of one of the popes. Something can be discovered in more detail of the methods of a restoration made in the late twelfth century, in St Peter's, by command of Innocent III. We are told by the *Liber Pontificalis*: 'Hic renovavit absidem beati Petri apostuli ex musibo, quod dirutum erat', 'This pope restored the apse, in the basilica of the Apostle St Peter, in mosaic. It had been in ruins'. The mosaic as a whole no longer exists. But Wilpert examined the pictorial record of it which has survived, and he was able to show that the form of the original was preserved almost in its entirety in Innocent III's restoration[35]—that this was, in fact, a true restoration, not a replace-

176, 177

ment with new work. The figure of Innocent III himself was introduced, with the 'Ecclesia Romana' balancing it on the other side. The heads of these two figures survive. Another small addition made by Innocent III, of a nimbed dove, survives also as a fragment. The representations

29

of Jerusalem and Bethlehem had presumably almost disappeared, to judge from the surviving drawings, and new designs had to be produced for them. It is difficult otherwise to explain the oriental air which the two groups of buildings have in the pictures made of the mosaic, in contrast with the many other representations of Jerusalem and Bethlehem that have survived in a similar position. But that is the full extent of modernization or addition. The fourth-century fragment, representing St Paul, from this mosaic was preserved by Innocent's craftsmen almost intact, in spite of what has sometimes been said (for example, by de Rossi[36]) about its alteration. What could be saved evidently was retained; and the new material must have been in odd contrast with its surroundings. A dove (a very different bird from Innocent's mentioned above) that has also survived among the classical fragments in the Vatican has sometimes been said to come from this mosaic. But there is no obvious place for it in the Renaissance sketch that records the mosaic, and technically it goes not with the St Paul but with a magnificent head of a cherub, similarly made of small *tesserae*, whereas those used for the St Paul are larger. Both come from some unidentified classical source.[37]

Some time before Innocent III's work in St Peter's was done, the first of the surviving comprehensive replacement schemes was undertaken, that in S. Clemente. Here the structure of the apse to be decorated was new, since the ancient apse was destroyed to make room for the larger church, built at a somewhat higher level than the earlier one. It appears that an antique design, taken from the old apse, was adapted for a new and, as it were, autonomous mosaic. The great scroll pattern springing from an acanthus root comes from the ancient work,[38] as does much of the detail, but the central group of the crucifixion was new. The original centrepiece was probably a cross, not a crucifixion. The result may be regarded as one of the finest in the whole Roman series, one in which the effects of the medium are brilliantly exploited. By the time the next two replacement mosaics were made in the last decade of the thirteenth century, 160 years after the S. Clemente mosaic, the art of the mosaicist was already beginning to be prejudiced by a desire to achieve the effects of painting, and, splendid though Toriti's work in the apse of Sta Maria Maggiore is, it lacks the feeling for the medium which is the great quality of the S. Clemente mosaic. It may be significant that Toriti calls himself 'pictor' in the inscriptions in Sta Maria and St John Lateran. Painting was his *métier*. What he seems to have done in these two mosaics was to cannibalize most successfully the ancient work which he was replacing. He may actually have used some of the antique materials, in addition to the 'miraculous head',[39] which he preserved intact, and he certainly reproduced much of the detail. Nicholas IV's inscription in St John Lateran refers to the restoration of the ruined apse and its 'ornamentation with mosaic', and goes on to state that he caused the miraculous image 'to be renewed and put back in its place' (or possibly to be 'put back in its place without damage').[40] We have, therefore, to guess the extent to which the rest of the design was new. Clearly the smaller figures inserted among the main range on each side of the cross belong to the new design. But much of the remainder, so de Rossi believed, Toriti may have owed to his ancient predecessor.[41] A similar process went on with the apsidal mosaic of Sta Maria Maggiore, where the view generally taken is that the splendid scroll pattern on each side of the central figures is substantially from the antique work, as the lower border clearly is also. If the word 'cannibalize' is used of these mosaics, it is in a sense in which it could be applied with equal fairness to Shakespeare's adaptations of Plutarch. A new and magnificent creation is in no way worse for incorporating extensive material from the source of its inspiration.

It would be of the greatest interest if we could know what was remaining of the mosaic of Sta Pudenziana when it was restored by Renaissance craftsmen. The scale and placing of the evangelist symbols, of which enough remains from the late fourth or early fifth century for certainty on these

IX

II

181

5

VIII

XXIX
62, 64–66

two points, shows that the original work was far larger than the existing remains at first sight suggest, and these huge symbols, showing against the deep blue sky, must have been an extraordinarily impressive feature. Not only was the vault of heaven represented far more grandly than the existing mosaic suggests, but also, no doubt, all twelve apostles were seated below. If the restorers cut down the size of the mosaic unnecessarily, they have much to answer for. But it is more likely that damage along all the edges was already too extensive to make full restoration possible. In detail their work, which according to de Rossi was done in plaster, may have been more than usually satisfying, since they were handling one of those antique originals towards which the age was sympathetic. Camuccini restored the work again, with immense care, in the nineteenth century, replacing the Renaissance plaster repairs by mosaic. There is a certain softness

42, 44   in the technique of the original artist, seen in the splendid heads of St Peter and St Paul, and those of the women, whoever they represent, standing behind them, which contrasts with the harsher

43   competence of the restorers. In the left-hand group, most of the heads are substantially antique. But the head in the middle (that on the left of St Paul) shows clearly where the forehead and edge of the hair have been renewed in the harsher technique: the eyes are much more staring, and the pouching under the eyes is much more emphatic, than in the neighbouring faces. Below

44, 45   the eyes the work on this head looks early. On the other side the contrast between Peter's head and the fine but not antique head of the apostle next to him is at once apparent. Unfortunately the central figure of Christ seems to me to have been so much restored at various periods that it is aesthetically a muddle. It may be doubted whether there is any hope of recovering from it anything more than the general outlines of the ancient artist's work.

The sixteenth and seventeenth centuries saw the destruction of several great mosaics, the loss of which is now universally lamented, and for which the important work of recording mosaics, undertaken from time to time at this period, is only a partial compensation. A single marvellous

VI   fragment of Giotto's *Navicella* is a reminder that the extraordinary reputation this work enjoyed

222   during the later Middle Ages was fully justified. The *Navicella* was elaborately recorded before

221   its destruction. But the version of it recreated a few decades later is a poor travesty. The destruction of mosaics in the dome of Sta Costanza in 1620 (a few years before the *Navicella* was finally destroyed, though it had already suffered drastic modification by that date) was also a major disaster, and here the detail of the existing sketches is often unreliable and based on the artist's imagination. Some of the nave mosaics of Sta Maria Maggiore, destroyed at about this date in order to provide a finer approach to the Sixtine and Borghese chapels, were already in a state of ruin,[42] and here the end may be thought in any event to have justified the means, as perhaps also in the case of the later damage done to the façade mosaic when a new and splendid façade was built. But the reasons were often less cogent—an individual's whim or a transient fashion. Gregory XIII altered one side of the mosaic in SS. Cosma e Damiano apparently in order to introduce into it the figure of a greater holder of his own name than himself. Alexander VII, a

XII   few generations later, removed the new figure and restored a representation of Felix IV, an obviously mid-seventeenth-century figure in sixth-century surroundings. Byzantine emperors would, more simply, have remade the heads and renamed them without touching the figures as a whole.[43]

This was a time when the claims not only of great architecture, but of small architectural frills also, were paramount, and the new ceiling in S. Clemente, or the balconies on the triumphal arch of Sta Prassede, were allowed to prejudice seriously the effects of works whose interest was considered in that period to be mainly antiquarian. When the triclinium of Leo III was destroyed in

VI St Peter's, old basilica. Roundel, showing the head of an angel. An original fragment, now in a church at Boville Ernica, from the border of Giotto's *Navicella* (perhaps *c.* 1300).

the eighteenth century, an attempt was made to preserve the mosaic. It proved impracticable to restore it and, instead, a new architectural feature was built, to be decorated with a copy. This work, the so-called *Tribune of Benedict XIV*, represents stylistically the nadir of the art of restoration. It gives the iconography of the original, but little more. Nevertheless, the awareness shown of the need somehow to preserve the monument is in itself significant of changing attitudes.

186   Thereafter standards rapidly improved. Some of the work in the apse of S. Paolo is an impressive testimony to the skill of the designers of the late eighteenth or early nineteenth century, as is the version of Toriti's mosaic produced for the apse in St John Lateran in 1884. It is, however, a tragedy that the 'miraculous head' was not replaced in its original form in this restoration. Both these schemes provided, in fact, modern versions of older works. Work on the vault mosaics in Sta Costanza (1834-40), by Camuccini and his assistants, was different in character, in that it was essentially the repair of the old work rather than its replacement by new. In detail, much that was missing had to be supplied in new materials. But Camuccini was helped by the fact that the patterns are repeated on each side of the circular colonnade. What was missing on one side could often still be seen intact on the other. And his attitude to the task as a whole is shown by his refusal to remake the mosaic of the recess over the sarcophagus. The scheme there, a white ground with black stars, and the ☀ in a medallion in the crown of the arched recess, was known, was very simple, and a substantial fragment remained. But he argued that restoration in this arch would lead to the creation of virtually a new mosaic. In general, his work in Sta Costanza is triumphantly successful.[44]

When sixteenth-century restorers decided to replace sections of mosaic that were missing, they normally worked with plaster artificially scored into sections to represent the cubes of mosaic.
24   This technique was extensively used in Sta Maria Maggiore; and a number of the nave mosaics were completely replaced in this way, the designs bearing no relation to the original though the incidents shown may have been the same. Sections of mosaic which have been repaired by this technique are always instantly recognizable. The easiest way to replace an individual missing *tessera* or a small group that has been lost is to apply surface plaster. Clumsy, unsuitable repairs of this kind were often made in Sta Maria Maggiore and in many other chuches. A photograph (see Plate 22) showing the double panel representing the incident of the Quails in the Desert, and taken before the last major repair work was done, shows many patches of such first-aid. They appear in the photograph simply as blobs of white or grey. The photograph also shows repairs done with new *tesserae*, such as three small patches near the lower edge of Moses' tunic in the upper half, and much larger patches of new gold *tesserae* by the upper right-hand and lower right-hand edge. These, with the metal ties which were used when the mosaic surface was coming away from its bed, and which were often coloured to make them less visible, are mostly comparatively modern in date. In the upper register alone at least seven ties can be seen, and at least three in the lower. In the most recent restoration (1927) all these makeshift devices were eliminated and
IV   the mosaics were secured again in their beds. Missing sections of mosaic, in this phase of restoration, were replaced with coloured plaster, and outlines were sketched in roughly so as to give the general scheme of the design. But no attempt was made, by scoring the plaster, to create the illusion of a mosaic repair. It is a fairly satisfactory compromise; though those mosaics which have been restored with actual mosaic *tesserae* (like the one representing the meeting of Abraham and Melchisidec, in which most of the right-hand side is new) certainly give a pleasanter, if in detail a more misleading, result.

When restoration of any kind is being identified, obviously questions of style and technique are vital. One of the illustrations shows a fine fifteenth-century fragment representing the head of St Bernard of Clairvaux. In this work the original structural lines in the setting of the *tesserae*   27 were brilliantly used, in the manner described above, to suggest the physical structure of the cheek and of the drapery. It will be apparent at once that the restorer did not follow these structural lines: over the ear, and to the top of the head slightly to the left above it. The lack of structure in the arrangement of the *tesserae* here is conclusive indication of damage which has had to be repaired; and, though the work is well done, it can be proved from earlier photographs that a large part of the back of the head is modern. In the case of the eighth-century Christ in the *confessione* of St Peter's the argument will run rather differently. For there the character of the   III original work was rougher, and it is the relatively neat finish of the left-hand side of the work, including the right shoulder and right arm of the figure and the background above the right shoulder, that give rise to suspicion. Here we are fortunate in being able to identify at least one more work by the same notable artist, and though that too has now suffered restoration, a good   108 idea of his style can be formed. It may be confidently assumed that the *Confessione* head at least still substantially represents his original work, even though it has been completely reset, and has acquired in the process that unsatisfying modern slickness which it is so difficult to avoid.

The group of mosaics which has suffered most through restoration is that in S. Paolo fuori le Mura. The triumphal arch dates from the time of Galla Placidia, in the second half of the fifth   185 century, and though it has been held that the inscription which associates the arch with her refers to its structure rather than its decoration, there is no doubt that the original decoration was made not long after, if not at, that period. The great mosaic of the apse was made by Venetian craftsmen in the first half of the thirteenth century. Five original thirteenth-century heads, one the large head of St Peter, who stands in the mosaic on Christ's left, have been preserved. Their condition is good, and it is puzzling that the mosaic from which they come was scrapped. There seems to be evidence that these heads had been removed and the new mosaic already put in place before the fire of 1823. In the drawing made immediately after it, the strange head in the roundel of the triumphal arch also appears in its present form. This seems likely to be   183 the result of many restorations at many different periods, but can be only a travesty of the original. It was not, then, the nineteenth-century restoration after the fire, but work done before it (though probably not long before), which deprived the church of its Veneto-Byzantine original in the apse; while time and the determination to keep the mosaic as an effective decoration account for the changes which in the course of many centuries have destroyed the quality of the triumphal arch mosaic.

A third series of mosaic decorations, made originally for the façade of the church by Cavallini in the early fourteenth century, and which by the date of the fire were already largely ruined by decay, were taken down and the arrangement was replanned so that the mosaic could be placed on either side of the space between the triumphal arch and the apse. Here again there is virtually nothing left of the original work. Only in one or two figures can traces of Cavallini's style be detected. Some authorities have held that one or two original pieces of the apsidal mosaic have survived *in situ*, incorporated into the modern version, in the lower section of the mosaic near its centre. A difference in style is indeed apparent in these central figures in the lower register. But the sad truth is that none of these mosaics (the relics of the Cavallini façade mosaics, the apsidal mosaics, or the mosaic of the triumphal arch) can be taken seriously as an example of the work of the period in which the originals were made. They are of considerable iconographical importance, two of them at any rate faithfully preserving the earlier scheme. And the view may be taken that the apsidal mosaic is a fine work in its own right. But the mosaics are far removed from their originals.

No comparable holocaust of restoration has taken place elsewhere, though of course elaborate schemes of mosaic decoration, as in Sta Sabina or S. Stefano Rotondo, have been almost wholly lost. In many mosaics (as in the apse of Sta Prassede, or the three central figures of the façade mosaic of Sta Maria in Trastevere) resetting has given a certain hardness of line, without prejudicing the original work further. And many others have some patches of restoration that are unhappy.

These observations show that complex questions of authenticity arise in the study of Roman mosaics. Nor is this problem confined to Rome. In Ravenna there are analogous difficulties, and also in Istanbul, though there the restorations or new versions are often of a much earlier date than most of those discussed above. The implication, for the Roman material, is not that it must be dismissed as unauthentic and therefore unimportant, but that a close examination is necessary, work by work, before we accept a mosaic at its face value. The student's task will be to assess the facts for every mosaic he examines. Can he accept (as I should judge he may, exceptionally, in the chapel of S. Zenone in Sta Prassede) not only the authenticity of the general scheme as it now appears, but also the authenticity of the craftsmanship, using his observations of the actual methods of setting to distinguish between this mosaic and others, or, indeed, between the work of one craftsman and another, in this chapel? Or can he, as will much more often be the case, accept the authenticity of the general scheme, while rejecting in detail, because the mosaic has been reset, the evidence of the present setting of the *tesserae*? This is how I myself would regard the apsidal mosaic of Sta Prassede. In the chapel of St Venantius in St John Lateran, it is possible to study in detail the results achieved when a mosaic has been entirely reset by the expert methods now in use. In that case I would certainly hold that the existing mosaic gives an excellent idea of the original—and, indeed, of the technique of the original. But if, by studying the mosaics in their present form, we attempt to distinguish between the work of one seventh-century craftsman and another, we may find ourselves falling into the trap of one who tries to use Wilpert's great book on the Roman mosaics for this purpose.[45] Where the Sta Maria Maggiore mosaics, for example, are concerned, such a person finds himself convinced that two works are by the same craftsman, only to discover that the technical similarities reside in the colour plates in Wilpert's book, and not in the works themselves. In the chapel of St Venantius, uniformity of style is due to restorers, imitating skilfully the technique, but not preserving what Otto Demus calls the 'handwriting', of the craftsmen. We may reach the conclusion, in the case of Sta Pudenziana, that though no accurate impression of the general scheme can now be formed, owing to the drastic surgery (which may have been inevitable) that was carried out in the sixteenth century, yet here and there enough remains of the original work to enable us to distinguish between artist A and artist B. We shall find that even though parts of the façade mosaic of Sta Maria in Trastevere have been reset, the styles of the original artists are so distinctive as to make possible the categorizing of the work by different phases and different hands, and so on. The results will show that for a large number of the mosaics we can form a good impression of the artist's original intention. And the series remains unique in extent, stretching as it does right back into classical antiquity, and impressive in the number of masterpieces that it includes.

124

139

v, XIX, XXII,
XXI

124, 97–104

42–45

139–147

1 *Natural History*, bk XXXVI, ch. lxiv.

2 Most of the mosaics in the National Museum in Naples were taken from houses overwhelmed in the eruption in which Pliny himself was killed. The vast majority, so far as I can judge, are made entirely of natural materials. In a few, *tesserae* of opaque glass are used for some colours: I have noticed reds and ochres.

3 The Mosaic of the Doves and those which belong to the same group can (exceptionally) be dated with some confidence. They are from Hadrian's great villa, and so were made perhaps in the first half of the second century AD, though the possibility of their having been brought from elsewhere cannot, of course, be completely excluded, and, if this was the case, they might have been made much earlier.

4 *Mosaik von der Antike bis zum Mittelalter*; German ed., trans. from Norwegian, Munich 1960, pp. 14 and 47.

5 Ibid., p. 14.

6 *Theophilus de Diversis Artibus*, ed. C. R. Dodwell, London 1961. The two references to mosaic in Isidore of Seville's *Etymologiae* (XVI, xvi, and XIX, xiv, in the Oxford Classical Text edition) unfortunately give no further clarification. One mentions the suitability of coloured glass for pictures; the other alludes briefly to the construction of *lithostrota* from *tesserae* variously coloured.

7 'Nuove osservazioni sulla tecnica dei mosaici romani della basilica di Sta Maria Maggiore', *Riv. di Archeol. Crist.*, XI, 1934, pp. 51–72.

8 These portrait glasses are an alternative possible interpretation of the 'pictures' mentioned by Theophilus. But, as far as I am aware, none survive that could be considered contemporary with Theophilus.

9 Professor E. V. Sayre, of Brookhaven National Laboratory, told me that cubes from Sta Sophia that he had examined were of solid, opaque or clear glass, with an embedded layer of gold or silver foil. While he had not found glazed terracotta in this context he said this might be only because of the nature of the samples he had had. Glazed terracotta, or pottery, is the normal material for the 'mosaics' with which the Muslims decorated their mosques during the later Middle Ages. But these are not mosaics in the accepted sense of the word, since on a single tile there are often three or four colours and several different elements of pattern, while individual tiles are normally several inches square. Glazed *tesserae* of earthenware were used by restorers in Sicily in the seventeenth century; cf. O. Demus, *Mosaics of Norman Sicily*, 1950, p. 110.

10 To determine for certain whether *tesserae* are natural or artificial seems sometimes impossible without chemical analysis. But artificial material can often be distinguished by slight pitting, the result of an oxidizing process. Also, it fractures into a faint curve, while stone can be cut to a flat surface.

11 The backgrounds of the Sta Costanza mosaics were said by G. B. de Rossi, on V. Camuccini's authority, to be not of enamel or glass, but of palombino marble ('Sta Costanza', fol. 9, verso, in *Musaici cristiani e saggi di pavimenti delle chiese di Roma anteriori al secolo XV*, Rome 1873–99).

12 It is similarly used in a mosaic of about the same period found in Antioch. See L'Orange and Nordhagen, op. cit., p. 64 and Plate 29.

13 There is, however, reason to think that this niche may not have been the original site of the sarcophagus; see p. 61. But it stood in this part of the building.

14 See pp. 73–74 for a discussion.

15 The exception is, in fact, only apparent in this example, though the area of gold is greater; the sky above is not gold and thus marks itself off from the gold background. This strip of sky is substantially original.

16 Op. cit., pp. 51–56.

17 For example, in Sta Prassede: EMICAT AVLA PIAE VARIIS DECORATA METALLIS PRAXEDIS. . . . 'This, the church of the revered Praxed, shines with its ornament of many-coloured metals. . . .' See also, in Sta Agnese: AVREA CONCISIS SVRGIT PICTVRA METALLIS. . . . 'This picture stands up aloft, golden with neatly cut cubes of metal. . . .'

18 Except in floor mosaics, with which this book is not concerned.

19 In the very early Christian mosaic with the vine scroll recently re-discovered under St Peter's, the sketch seems to have been in various tones of grey and to have been full enough to be precisely followed. See B. M. A. Ghetti and others, *Esplorazioni sotto la confessione di S. Pietro*, 1940–49, vol.

I, pp. 41–42. For the method of fixing to the masonry, see L'Orange and Nordhagen, op. cit., p. 60.

20 This upper layer of mortar had to be laid in sections, since it had still to be moist when the *tesserae* were set in it.

21 Op. cit., p. 60.

22 J. Wilpert, *Die römischen Mosaiken und Malereien der Kirchlichen Bauten vom IV bis XIII Jahrhundert*, 4 vols, Freiburg 1916.

23 For an example (apparently fifth-century) outside Rome, see A. Bellucci, 'Le catacombe di S. Gaudioso e di S. Eufebio a Napoli,' *Riv. di Archeol. Crist.*, XI, 1934, p. 90. In the chapel of St Venantius the sketches were in black and red; see the article quoted in Notes on the Text IV, 17.

24 Plate 89: the archbishop's chapel, Ravenna.

25 Plate 96: the church of St Martin and St Sylvester; our Plate 2.

26 On these *emblemata* in classical mosaics, see L'Orange and Nordhagen, op. cit., pp. 43–45.

27 See, for example, C. Cecchelli, *I mosaici della basilica di S. Maria Maggiore*, Turin 1956, pp. 75 et seq.

28 See p. 70.

29 See G. Astorri, 'Nuove osservazioni sulla tecnica dei mosaici romani della basilica di S. Maria Maggiore, *Riv. di Archeol. Crist.*, XI, 1934. He thinks that this was so on the triumphal arch in Sta Maria Maggiore.

30 In the Piazza Armerina mosaic, the pointing is more apparent than in the examples in St Peter's or in Antioch. But the important feature which they all share equally is that no attempt has been made to conceal the division between one *tessera* and the next, whether the pointing is obvious or not.

31 Op. cit., p. 60.

32 See also L'Orange and Nordhagen, op. cit., p. 66. This technique is also found in the mosaics of St Sophia and St Eirene.

33 G. Mathew, *Byzantine Aesthetics*, London 1963, p. 29.

34 See C. Bertelli, 'Un antico restauro nei mosaici di Sta Maria Maggiore', *Paragone*, March 1955, pp. 40–42; see also p. 79 of this book.

35 Op. cit., I, pp. 361–367.

36 Op. cit., 'Mosaico dell' abside di S. Pietro' (fasc. XXVI).

37 The possibility has to be considered that these might be stray fragments from the original mosaic of the apse in St John Lateran. But the form of the dove I think eliminates this possibility. And the technique is entirely different from that of the St Paul. This is not conclusive, however, since in a large mosaic considerable differences sometimes occur.

38 See the discussion of this scroll on p. 248.

39 See p. 70.

40 The words are 'integrum reponi fecit'.

41 The definitive article is that by J. Wilpert: 'La decorazione Constantiniana della basilica Lateranense', *Riv. di Archeol. Crist.*, VI, 1929, pp. 53–150. See p. 70 of this book.

42 See the drawings reproduced in Cecchelli, op. cit., Plate XI. Out of six half-panels one is recorded at that time as entirely modern, as is a substantial part of a second.

43 As the Empress Zoe did when she remarried. See A. N. Grabar, *Byzantine Painting*, trans. S. Gilbert, Geneva 1953, p. 102.

44 H. Stern expressed a more critical view in 'Les Mosaiques de l'église de Sainte Constance à Rome', *Dumbarton Oaks Papers*, XII, 1958, p. 192. But he compared the existing mosaic favourably with a Renaissance drawing of what remained of that section.

45 More subtly, he may fall into the same trap when studying Cecchelli's book (op. cit.) on the mosaics of Sta Maria Maggiore. Two of Wilpert's plates of the nave mosaics have been reproduced by Cecchelli in his book as Plates XVI and XXX. In Cecchelli's book they immediately strike one, quite wrongly, as being by the same hand.

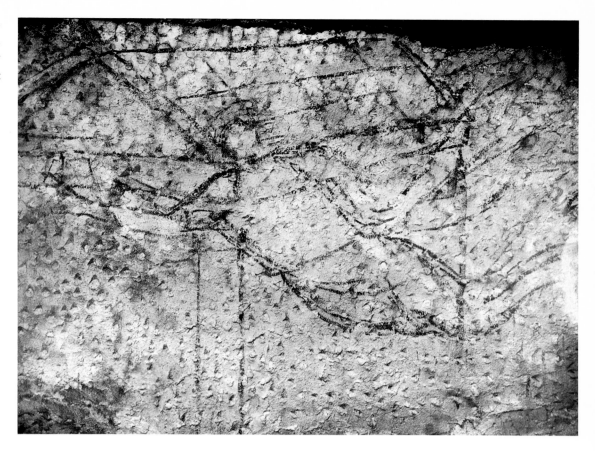

1 Sta Maria Maggiore, mosaic of the triumphal arch (*c.* 435). Preliminary sketch on the lowest layer of mortar.

2 S. Martino ai Monti, crypt. The mortar shows the imprint of missing *tesserae*.

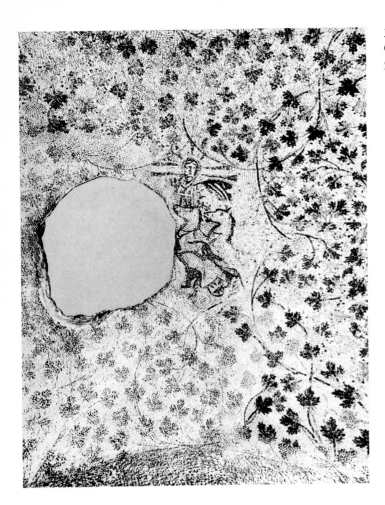

3　St Peter's, cemetery below the church. Christ ascending in a chariot, as the Sun God (third century).

4　St Peter's, cemetery below the church. Detail from Plate 3.

5 Vatican Grottoes. Head of a cherub (provenance unknown; late classical period).

6 Sta Pudenziana, mosaic of the apse (*c.* 400). Detail.

7   Sta Maria Maggiore. Detail from mosaic panel (see Plate 59) in the nave (early fifth century).

8 Sta Maria Maggiore. Detail from mosaic panel (see Plate IX) in the nave (early fifth century).

9 Sta Cecilia in Trastevere, mosaic of the apse (ninth century, first quarter). Sta Cecilia and her husband.

10 Imperial Palace, Istanbul. Detail from a pavement (late classical secular work).

11 Piazza Armerina, Sicily. Detail from a pavement (late classical secular work).

12　Sta Maria Maggiore, mosaic of the triumphal arch (*c.* 435). Three heads from the Presentation scene.

13   S. Vitale, Ravenna. The Byzantine emperor Justinian (sixth century, second quarter).

14 Sta Maria Maggiore, mosaic of the triumphal arch (*c.* 435). Head of the Virgin in the Presentation scene.

15   Hagios Georgios, Salonika. Head of a saint (Byzantine; dated by L'Orange and Nordhagen *c.* 400).

16 Hagios Georgios, Salonika. Head of a saint (Byzantine; dated by L'Orange and Nordhagen *c*. 400).

17 S. Lorenzo fuori le Mura, mosaic of the triumphal arch (sixth century, fourth quarter). Head of St Lawrence.

18   S. Lorenzo fuori le Mura, mosaic of the triumphal arch (sixth century, fourth quarter). Head of St Paul.

19   Cathedral, Cefalu. Detail from Sicilian–Byzantine mosaic:
St John Chrysostom (mid–twelfth century).

20 S. Paolo fuori le Mura, mosaic of the apse (Veneto-Byzantine; *c.* 1225).
Surviving original head of an apostle, now in the Vatican Grottoes.

21   Sta Maria Domnica, mosaic of the apse (ninth century, first quarter). Head of an angel.

22   Sta Maria Maggiore, mosaic panel in the nave, No. 22 (early fifth century).

23 S. Vitale, Ravenna. Band of decoration, with busts of Christ, St Paul and St Peter (mid-sixth century).

24   Sta Maria Maggiore, mosaic panel in the nave, No. 2 (early fifth century). Abraham and the angels.

25 Vatican Grottoes. Head of an angel, once attributed to Giotto, but in fact a version, made in 1727, of the head shown in Plate 26.

26 St Peter's, old basilica. Roundel, showing the head of an angel. An original fragment, now in the Vatican Grottoes, from Giotto's *Navicella* (*c.* 1300).

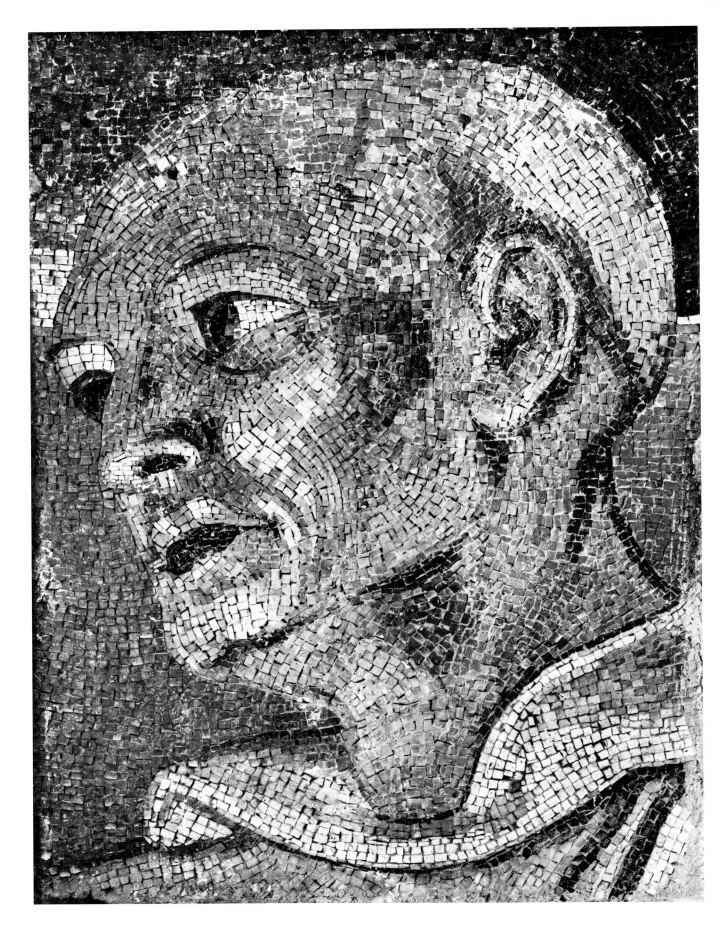

27   St Peter's, old basilica. Head of St Bernard, now in the Vatican Grottoes (fourteenth–fifteenth centuries).

1 The first stage in the making of a wall mosaic. A rough design has been sketched in the mortar, which has been pitted later in order that a second layer of mortar can be keyed into it. See Plate 55 for the final version; the position of the angel in relation to the *aedicula* has been changed, but its poise in the air remains as in the first sketch.

2 As well as the imprints where missing *tesserae* were originally bedded, the plate also shows traces of the frescoed design on the uppermost layer of mortar (seen especially in an area stretching down from the shoulder over the chest to the wrist, and in the face). Both these features, where they are available, can provide important information for the restorer.

3, 4 In the lower left-hand part all the *tesserae* have been lost, only the frescoed design in the mortar being visible. (The hole was made by those who originally discovered the mosaic during the Renaissance period, coming into the vault from above.)

5 The use of smaller *tesserae* for the face, and the elaborate, painterly modelling thus made possible, are typical of one type of fine classical work. This head is probably from the same mosaic as the dove shown in Plate 181. Unfortunately, nothing is known of the provenance of these fragments.

6 The four heads are original work, largely un-restored, set flush with the mortar in a smooth surface. A large triangular area shown in the lowest third of the plate, to the right, including the hands, and almost all the central figure's drapery, are modern.

7 The texture of the surface is now looser than in earlier mosaics, and the work is beginning to assume the character of an incrustation. The work lines are still plainly visible. The fine effect largely depends on the *tesserae* being large enough for individual units to tell as single elements of colour, in contrast with the chiaroscuro shown in Plate 5.

8 The work lines are strongly marked (contrast this plate with plate 9).

9 The figures are now hieratic and unearthly, and the work lines almost non-existent except in patches of restoration (for example, the forearm

on the left and the patch in the lower part of the dress on the right).

10, 11 The neat work lines are everywhere apparent. Areas of colour are blocked in without chiaros-curo. The surface is closely knit.

12 The texture of the surface is loose. The *tesserae*, tilted in various directions, tell as individual points of colour. The condition is original, except for a band of consolidation across the chests of the two right-hand figures.

13 The *tesserae* used for the flesh are smaller than those shown in Plate 14. Apart from the jewels (rendered in mother-of-pearl) the *tesserae* are, however, apparently of glass, as is shown by the pitting visible in several of them. In true By-zantine work, they would probably already have been of stone at this period. There is some draw-ing (contrast Plate 14) in the lines of the face.

14 The *tesserae* are of glass, even for the jewels. The texture is even looser than in the head of Justinian (Plate 13), which, by contrast, has something of the late classical or Byzantine regularity of struc-ture. The head is original work, but some areas (near the base of the plate) may have been reset.

15, 16 The work lines, used to suggest the lines of the physical structure of the face, are a notable feature. Small *tesserae*, apparently of stone, have been used to represent the flesh. There is in these heads a classical softness and delicacy of modelling which are in contrast with, for example, the hieratic character of the head shown in Plate 19. But, in contrast with Plates 13 and 14, Byzantine tech-niques are here manifest.

17 This head is by an artist working in the Roman style. The *tesserae* used for the flesh are fairly large, and are of glass. The style of the setting is impressionistic.

18 This head, though made for the same church and at the same period as the one shown in Plate 17, is by an artist working in the Byzantine tradition. The *tesserae* used for the flesh are far smaller, and are apparently of stone. There is some orderliness in the work lines of the face.

19 This portrait, though strongly individualized, is nevertheless hieratic. The small *tesserae* used for

the flesh are set with brilliant precision; the work lines and the strong highlights have been used to interpret the structure of the face.

20 The apostle represented seems to be St Thomas. Here, as in the portrait shown in Plate 19, there are marked highlights and work lines which suggest the structure of the face; but the craftsmanship is less distinguished.

21 Fine and characteristically Roman work. There is probably a small repair, excellently done, below the chin on the left. The texture of the surface is very loose, and there are no work lines. The material is glass.

22 Three hands seem to be represented, the lower register (left-hand side) being by one artist, the upper register by another, while the work (linear in character) on the right of the lower register may be a poor ninth-century restoration. For the linear drapery, compare, for example, Plate 9.

23 The heads of St Paul and St Peter seem to be iconographically in the tradition followed by Roman artists; insufficient evidence is available, it seems, to determine whether, at this early date, it was standard in the east also. The head of Christ may have been closely similar to the original of the triumphal arch roundel in S. Paolo fuori le Mura (compare Plate 185, top centre).

24 The restorations at the foot of the panel, on either side, and among the foliage above the head of the angel on the left (lower register), were carried out in plaster, scored to imitate mosaic. The artist responsible for this panel is the one whose style approaches most nearly that of the work on the triumphal arch (compare with it Plates 57–59); the artist of those mosaics, however, seems not to be identical with this one. For an example of work, in the nave series, by the artist who executed this panel, see Plate 46.

25 This head was actually built over the head shown in Plate 26, and the inscription made at the time of the 'restoration' described the head as Giotto's work.

26 This head was recovered in modern times from its position behind the later version shown in Plate 25. See Plate VI for another original fragment, nearer to its original condition, from the *Navicella*.

27 Though this head is in many ways characteristically western, the artist has used the work lines to bring out the structure of the face in the Byzantine manner (compare, for example, Plate 19). Where there are restorations the precision of the work lines has been lost: for example, a little above the right eye; at the top of the head between the left eye and left ear; at the back of the head.

II

THE ANTIQUE OR
CLASSICAL PERIOD

THE EARLIEST CHRISTIAN MOSAIC surviving in Rome is that which in recent times has been rediscovered, having been seen long ago by a sixteenth-century investigator, under St Peter's. 3 Its characteristic is its understatement of any specifically Christian 'message'. The symbols it uses are of the kind which graced many earlier pagan burials: symbols of an immortality in which the dead would be richly provided with the delights of Paradise. The same is true of the great series of mosaics in Sta Costanza, so much so, indeed, that in medieval times it was called a 'Temple 34–39 of Bacchus'. From this the art develops until it comes to embody the most grandiose proclama- I, VII tions of Christian faith, expressed first in the mosaic of Sta Pudenziana, of which only a fragment 6, 42–45 (the edges heavily cut back in size, the great series of seated apostles reduced to a small fraction of its former spread) now remains. This set the fashion for a number of mosaics which, when the use of gold became more usual, were more and more splendid in appearance. As such splendours developed, the neatness and precision of classical style gave way to new objectives. The aim of the apsidal mosaic became not to decorate, but to dominate, as the theophany of SS. Cosma e XI, XII, XIII Damiano still dominates, and must have done even more powerfully before the mosaic of the twenty-four elders, on each side of the apse, was virtually destroyed. In the notes which follow, the development of these changes is traced, and an attempt is made to show what elements of classical style came to be incorporated in the medieval Roman tradition; to show also those which came to be regarded as having too strong pagan associations, and so were discarded till interest in them revived at the Renaissance.

ST PETER'S: TOMB MOSAIC IN THE CEMETERY BELOW THE OLD BASILICA
Christ, apparently heavily bearded, a halo behind his head, the arms of the Cross suggested on 3 each side of the head, rays as of the sun spreading behind his head, a cloak flying out over his left shoulder, is shown as if he were the Sun God: in a chariot, of which only one wheel is visible, drawn by two prancing horses. This makes the bearded face a striking detail, since whatever the precise date of the mosaic, it was done at a time when many representations of Christ were beardless, and to show him thus might have linked the representation more closely with those of the Sun God. In the background, against a ground of dun-colour, the trailing branches and leaves of a vine, the leaves in a dark and a lighter tone (the dark being thought of as the lower). This vine,

viewed like those that are trained overhead to give shade as well as fruit, is not in the line of development of the vine-cum-acanthus scroll which was to become so important a feature of Christian mosaic designs.[1] Though the branches intertwine, they make no formal repeated pattern. The plant is represented naturalistically.

It is interesting to compare with this the 'inhabited' vine scroll in Sta Costanza, which shows its development from a design such as that on the mosaic floor of the Baths of the Seven Sages at Ostia in three respects: it springs from a root of acanthus pattern; it burgeons into fronds, some of which bear no botanical relation to the vine, though others do; and it is inhabited by birds and beasts. The artist of the Sta Costanza vine ensures that we do not mistake its character by introducing the bunches of grapes, and the scene is, in fact, a grape harvest. But its links with the more formal scroll are unmistakable also.

By contrast, the grapes are not visible on the St Peter's vine; but the naturalistic representation is sufficient without them. The design is taken from the vine itself, not from a conventional pattern. The artist's purpose was to represent the growing plant, not to develop a conventional decorative pattern originally based on it; and there can hardly be any doubt that, early as this is, the vine is already symbolic, the association being with the imagery of the 'true vine' in the Fourth Gospel.

Technically, the mosaic is of considerable interest, since the upper layer of mortar is largely intact even where the *tesserae* have become detached and are lost. The detail has been painted on it in fresco for the mosaicist to follow.[2] The wall mosaics adjacent to this have lost their *tesserae* completely, but the fresco designs can still be seen plainly.

There are also sections of the vault mosaic from which the *tesserae* have disappeared, leaving the design on the plaster still visible. (One such section is the lower half, on the left-hand side, of Plate 3.) In the original, what appears in the photograph as the linear character of the centre-piece is not nearly so strongly marked. The 'lines' are, in fact, shadows; there is a considerable depth of *chiaroscuro*. There is some yellow 'gold' (probably not gold-leaf, but colour) about the figure of Christ. A third-century date for this mosaic seems now generally accepted.

Fig 1 Mosaic floor of the Baths of the Seven Sages, Ostia. Detail.

39

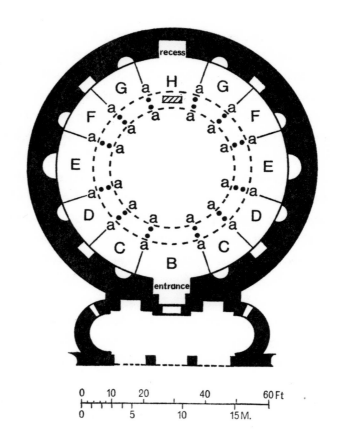

Fig 2 *Diagram of Sta Costanza, showing the arrangement of the mosaic patterns in the vault, in relation to the entrance and the sarcophagus.*

a a   pairs of linked pillars carrying the drum of the dome

B–G   mosaics of the vault

  B   plain pattern

  c   dolphin pattern

  D   Cupid and Psyche pattern

  E   vines, and *putti* vintagers

  F   roundel pattern of figures and heads

  G   Paradise pattern

  H   probable position of the sarcophagus in antiquity

STA COSTANZA

This church was built in the fourth century as a mausoleum for Constantina, the daughter of Constantine, and her body was brought back here from Bithynia on her death in 354. The mosaics may have been finished by that date, though those in the small apses were possibly added later. Architecturally, the interior of the church has remained virtually unaltered: in form circular (this being a characteristic of the imperial mausolea), with an inner ring of columns supporting a small dome, and creating, with the outer walls, a curved colonnade within the church. The surviving mosaics are in the barrel vault of this colonnade, and continue round it. A further series, with scenes from Genesis and from the New Testament, once decorated the drum of the dome.[3] The focal point of the church was the porphyry sarcophagus of Sta Costanza which stood astride the circle formed by the pillars of the colonnade immediately opposite the entrance, on the far side of the church; and the design of the decoration leads up to this centre-piece. The actual sarcophagus is in the Vatican Museum, but a full-size cast, coloured like the original, has now been placed in the church and gives an idea of the importance of this magnificent object in the architecture and decoration of the building. The vaulted recess above it[4] contains the remains of a pattern of stars, black on a white ground; traces of what was the gold of a ☧ symbol can still be seen.[5] The carvings on the sarcophagus represent *putti* harvesting grapes, and are echoed on one section of the mosaics.

It is possible to regard these mosaics (which were, in fact, extensively but very well restored early in the nineteenth century[6]), simply as an antique decorative scheme dating from an age when Christian art as such had hardly begun to exist. In many ways they resemble decorations found in pagan buildings long before the time of Constantine. The vine symbol, in particular, was used to suggest the joys of immortality in the Dionysiac mystery cults and need not be Christian in intention. But the main lines of the symbolism in this instance seem clear (the Christian element

35

28

having been more obvious when the mosaics of the dome still existed) and to question the Christian intention of the series in the vault of the colonnade seems paradoxical. The mosaics in the bays on each side correspond, so that whether we go round the colonnade to the right or to the left towards the tomb, we encounter a similar series of panels in the same order. Those by the door are simplest, a delicate geometric pattern in blue and white. Wilpert noticed in it the *crux gemmata* (jewelled cross), which, typically of this scheme of decoration, could be intentional, but might be an accident of the pattern. The mosaics nearest the sarcophagus are incomparably more elaborate and richly coloured, with fruits, birds, vessels of all kinds for pouring water, and an umbrella-like object that seems also to be a fluted vessel. It and other vessels scattered through this design are perhaps symbols of purification, and the fruits suggest the garden which is the meaning of the word 'Paradise', while birds symbolize the power of the soul to rise above earthly things.[7] In these two corresponding bays of the mosaic alone, next to the sarcophagus, touches of gold are used with great effect to enhance the richness of the symbolism. Thus the journey from the entrance to the sarcophagus leads from the ordinary and worldly, through the vine harvest (which is death, or perhaps more precisely the Last Day; the symbol comes probably from Revelation xiv. 17–20) represented in the intermediate panels, to the sarcophagus.

I, 36, 37

The extent to which the reading of symbolism into the other panels would be justified is a matter for discussion: whether there is an allusion to the Christian fish symbol in the four dolphins, heads together, tails away like the spokes of a wheel, in the second section of the vault, or whether these are simply decoration; similarly also, whether the figures of cupids and psyches are allegorical and why the birds and lambs are associated with them.

38

In the harvest section that follows the vine is surely the True Vine, Christ (this, as a Christian motif, having already appeared in the earliest Christian catacombs of the first to second centuries). Among the branches are *putti* picking grapes. In some corners more *putti* are treading the grapes, and the juice is flowing out of the tank in which they have been placed, while elsewhere others again are leading ox-carts that contain the harvested fruit. While many of the fronds in this scroll are vine fronds and the vines botanically plausible, with bunches of grapes showing here and there, other fronds are of a different character, and at the root of the stem are traditional acanthus leaves such as can be seen on earlier classical decorative scrolls.[8] Leonardi[9] shows that to the early Fathers the vine harvest signified martydom; but he thinks that in the graphic arts the vine was simply adopted, for Christian use, as a symbol of joyful immortality. But it is hard to believe that it had failed, by this date, to acquire 'overtones' from St John's Gospel. The detailed activities of the *putti* do not matter. But the idea of the harvest, the end of one life and the beginning of another, is central. The identity of the figures (head and shoulders) in the centre of each of these harvesting scenes is uncertain. The view that they are Constantina and her husband is a possible one. Almost certainly one is a man, the other a woman. They have some similarities with the Sta Pudenziana heads, discussed below, which are some fifty years later. The pattern of heads and busts in the next section seems to be purely decorative.

VII   Sta Costanza, mosaic in the vault
(mid-fourth century). Cupid and Psyche pattern.

28   The huge and most splendid porphyry sarcophagus mentioned above is the focus of the decorative scheme. On it, again, while the main design of the *putti* and grape harvest might be purely decorative in intention and without religious significance, in the context of the peacocks (one of the most widespread of Christian symbols later) and lambs, it can hardly be doubted that sarcophagus and mosaics were designed in association with a definitely Christian intention.

40-41   Apart from the mosaics in the vault, there are two, sometimes thought to be much later, which decorate two small apsidal recesses within the side walls. Wilpert, however, considered them to be approximately contemporary with the mosaics in the vault, and he is surely right. The dun background and the absence of gold create a strong presumption of an early date. The metallic *tesserae* used in the festoons of fruit that edge these mosaics were perhaps all added by a restorer, the original having been yellow. The low pitch of the apse distorts figures that seem always to have been curiously rough in execution, but may have lost much of their original character through restoration. That the original workmanship was somewhat more elegant can be inferred from the fine quality of some of the rich decorative work in the borders. These two mosaics are at a level which made them an easy prey for the restorer. One shows Christ more heavily bearded and older than in the other, seated on the globe of the Firmament against a background of fruiting palm trees, receiving someone whom Wilpert interpreted as St Peter, who approaches from the right in an attitude of humility. The scene is generally taken as the *traditio clavium* or handing over of the keys. Christ holds out some object (its identity being obscured by restoration) in his right hand. In Wilpert's view, this was originally the key of Peter. But the clothes of the figure seem feminine. W. N. Schumacher, in the second of two articles on these two apsidal

40   mosaics,[10] puts forward a different theory. He points to the lack of balance in the design as it remains at present (having suffered a number of restorations) and believes that its asymmetry is due to the disappearance of a balancing figure on the right. The difficulty about this view is the fact that the axis of the figure of Christ is not central to the design, but has been shifted substantially to the right—not far enough, perhaps, to give a balanced composition, but too far for us to imagine a figure on the right-hand side taking its place easily in the design. It would seem to be most unusual, indeed without precedent in the mosaic series, for a saint or martyr (for example, St Agnes) to approach the Almighty without a sponsor. The problem may be without a solution, the original design having disappeared without leaving sufficient trace. It is possible that a restorer at some period had in mind the notion of St Agnes approaching the heavenly throne. A more precise interpretation is now impossible.

41   The subject of the other apse mosaic has also been a matter of controversy. St Peter and St Paul are shown approaching a youthful, though bearded, Christ, holding his right hand open in bestowal. In his left hand is a scroll, which falls into the arms of Peter. Both apostles are represented as in extreme old age, bent almost double; Peter's age especially seems to be emphasized in contrast to the youthfulness of Christ. In the original the figure may have been beardless. In the existing version a beard seems to be intended. Christ is shown standing on the clouds above a hill from which as usual flow the four rivers of Paradise. The huts to right and left seem to be forerunners of the cities of Bethlehem and Jerusalem, regularly represented in the right- and left-hand corners of later apsidal mosaics in Rome; the four sheep presumably represent the flock of apostles, the fruiting palms the riches of Paradise. The difficulty lies in the wording on the scroll, which at present reads DOMINVS PACEM DA. Wilpert took the scene as the *traditio legis* and believed therefore that the original must have read DOMINVS LEGEM DAT, as in the inscription of the analogous and magnificent (though largely ruined) Naples mosaic of about this date, in the cathedral

baptistry. Schumacher makes an unanswerable case for this view.[11] He shows both the association of the theme with representations of pagan imperial ceremony, and its connection with the theme of the St Peter's apse. Incidentally, the type of St Paul is here close enough to an unusual head on a sarcophagus, dated by Gerke about 380,[12] for that to be considered perhaps as evidence for a similar date for this mosaic.

The strongest argument for a later date for these two mosaics is the difference in intention between them and the mosaics of the vault. These are explicitly religious. It seems, indeed, certain that the mosaics of the drum were also religious, the scenes in the lower register being from the Old Testament, those above from the New.[13] To judge from the drawings which record the drum mosaics, that scheme was 'humanistic' like the mosaics of the vault, the framework within which the pictures were displayed being elegantly non-Christian, even though not positively pagan, the only visual hint of the supernatural being the halo which Christ seems to have worn in the one New Testament scene of which a fairly close record survives. The mosaics of the vault, as we have seen, are probably symbolical, but could be purely decorative. But the two apsidal mosaics proclaim a Christian message, and were designed to do this rather than to form an element of the rich decoration, of which the mosaics of the drum, because of their idiom and their pattern, formed, by contrast with these, an integral part. The explanation may be that they were made twenty or thirty years after the mosaics of the vault, perhaps after the burial of Constantina in the mausoleum which had been built for her during her life.

Sta Pudenziana

The mosaic in the apse is the remains of late fourth-century work. Part of an inscription was still legible in the sixteenth century; de Rossi reconstructed it in the form SALVO INNOCENTIO EPISCOPO ILICIO MAXIMO ET . . . PRESBYTERIS LEOPARDVS PRESB. SVMPTV PROPRIO . . . MARMORIBVS ET PICTVRIS DECORAVIT, 'When Innocent [Innocent I, Pope 401–17] was bishop [of Rome] and Ilicius, Maximus and . . . were presbyters, Leopardus the Presbyter made these decorations of marble and of pictures'.[14] A stone inscription also existed which mentioned Pope Siricius, in whose reign (384–99) the work was evidently begun. The mosaic was repaired by Pope Adrian,[15] whose monogram was at one time incorporated in the mosaic; but none of this medieval work is identifiable.

As originally constructed, the mosaic was far larger than at present. The huge Evangelist symbols against the sky must have been immensely impressive, and to imagine them standing free (not severely clipped as at present), with the cross towering up in the centre, gives an idea of the size of the mosaic in its original form. It certainly included all twelve apostles, though the outermost on both sides had disappeared by 1588, when the first picture of it was made. At that date it was still deep enough in the centre to show the feet of the Agnus Dei. On each side of the two central apostles, a cornice was built up in 1588 to conceal the damage to the lower edge. It was removed later when the High Altar was built.

The two figures behind St Paul and St Peter have been variously interpreted, sometimes as the Churches of the Circumcision and of the Gentiles,[16] in which case it is to the two apostles that they are shown holding out their wreaths. In the original design, however, with the whole range of twelve apostles shown, they were less conspicuous than now; they might be the two sisters, Sta Pudenziana and Sta Prassede, holding out their martyrs' crowns towards Christ. He is seated on a throne, above the range of the apostles. His right hand is extended in blessing and in his left hand is a book inscribed DOMINVS CONSERVATOR ECCLESIAE PVDENTIANAE. It is to be noticed

6, 42, 44

45

that apart from the central figure ('Christ the Philosopher' teaching his apostles as after his resurrection, but still, as it were, almost on the same plane as they), two other Christological elements were included: the Agnus Dei below and the cross itself. The dove also formed part of the design (below) and so probably did the Divine Hand in the crown of the apse.

A difficulty about the identification (which is, nevertheless, certain) of the apostle on Christ's right as St Paul is that his open book contains the first words of the First Gospel. This Gospel should belong to the Ecclesia ex Circumcisione and St Peter, if it belongs anywhere other than to St Matthew himself. The fragment of apparently older work in the centre of the pages seems enough to identify the Gospel. But G. B. de Rossi gave reasons for thinking that the inscription on the book was originally entirely different, basing his opinion on a drawing of the fragment in the apostle's hand made by J. M. Suarez, in the seventeenth century. Suarez thought the inscription was concerned with the founding of the church and the officials associated with it, and perhaps ended with a date. (HONORIO AVG IIII ET EVTYCIANO COS, 'In the consulship of the Emperor Honorius, Consul for the fourth time, and of Eutycianus'.) If this is so the words of St Matthew are an arbitrary insertion, surely before Camuccini's work in the first half of the nineteenth century, for his standards make it most unlikely that he would have been responsible for an invention of this kind. The mosaic (or the fragment of mosaic left after the architectural alterations of 1588 had been carried out) was restored, at that time, in plaster. We should accordingly have to assume the insertion of this verse at a later date by some ecclesiastical authority interested in St Matthew.[17] Most of the original work now remaining is on the left-hand side of the mosaic.

Above the arcade of pictured windows that forms the background of the figures are rows of decoration in green and gold (the motif being intended to represent the tiles of the roof) and the figure of Christ in the centre. Above the tiles of this arcade there are, on each side, groups of buildings represented with remarkable naturalism[18] (contrast, for example, the 'Jerusalem' and 'Bethlehem' in Sta Maria Maggiore, only a little later); above them is the sky, with striations of blue, pink, red, brown and gold, and in the centre, on what might be a rocky hill (immediately behind the head of Christ, which is surrounded by a gold nimbus), an immense jewelled cross. On both sides of this, in the sky, are the symbols of the evangelists, from left to right the angel of St Matthew, the winged lion of St Mark, the winged bull of St Luke, the eagle of St John. The figure immediately on Christ's right is, as we have seen, St Paul; that on Christ's left, with the greenish cloak, is St Peter. In the figures on Christ's left, little that is original remains, except the head of St Peter himself, and the martyr's crown (in the hand of St Praxed) held above it. The rest is modern. On Christ's right, more early work remains: the head of the apostle next to St Paul may be partly restored, but the others are intact; the shoulder of the same figure is a restoration, as is the hand of St Paul; otherwise, up to and including the symbol of St Mark, this side is still mainly fourth-century work. The figure of Christ is a patchwork of restoration, the left-hand side of the throne being original, the right-hand side apparently restored; and it has been too often repaired for us to discover what was there at first. His cloak has the monogram 'L'; his tunic (like the tunics of the other figures) bears the *clavus* in different colours. The amount of colour in the apostles' clothes would certainly not have been used at a later date, when tunics and cloaks came to be executed in white. The splendid series of original heads that remain—St Peter on Christ's left (the only original head on this side), St Paul on his right,[19] the figure standing behind St Paul, and the three figures further to the left (that is, next to St Paul)—are reminiscent of classical portraiture, as is a head, executed in a strikingly similar technique, in Sta Costanza. Even in this limited group, two hands can be distinguished at work in Sta

Pudenziana. In the work of one, the abler of the two, the sharp black shadows are already tending to become outlines. This is noticeable in the profile of the noble St Paul, where the nose is precisely outlined, rather than its shadow suggested; in the next head (though it is by the same hand), the dark line which sets the shape of the nose on the face is within a light shadow, and the artist has forborne to use a sharp line on the other side of the nose. The drawing of the two heads farthest to the left is more tentative. The third in this group, though partly original, has unforunately suffered some damage on the forehead and elsewhere, which obscures its quality. The lines in the first two heads, where they exist, are dotted, rather than continuous. If the group as a whole is compared, on the one hand, with the earlier portrait head in Sta Costanza with its blotchy technique and its rejection of outlines, and, on the other, with the work of the Aphrodisius mosaic in Sta Maria Maggiore, in which outlines are becoming more pronounced, one tendency in stylistic development from the mid-fourth to the mid-fifth century can be observed. 39, 56

In terms of its general intention, the mosaic is the first, or at any rate the first surviving, of a new type; its designs are planned to be something far more than symbolic decoration. Not only the narrative parts of the mosaic, but also the evangelist symbols (symbols though they are), are part of this new intention, in that they are designed not simply to be evocative, like the lamb or the peacock of some earlier works, but to impress an idea (in the case of the evangelist symbols, no doubt that of the supreme importance of the four canonical Gospels). So here, though the techniques remain classical, though the character of the portraits is close to that of the two portraits in Sta Costanza and to many others in pagan classical works, the mosaic as a whole marks the beginning of a new era in Christian art. It is one of the most fascinating mixtures of old and new that is to be found among the mosaic decorations of these churches.

ST PETER'S: CONSTANTINIAN FRAGMENTS IN THE OLD BASILICA
The façade of the old basilica of St Peter's was decorated with a mosaic representing the twenty-four Elders of the Apocalypse. This mosaic was undoubtedly the ancestor of the many versions of the theme which were set up in the churches of Rome during the Middle Ages, often on the triumphal arch. Their treatment in surviving examples is almost invariably highly conventionalized, the single exception being a tiny fragment of early work from such a series, discovered in Sta Maria Maggiore.[20] No fragments exist of the St Peter's version. It may in fact have dated from the reign not of Constantine but of Pope Leo I about a century later.

There was, however, an apse behind the altar of St Peter decorated with a mosaic;[21] and the character of this is better known, since before its destruction a representation was painted in fresco 29 in the Grottoes, while there are also sketches in two Vatican MSS.[22] The mosaic had three registers: the lowest carried the inscription; the next showed sheep, representing the apostles, emerging from Jerusalem (left) and Bethlehem (right). When the mosaic was repaired by Innocent III he inserted in this register a figure of himself on one side of the Agnus Dei (left), and on the other a second figure, a woman (right) representing the Ecclesia Romana. The two heads of these figures 176, 177 survive with another small fragment, the Dove which was Innocent III's badge.[23] This thirteenth century work is bold and highly stylized but must have jarred uncomfortably with what remained of the original.

Above, in the upper register, were Christ between St Peter and St Paul, Peter on Christ's left, Paul on his right. Neither had the attributes which were to become traditional (St Peter's keys and St Paul's sword), nor was the iconography of the portraits of the type which later became established, though both were labelled. On each side was a fruiting palm tree, and on the ground, much smaller in scale, were four pairs of tiny figures and a single figure at each end, called by Schumacher *genie*. Below were the four rivers of Paradise with deer drinking from them; above, in the crown of the apse, was the tabernacle or tent of Paradise, with a small Greek cross in the apex. The form this tabernacle took is well represented by that in the mosaic of S. Paolo, which was an almost exact copy of it. The border of the mosaic was a classical pattern, the motif developed out of two urns or chalices, but the ornament in general was quite unlike the pattern of flower festoons which came to be adopted conventionally in later apsidal mosaics in this position. There was apparently no special feature (as there regularly was later) where the ornaments met at the summit of the apse; this border was thus not divided into two sides, but was a continuous design.

186

The interest of this work lies partly in its anticipation of and differences from the pattern of apsidal mosaics which was to become conventional in Rome. Elements that constantly recur are the band of inscription below and the flock of sheep representing the apostles, the four rivers of Paradise and the drinking deer, and the tabernacle or tent of heaven above. But in no surviving mosaic do the little figures representing the rest of the apostles (dwarfed by Peter and Paul) recur, while the border is also *sui generis*. This particular ornament could only have been used in classical times or during the Renaissance period. There is no intermediate period when such a design would have been in place.

A single fragment from what is, I believe, the original part of this mosaic still survives. It is the half figure of St Paul. He faces half right, the right arm held out across the body, the hand extended to lead the eye to the central figure. This fragment is sometimes said to come from the Oratory of John VII; but the precision of the setting, the modelling and absence of bounding lines makes this date impossible. The style is unusual, perhaps without close parallel in Rome, though two mosaic heads from the catacombs of St Ciriacus, reproduced by G. B. de Rossi,[24] seem to me, judging from his large-scale illustration, to have resembled it in technique. De Rossi was himself puzzled by this fragment and regarded it as so much restored as to have lost its authenticity. One's first impression might indeed be that it was seventeenth century. But this is a dangerous conclusion to reach without reasonable evidence for it, since it was to the antique that painters were looking for their models. They worked designedly in the antique manner. Moreover, this head seems to date from a period before the traditional iconography of St Paul, already seen in Sta Pudenziana, was securely established. One would not expect a seventeenth-century imitator to do otherwise than follow the traditional portraiture. The type then is a strong argument for an early date, which means that the credentials of the fragment deserve serious examination.

III, 31

Its documentation consists simply of an accompanying inscription. It was saved from the destruction of the old basilica in 1631. It came from the 'Apse of Innocent III before the High Altar' (IN APSIDE INNOCENTII PAPAE III ANTE ALTARE S. PETRI HIC MDCXXXI AFFIXA) and represents St Paul. Fortunately the design of this apse is known from a number of sketches made in the sixteenth century. These were studied by Wilpert, who came to the conclusion, no doubt rightly, that the mosaic of the apse had been restored, not created, by Innocent III. In his view, the restorers preserved the original character of the mosaic. Certain parts were missing, and they had to be replaced. These seem to have included the two 'cities' of Jerusalem and Bethlehem which, in the surviving sketches, have an orientalizing character foreign to the earlier mosaic. They look almost as if designed for the Brighton Pavilion. But the main figures remained intact, and this fragment seems to be one of them. When one compares it with the design as preserved in the fresco, one sees an almost indisputably close correspondence.

29

To examine it in detail is to assure oneself immediately of certain points. The gold background, wherever it comes from, was not put there by the man who worked on the head. The work on the head is of great refinement, the *tesserae* set so close that one could hardly insert the blade of a penknife between them. The surface is that flat surface so much admired in antiquity (and again, of course, during the Renaissance). The materials used in the head and draperies are natural marbles. By contrast with the flat surface of the figure the gold is an 'incrustation' on the surface. It is most interestingly manipulated, the work lines around the head forming a circular pattern which is eccentric to the head itself and the halo, and which thus gives the suggestion of a glow emanating from the apostle's face. The early gold *tesserae* are sometimes of red glass, sometimes of very dark glass, rather large in size, very irregular in shape. Above Paul's right shoulder there is a patch where they have clearly been lost, the new patch reaching up into the halo and as far as the neck. There is more renewal of the gold background on the lower right-hand side of the figure. There seems to be a patch of restoration above the ear and another on the drapery between the wrist and the beard, this patch perhaps extending on to the back of the hand, now somewhat awkwardly placed in relation to the fingers. The most likely explanation of these facts is a fairly straightforward one. The mosaic in its original mid-fourth-century form had a background not of gold, but perhaps of whitish-grey, perhaps of dark blue;[25] a century later it was embellished by a gold background. There were no doubt extensive later repairs to this background as a whole in Innocent III's restoration. But his artists were able to leave the figure itself almost untouched. The newest gold dates presumably from the 1631 setting. A group of *tesserae* were missing above the elbow in the fabric of St Paul's mantle; there the surface was consolidated without any new *tesserae* being inserted.

It is worth while comparing this figure with another fragment which was extracted from 110 the ruins of the old basilica and mounted at this same date, 1631. It comes, so its inscription tells us, from the ciborium in the oratory of John VII. Unfortunately it was badly damaged by the time it came to be moved. The two kneeling figures on each side of the Virgin are sadly battered, and the lower part of the mosaic has suffered extensively. An early break can be traced right across the central figure. But the part that is best preserved is the head and shoulders of the Virgin and the head of the Child, a remarkable illustration of a technique very similar to the Byzantine techniques practised later: the *tesserae* are very small, worked in neat lines, much of the material used being apparently natural, and not glass. The repairs to the lower part look as if they had been done long before the seventeenth century. The gold *tesserae* certainly did not come from the same workshop as those used in the St Paul.

Here then are two early mosaic fragments, consolidated and preserved at the same date, as relics of what the old basilica contained. They are wholly different in style; and the differences have been preserved by some seventeenth-century antiquarian whose standards are also perhaps apparent in the John VII fragments. Thus I find the view that the St Paul is substantially a seventeenth-century work impossible to accept,[26] especially as it seems to involve a seventeenth-century artist working within a border of much earlier, incrusted, gold *tesserae*. Though the technique of the head is unusual in Rome, it can be closely paralleled elsewhere, mainly in work from the east, with the same blocking-out of areas of colour and the same insistence on the methods of mosaic rather than of painting. The artists do not attempt to make subtle gradations of light and shade by using *tesserae* so small that they make no individual, only a mass, effect; here the individual units speak for themselves. The greens or reds or blues are clearly 'mapped out', so to speak, as they are in the third-century example from Antioch illustrated in L'Orange and Nordhagen.[27] In their fourth-century example from Antioch,[28] the *tesserae* are fitted together with greater precision, as they are in this St Paul, so that the mortar lines are less obtrusive. In the floor mosaics in the palace at Constantinople we see this same definite mapping out of areas of colour (rather than elaborate *chiaroscuro*) and a similar precision in the setting of the mosaic units. The conclusion may be thought to be justified that this is the remains of classical work from the Constantinian apse (which Innocent III restored), the figure being substantially intact, and that the surrounding, but later, gold background, technically so different from the work on the figure, has complicated the issue when this fragment has been discussed in the past. It is a confirmation of the early date that this portrait does not conform to the pattern that became traditional for the portraiture of St Paul, a pattern that was not established till the second half of the fourth century.[29]

Two other Constantinian fragments remain, each of exceptional quality, but neither can be
5   placed in any of the known schemes. One is the magnificent head of a cherub, the other (closely related to it in technique, since both are made overall of exceptionally fine *tesserae*) represents a
181   dove. These two are specimens of the technique which we have contrasted above with that of the St Paul, the individual elements being so small that the effect of each is lost in that of the whole, with the result that the most delicate gradations of colour, light and shade are possible. A swan,
182   often linked with the dove,[30] is not in fact a classical fragment remodelled in the twelfth century by Innocent III's restorers, but a fragment from the apsidal mosaic of S. Paolo fuori le Mura.[31]

St John Lateran: the head of Christ in the mosaic of the apse. S. Paolo fuori
le Mura: the head of Christ in the mosaic of the triumphal arch
The mosaic in the apse of St John Lateran has suffered many vicissitudes. It is one of the two bearing the 'signature' of Toriti, who recreated the mosaic of the apse as a whole in St John Lateran, as he did also that of Sta Maria Maggiore, in the last decade of the thirteenth century. There is wide agreement that, in both churches, he followed the general lines of much earlier work (of the late classical period[32]) and that, in both mosaics, some of the original detail was copied pre-
VIII   cisely. It was believed in the later Middle Ages that the head of Christ originally appeared miraculously in the Lateran apse. In the record of Toriti's restoration, his patron refers to putting this head in its place 'unharmed' (or perhaps 'renewed'; the phrase is VVLTVM INTEGRVM REPONI FECIT). But the legend has a significance beyond that of the sanctity of the 'portrait'. A contemporary record gives the information that in the thirteenth-century reconstruction the portrait was found to be constructed on its own independent bed of Travertine marble.[33] This feature no doubt lies behind the story of the sudden 'miraculous' appearance. When the portrait was originally put in its place, it was already a complete work in itself. The apsidal mosaic was taken down and rebuilt, in its entirety, in 1884, in connection with the extension and rebuilding of the apse. Yet even in our photograph, the lines of the independent bed, sloping down by each side of the head to a point outside the shoulders, can be seen, and the *tesserae* of that part of the halo (a halo lacking the cross,

VIII   St John Lateran, main mosaic of the apse.
The 'miraculous' head of Christ. Detail from a version made in 1884
of Toriti's mosaic, itself based on a classical original.

as in other early examples) have a different quality and seem to be set more roughly than the rest. In this modern version also, therefore, the head was build into the mosaic as an *emblema*.

We ought to have here, then, an actual ancient fragment incorporated in a work that is as a whole much later: an example (the only one in the whole series of Roman Christian mosaics) of the use of the *emblema* technique which was developed for expensive work in classical antiquity. But unfortunately the nineteenth-century restorers failed (as Wilpert showed, in an article[34] which also conclusively established the relationship between Toriti's mosaic and its classical predecessor) to preserve the relic that had survived a major restoration before, and we are forced to rely for our knowledge of it on an old photograph published in 1901, after the loss had been

32 sustained. And in a somewhat earlier engraving, fortunately more detailed than the photograph, the lines of the original *emblema* can again be seen, as they can in the modern substitute version which was worked in the same technique. The head seems to have been close in appearance to that in Sta Pudenziana, its equable expression a curious contrast to the tortured anxieties of the portrait that came to be substituted for it. Only in the chapel of St Venantius, in the baptistry adjoining the Lateran church, the Christ with its even, untroubled air seems to depend directly on it. The conception it represented became unfashionable and was usually replaced by something grim and austere. In technique, if we can regard as authentic the network of *tesserae* shown in the engraving, its closest relative may be the fragment from the Constantinian apse.[35]

185 The roundel in S. Paolo, the original of which was later, perhaps by as much as three-quarters of a century, than the St John head, may have been one of the first examples of this different fashion. The S. Paolo roundel had certainly assumed its present form, or something near it,

183 before the fire of 1823; the sketch made after the fire shows the roundel clearly. It seems probable that the original head also had some quality comparable to the grim, ascetic expression of the present version. Because of the strange idiom the head has been supposed to have been the work

23 of Syrian craftsmen. A roundel made somewhat later in S. Vitale, Ravenna, also shows the hand as being disproportionately small, almost deformed, and in this respect perhaps echoes the original in S. Paolo. For even though there is evidence[36] that, in the seventeenth century, part of the S. Paolo mosaic, showing the hands, was already missing, there may have been impressions in the

XI mortar, if that survived, to justify the restorer's version. In expression, the Christ in SS. Cosma e Damiano, the next important mosaic in the Roman sequence, resembles the head in the S. Paolo roundel more than the Lateran head. Yet it emphasizes not so much the austerity as the tremendous power of Christ; in spite of Hoogewerff's view, it seems to me to belong to a different climate of thought from that of the image that we can reconstruct of the 'miraculous head', and Hoogewerff's suggestion that it is directly derived from the 'miraculous head' seems to me unlikely.

32 M. Gerspach's engraving of the 'miraculous head' gives some notion not only of the expression but also of the structural lines into which the *tesserae* were worked, and can be taken as some evidence of its technique. The larger *tesserae* of the background on the right-hand side can hardly be simply imaginary, and they represent almost certainly an early repair. In general, the *tesserae* were evidently, as pointed out by E. Munz, a French observer[37] who saw the mosaic in 1876, 'fort gros'; and his phrase reinforces the impression which a comparison of the engraving with the

31 St Paul fragment from the old basilica of St Peter's creates. The 'miraculous head' perhaps had a gold halo from the first. The *tesserae* were large; the colour was mapped out in substantial areas, as in the case of the head of St Paul, not worked with tiny units into almost invisible gradations of light and shade; and the work lines were probably visible.[38] The technique of the two suggests

that they were close in date. If the St Peter's mosaic was fourth-century in date, this was also; if fifth, this must go with it. The S. Paolo roundel was wholly different from them both, in intention as well as technique.

STA MARIA MAGGIORE: THE FIFTH-CENTURY MOSAICS

Three groups of mosaics in Sta Maria Maggiore have an interest for the study of antique classical style: (*a*) the framed panels in the nave, of which twenty-five still survive, some much damaged; *46–54, 55–60* (*b*) the mosaics on the triumphal arch; (*c*) the main mosaic of the apse. This last is a signed work **XXVIII** by the artist Toriti (calling himself in the inscription 'pictor', the painter), and was made under *197–199* the patronage of Cardinal Colonna and Pope Nicholas IV (1287–94). But it is now generally accepted that the artist was to a large extent following the lines, and to some extent using the detail, of the antique classical mosaic originally constructed in the apse in the fifth century, in the time of Sixtus III (the XYSTVS EPISCOPVS whose name appears on the triumphal arch). This mosaic of the apse will be discussed in terms of the later date. The classical border is separately treated here,[39] but it is worth emphasizing that, while only (*a*) and (*b*) are considered at this point, (*c*) and its related mosaics, which throw light on the classical style of the fifth century, must be taken into account in any full assessment of this.[40]

There has been an increasing disposition in recent years on the part of some authorities, and of C. Cecchelli in particular, whose book[41] on the mosaics of the church as a whole was published in 1956, to regard groups (*a*) and (*b*) as belonging to the same period, namely, the reign of Sixtus III, as against earlier views that the nave mosaics were so different in style from the triumphal arch mosaics that they must be assigned to a distinctly earlier period. As mentioned elsewhere,[42] the mosaics of the nave were made on independent beds, and therefore were probably not constructed *in situ* on the wall to which they now belong, though they may of course have been made for it, if not on it. Such a technique was commonly used for fine mosaics in earlier antiquity, especially for elegant centre-pieces (*emblemata* or insets), which were embodied in patterns produced by less expensive craftsmen. Some of those who have held the view that the nave mosaics were earlier than those of the triumphal arch have believed that they were made for a basilica earlier than the present one, and were among the elements of this earlier building incorporated by Sixtus III when he rebuilt it. Others have doubted whether an earlier basilica on this site existed, and have supposed that the nave mosaics were made for a different church and removed here, as the independent bedding would make possible, by Sixtus.

Neither of these views commended themselves to Cecchelli, who rejected unhesitatingly the archaeological argument used to support the hypothesis of mosaics introduced from elsewhere. His view was that the two series, are, roughly at least, contemporary; that stylistically there are some close similarities; and that some general stylistic differences (which are admitted to exist between them) can be adequately explained by the completely different type of subject. Thus the triumphal arch mosaics are concerned with the Annunciation and with the childhood of Christ. But their treatment of the theme is unusual. There is no scene of the Nativity. In the Epiphany scene, where Christ is usually represented on his mother's knee, he is here shown seated by himself on a large throne. He is attended by angels. His mother is sitting independently on his right and a second female figure in a dark mantle, whose place seems to be set farther forward than that of the Virgin, is on the other side of the child. This second figure is represented on a slightly larger scale *55, 59* and therefore seems to be of even greater importance than the Virgin. She is regarded by Cecchelli as representing Divine Wisdom.[43] Others have seen in her a representation of the Church, and have compared her with the two figures of the churches in Sta Sabina (see Plate 74). E. Mâle, in a characteristically brilliant passage,[44] reads this whole scene as a condemnation of the current heresy denounced by the Council of Ephesus: that is to say, it shows the Child already as divine, belonging to a different order of being (as it were) from that of his mother; and it therefore discards, by implication, the view that divinity entered into him only at his baptism. Whatever the right interpretation of the second figure, there is no doubt that the treatment is intended to stress the divinity of the Child.

Another unusual scene seems to have a similar intention. It is taken from one of the apocryphal Gospels and shows an incident of the flight into Egypt, in which a pagan ruler, Aphrodisius, recognized Christ as divine. The theme of the triumphal arch mosaics as a whole is therefore the divinity of Christ in childhood. He is shown accompanied by a sort of court of angels. And it is fairly argued that such a theme calls for a different treatment from that of episodes in the lives of the Patriarchs Abraham, Isaac and Jacob, and of Joshua, which are the subject of the nave mosaics. Our problem therefore becomes a matter of degree. How different in style and technique is the one group from the other?

The artists of the mosaic of the triumphal arch
If we could find the same hand at work somewhere in both series, that would be almost un-answerable evidence of their being contemporary. But there appears to be no overlap. We can, I think, identify at least five hands in the work on the triumphal arch, and perhaps eight, very tentatively, in the nave mosaics—all different from the five of the triumphal arch. Though there are some important resemblances, the differences seem to me to be even more striking.[45]

Two elements in the classical tradition, readily identified in much of the work of this period, we shall find recurring in both series of mosaics: the impressive feeling for solidity (a sort of third-dimensional quality), and the sense of individuality. The artist of the Annunciation section shows the first finely in the solid modelling of the angels' drapery (Plate 58). The heavy, rounded folds have an almost tactile quality. The face of the angel on the right (Plate 58) again shows this feeling, of which we are also aware in the work of other hands (for example, in the body of one of Aphrodisius's attendants). But, besides these elements, a new quality of vision is em-bodied in the mosaics, a quality not observed in Sta Costanza or Sta Pudenziana, though it must be regarded as a legacy of the classical tradition. It was to become immensely important in the development of style in the ninth-century mosaics, and is a kind of impressionism, of concern with the effects of light. In the triumphal arch mosaics, Cecchelli associates this especially with

IX   Sta Maria Maggiore, mosaic of the triumphal arch (*c.* 435).
The city gate of Jerusalem. The sheep symbolize apostles.

the artist who executed the Presentation section. A detail, rightly famous and often reproduced, shows three heads of elders who form part of the audience of the scene. The regular patterns of *tesserae* out of which the heads would be constructed in a classical mosaic of the type which sought more solid effects, are here (at least so far as the faces are concerned) broken up, with brilliant results. The faces are individualized: younger on the left, older and heavier in the centre, not quite so old on the right. But the main interest is in the shifting, darting glance of the eyes, and a mobility of look which is achieved by what has been described elsewhere in this book as a sort of *pointilliste* effect. This artist was also responsible for most of the principal figures in the Epiphany scene.[46] The four faces of angels standing behind the throne show something of the scintillating quality described above. We see also, in the draperies, the characteristic use of white highlights (quite unlike the draperies of the Annunciation angels, where the marked idiosyncrasy is the use of solid, darker lines, often only a single *tessera* thick, in the furrows of the folds). This Presentation artist is often curiously content to represent hands in a strange, claw-like form (the Christ Child and the figure of Divine Wisdom in the Epiphany scene, and the right hand of Joseph, as he turns towards the prophetess, in the Presentation scene). These characteristics help to identify his work.

The faces and clothes of the main Aphrodisius group show the work of a third artist. A fourth, so different in style that I have sometimes suspected him of belonging to a different generation, was responsible for the Massacre of the Innocents scene. The rounded faces, straggling hair and wide-open eyes (features that are, here, not strongly individualized as between one woman and another) are unlike anything by the other hands, as is the dotted technique of outlining faces and helmets, for Herod and the soldiers round him. This artist, as Cecchelli says, has something of a genius for colour. His work is a forceful reminder of the fact that in any period when good work was being done, we must expect to find that varied styles have emerged.[47] The other Herod scene on the opposite side of the arch is by yet another hand. Here the characteristic is the dark outlining of one side of the face only, in order to give the impression of light and shade. The brilliant *pointilliste* technique is thus substantially confined to the work of one artist in this group, the Presentation artist, though the work of others, and particularly the Annunciation artist, at times has some suggestions of it.

Contrasts between the mosaics of the triumphal arch and of the nave
Before the question of the different artists at work in the nave panels is discussed, some more general points of contrast between these panels and the arch mosaics may be mentioned. The difference in the use of gold has been discussed briefly elsewhere.[48] In the nave panels (as in no other mosaics discussed in this book) not only do touches of gold highlight the mosaics (they do this also in Sta Costanza, and, far more lavishly, in Sta Pudenziana), but gold is used also in large patches, not to create the whole background and so to provide the dominant characteristic as it were of the *mise-en-scène*, but rather to add interest and variety. A singular example is No 18, the battle with the Amalekites. Moses and his two companions are the dominating figures in the scene. But the streak of gold positively avoids them, streaming down from the upper right-hand corner towards the middle of the picture.[49] More typically, as in the two scenes of No 23 (the lower scene being the carrying of the ark with the blowing of rams' horns round the city of Jericho; the upper, the fall of the city), it is a band of colour stretching across the background, but not reaching up into the sky. In one of the two scenes showing Abraham with the angels, it seems to be used deliberately to focus attention on them (in the lower half of the panel), but

equally deliberately it is avoided in the upper half. By contrast with the practice in the nave mosaics, on the triumphal arch a gold background is the rule rather than the exception—so much so that a casual glance at the arch gives the impression of a gold background throughout. This impression is not borne out by all the detail. But some scenes are set against a full gold background, and the general impression is, in this respect, completely different from that of the nave mosaics.[50] Though this might be explained by the difference of subject, it is at least a point that demands consideration.

There seems, however, to be a technical difference between the two series, which cannot be explained away,[51] and which is almost decisive in the question of period—almost, but perhaps not quite, for we can imagine the possibility of different workshops, possibly in different parts of Italy, being employed simultaneously on the two series. The difference is in the general method of setting the *tesserae*. A few among the mosaics of the nave, the work of vividly 'impressionistic' artists, represent some of the finest achievements in the idiom ever produced: for instance, the detail from panel No 11 also illustrated by Cecchelli.[52] In this, in his photographs from No 19[53] **IV** (which surely represent a pinnacle in the achievement of ancient mosaic) and in another detail **51** he gives, the texture of the surface is seen to be compact. As Cecchelli has observed, the *tesserae* are mainly squared. Irregularly shaped chips are comparatively unusual. With this is to be contrasted the far looser texture, the less regular form of each *tessera*, and the much more uneven surface of the triumphal arch work, as shown, for example, in Plates 12 and 14. It will be noticed that the technique shown in work on the triumphal arch in some details anticipates strikingly what was to be done a hundred years later in the Justinian mosaics in Ravenna. The resemblance **13, 14** is not as strong as it might seem at first sight. The Ravennate work is more orderly (in the working of the face, neck and forehead, for example); the drawing of the head is more elaborate (the varieties of tone used being greater) and more careful. In so far as the Roman work achieves an impression not only of the lights playing over the face but also of its structure, it does so by the most subtle suggestion of light and shade. One is basically a drawing; the other is not. There is no drawing at all in the face of the Virgin in the Roman mosaic. And the orderliness of the Justinian mosaic is seen to a far greater degree in some of the early Salonika mosaics. But, to return to the **15, 16** fundamental difference of technique between the nave series and the triumphal arch mosaics, this seems to argue a difference of workshop at least, and could be more naturally explained if there was also a difference of time. The flat, closely-knit surface of most of the nave mosaics belongs to the dying classical epoch. That of the Presentation artist, loosely knit and deliberately uneven, is something new.

Having said that, we must go on to say that the interest of the artists of the nave panels, like that of the Presentation artist (the texture of whose work is so different in detail), is also impressionistic. It is these vivid, momentary glances, varying intensely from individual to individual, captured by using single *tesserae* as points of light and of colour, that make the work at its best so effective. One sees this again and again on a miniature scale in the mosaics that show soldiers **28** marching or in battle. There is no question of simply repeating a pattern—as there is so often in medieval representations of the twenty-four elders, for example. One has the delightful feeling that these armies would never be in step, that the call for 'eyes front' would always fall on deaf ears. The use of these momentary effects of light and shade to individualize a figure or to characterize a scene is rare in classical mosaics. But something of the kind is visible in some of the Piazza **11** Armerina mosaics in Sicily, and in some of the mosaics of the palace floor in Constantinople. A **10** similar result is aimed at in certain paintings that have survived, such as the Pompeian Trojan

Horse.[54] These Pompeian paintings are seldom of first-class quality. But this one, and a considerable number of others, show that artists had been aware of, and had attempted to capture, those effects of light and variety on which the mosaic artists are here concentrating. In this interest, then, they show an affinity with an earlier classical tradition.

A final point to be noticed that again emphasizes the difference between the nave series, on the one hand, and the mosaics of the arch (which so often anticipate medieval practice), on the other, is the style of the festoons in the soffits of the triumphal arch. This is the first example in Rome of a pattern that was to become standard, both for the soffits of the triumphal arch and for the rim of the apse. The theme is always a festoon of flowers (sometimes including fruit; sometimes also small animals, and heads in roundels) growing out of a flower pot at the base of the soffit. What is remarkable about this, the first example, is that it is so highly formalized. Much later (in Sta Agnese for example, or S. Lorenzo) the festoon can still be surprisingly naturalistic. In this respect, also, the Sta Maria Maggiore triumphal arch mosaic looks forward to the medieval style. The contrast between it and the festoons of flowers on the vault of the chapel of St John in the baptistry of St John Lateran is striking.

61

75, 76

68, 69

Our provisional conclusions may be summarized thus. While both series of mosaics, those of the triumphal arch and those of the nave, belong to the late classical world, those of the nave represent a purer classical tradition, being technically far closer to the fine mosaics of earlier centuries. The impressionistic effect at which they aim was already recognizable, in mosaics and in paintings, as one of the objectives that the artists of antiquity sometimes set themselves. An analogous effect is aimed at by one of the most notable artists of the triumphal arch series who in this respect might be called the successor of the artists of the nave series. But he achieved the effect in different ways, and the variety of plane and the looseness of setting which characterize his work in particular, and that of his associates also to a large extent, mark out the triumphal arch mosaics as notably different from, and more prophetic of the future than, the brilliant nave panels. It cannot be claimed that these differences exclude the possibility of the two series being contemporary. But it seems probable, simply on stylistic and technical grounds, that the nave mosaics are the earlier. For the detailed study of the surface and for the discovery of exactly how many artists were engaged and how the work was divided between them, more photographs are needed. But there is no reason to think that in time the facts could not be established with a considerable degree of precision.

The hands engaged on the mosaics of the nave
For any full assessment of the style and the individual workmanship of the nave mosaics the photographic evidence is still inadequate. We must be content with far less than a full answer to such questions as the number of artists who worked on the series, and their individual characteristics. In the following pages, I attempt a rough estimate of the number of hands engaged on these mosaics. Though it is impossible to publish the available evidence fully in this book, I refer frequently to the plates published by Cecchelli and other authorities in order to indicate what I have in mind. The conclusions are significant, though tentative; and it seemed worth while therefore to summarize the process by which they had been reached even if I could not set the photographs in front of the reader. Cecchelli's book has several excellent colour plates, already mentioned, of details in the nave series; and it is mainly on them that I have relied in making the comparisons just discussed. By using this available material (and in it the Alinari and Anderson photographs, taken before the last restoration, are one important element; see below, in the section on the numbering of the mosaics), some few conclusions can be suggested.

78

Within this series also allowance must first be made for differences in subject. Nos 1–11, as we have numbered them, represent in the main only small groups of individuals. Often the scene is a tableau rather than a drama. With the scene at the Red Sea and the series of battle episodes having Joshua as their central figure, a different type of subject is essayed; the detail of faces and figures must sometimes be reduced to an almost miniature scale by comparison with those in other scenes, and the impression given, therefore, be to some extent different, even if the hand were the same in all cases.

It is also necessary to point to evidence of primitive restoration of the pictures themselves, not simply of the edges, evidence which seems sometimes to have escaped notice. The indifferent quality of panel 13, the arrival of the Quails in the Desert, has sometimes been observed (for example, Cecchelli's comment, 'mediocre composizione'). He does not, however, draw attention to the fact that there is work in three easily distinguishable styles in this one panel.[55] Apart from a restored section of background, affecting in part the tunic and mantle of the right-hand figure, the work of the upper half of this panel clearly belongs to the series. The faces and heads are close to those in the upper half of No 14, and must be by the same artist. But the three figures on the right-hand side of the lower half are equally clearly intrusive. They have no relation whatever to the impressionistic style, developed well, or not so well, by all the other artists of the series. The composition is linear and comparatively crude; and the two quails above their heads show as distinctly as the figures themselves that they do not belong to the rest.

It is difficult to date work as commonplace as this. But it is surely not post-Renaissance, and is most likely to be a piece of early patchwork.[56] The left-hand side of this lower half seems to be by a third hand. The faces, the poise of the individual figures, the texture and outlining of the hair, the treatment of the background behind the heads, the feeling for the material of the clothes, are in marked contrast with the upper half. But the baffled confusion caused by the arrival of the birds is vividly conveyed, and to this group Cecchelli's stricture by no means applies, though it certainly applies to the figures on the right. But the artist of the baffled group of figures is not represented elsewhere in the series, so far as can be seen, though his style is closely enough related to that of the remaining panels for it to be likely that he belonged to the same *atelier* as the other artists. This lower half suffered serious damage at an early date, and one large section at least, amounting approximately to the lower right-hand quarter, was replaced. It might be only coincidence that the rest of the lower half is by a different hand from the upper. The same seems to be true of No 24 (that is to say, the lower half appears to be by a different hand from the upper, the hand of the lower half being, I think, that represented in the next panel, No 25; Joshua's mantle, for example, seems to link the two). One suspects that in the lower half of No 24 Joshua's face (and possibly more of the panel) is perhaps an ancient restoration. But it does not seem to be the restoration alone that accounts for the different impressions, in colour and style, given by the upper and the lower halves of No 24.

The two panels with which the series now ends, Nos 26 and 27, have suffered so much that no conclusion can be drawn about their style. But the series on this side of the nave is on the whole in much better condition than that on the other, and some personalities seem to emerge. In the upper half of No 24, there is a fine contrast between Joshua, on the left, standing in an attitude of almost classical repose, the left knee slightly bent, and the feverish excitement of the troops on the right engaged in battle and the two messengers dashing back to find Joshua. The figure in the lower left-hand side of No 22 is strongly reminiscent of Joshua in No 23, and the angel in the upper half, differently posed, has something of the same quality. So has Moses, on the left in the upper half of

22

52

53

No 20; and so also have the two figures of Joshua in No 21. Several of these (and another in the group, No 23, not previously discussed because its figures are all on a tinier scale) are associated by a notable stylistic trick: the long, narrow, horizontal ribbons of yellow across the sky.

53, 54   Nos 20–23, then, and the upper half of No 24, seem to be the work of one artist. I shall call him for convenience the artist of Joshua and the Angel. An adjoining panel, No 19, is by an artist who shows similar traits, his work also having strong echoes of classical *motifs*. But the style here is much more powerful. This panel shows, in the upper half, Moses receiving the spies

51   returned from the promised land, and, in the lower, the attempted stoning of Moses. Moses' stance in the upper part of the panel is, in fact, close to what we have been examining in No 20. But the general effect is different, and the details of this artist reproduced by Cecchelli[57] show his superb mastery of the medium. It is likely that he was the artist of a panel not far from this which has disappeared but is known from an early sketch.[58] A figure of Moses in this, save for the fact that he carried a staff, must have been similar, almost line for line, with that of Moses when greeting the spies. Even if one supposes (as we should presumably do) that the design of the series as a whole was based on some similar series, made at an earlier date and almost certainly contained in a book rather than a building, the correspondence here, so exceptionally close, makes it clear

51   that the artist of the attempted stoning of Moses (No 19) was also responsible for the lost panel.[59] His quality shows at its best in the heads of the six men who are trying to stone Moses: the intense purposefulness of one in the foreground, the coarse brutality of another on the left, the cynicism of a third, are vividly represented. The *tesserae* are almost all squared; this factor adds enormously to the power of the result, both here and in the group of bronzed figures of the spies above, just returned from their mission, listening to the exchange between their spokesman and Moses.

7, 49   Another panel by this artist's hand (No 15) shows the crossing of the Red Sea. The Israelites are already on the far bank, and their enemies are being overwhelmed in the waters. Here again, the group of watching faces, with their strongly marked variety expressed with marvellous technical economy, represents a high-water mark of achievement in this or, indeed, in any medium. The same technical means, used by a lesser artist of the school in No 9,[60] gives a lively and amusing, but comparatively unimpressive, result.

    If the lost panel, and Nos 15 and 19, were all the work of this artist, there are several within the

22   sequence unaccounted for: the excited figures in No 17; No 16 (the panel restored in antiquity,
50   discussed earlier);[61] and No 18, showing the battle with the Amalekites, a single-subject panel which is in many ways a puzzle. A number of panels show battles or troops in battle array: No 17

52, 53   (lower half), No 18 and Nos 21–27. In No 18[62] the fighting warriors seem to have nothing whatever in common with those in the rest. Their equipment, such as corselets, helmets, spears (drawn here with a double row of *tesserae*) and shields (here often seen on the inside, with the carrying arm in front), differ in a variety of ways from those in the other battle scenes. The two fighting men on the left seem to be wearing some sort of chain mail. The man leading the file of the army on the right wears, it would appear, breeches, and the tightly fitting tunic of the companion immediately behind him should be compared with the loose kilts of the soldiers in Nos 24 or 25.[63] There are also some curious features in the way the *tesserae* are set (in a diagonal diamond pattern); and the absence of a white fleck in the eyes or faces is another stylistic feature unique in the series as a whole. The three figures at the top, on the other hand, fit into the sequence naturally. But as regards the battle scene as a whole, one must suppose not only a different source for the picture, but perhaps even an artist brought up in a different tradition. There is a puzzle here

x, 48   not likely to be explained. If No 13 (the child Moses) and No 14 (Moses' marriage with Zipporah)

X   Sta Maria Maggiore, mosaic panel in the nave, No. 13,
upper half (early fifth century). The young Moses before Pharaoh's daughter.

are by one artist, as they seem to be, this means that in thirteen panels on this side, in good enough condition to offer some chance of a critical assessment, there are something like six hands at work: the artist of the Young Moses, Nos 13 and 14; the artist of the Stoning of Moses, Nos 15 and 19; the artist of Joshua and the Angel, Nos 20–23 and No 24 (upper half); the artist of the Victory over the Amorites, Nos 24 (lower half) and 25 (both halves); the artist of the Battle with the Amalekites, No 18; and two others, the artist of No 16 (upper half) and the artist (probably a different one) of No 17. An assignment in the workshop, then, of two or three panels to each artist may have been approximately the average.

The average on the other side of the series seems approximately the same, though, since so many panels are in bad condition, certainty on this point seems even less likely to be achieved. The most remarkable panels are No 3 (showing the splendidly dignified parting of Abraham and Lot) and the fine but much damaged No 11, in which a magnificent detail[64] shows something of the same mastery, achieved by somewhat similar technical means, as the work of the artist of the Stoning of Moses. Even the least impressive panels, such as the coarsely drawn No 7,[65] or the commonplace Nos 8 and 9, leave us in no doubt of the impressionistic interest of the work as a whole. But none of the nave mosaics were executed by artists who worked on the triumphal arch; and the technical differences between the two series are most readily explained in terms of a difference of period between them.

The original edges, shape, frames and sizes of the mosaics of the nave
The exposed surface of the nave mosaics still bears evidence (often puzzling but possibly important) which throws light on the size, original shape and setting of the panels.

The original edges. No 19 is, in fact, the only panel which fits more or less exactly its eighteenth-century frame, the mosaic covering the full area available. Some of the panels were, from the first, edged with a mosaic border, of which substantial traces often remain. It consisted sometimes of a triple line, sometimes only a single line, of colour. The remains of it can be well seen in Wilpert's plate of No 3.[66] Here it consisted of an inner line of black *tesserae*, two *tesserae* thick ('double'), a single middle line of white, and an outer double line of red. In others it was simpler: a single line of white. In No 17[67] it is in part such a single line, doubled towards the top left-hand margin, though on the right-hand side of the mosaic there seems no trace of its having existed. Whether there was such a border in the panel or not, there are many instances (like No 17) in which the panel has clearly been enlarged at the edge with several inches of mosaic. In No 17 these additions to some extent take up the original colour, as can be seen along the right-hand edge. Sometimes, as in Nos 18 (upper left-hand edge), 23 and 24,[68] some attempt seems to have been made to extend the original design into this new area. In No 18, it looks as if, in both lower corners, there had been substantial damage before the enlargement took place, and the opportunity was used to repair it in mosaic which appears to be of the same texture as that of the new material on each side. The additions can hardly have been made in the sixteenth century, when the repairs were normally effected in plaster. Some payments were made for repairs in mosaic in the eighteenth-century restoration.[69] But we are often concerned here with material which Wilpert, an unrivalled judge, considered antique. For he distinguishes throughout his reproductions between mosaic material which, in his view, was antique and that which he thinks to be much later.

Another instance is worth examining in detail: No 13, the fine mosaic with two scenes from the childhood of Moses. The problem of the border is brought out by a comparison of Wilpert's

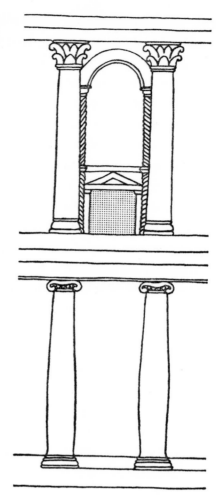

Fig 3 Pattern of the original niches framing the mosaics of the nave, below the clerestory windows, in Sta Maria Maggiore: based on an anonymous early sixteenth-century drawing (in Cod. Vat. Lat. 11257, fol. 18). Within the pilasters, narrow twisted columns framed the windows. The area of mosaic is shown by the dotted portion (compare Cecchelli, Plate XII). Note the bevelling at the top of the mosaic.

and Cecchelli's reproductions, the latter made after the most recent restorations. Where did the original margin on the left side come? Wilpert's reproduction shows that at some time the left-hand edge of the mosaic ran down along the outer edge of the thick white line of the *aedicula* under which Pharoah's daughter is sitting. The impression given at first is that all the material to the left of this line is later than the original mosaic (though doubtless antique). If the cornice, pediment and roof of the *aedicula* are examined in Wilpert's plate, it seems as if the whole of the left-hand side is a botched addition. According to this hypothesis, the triangular pediment remained untouched. The roof was modified (unsatisfactorily) so as to extend out to the new edge; and the cornice was extended, in a straight line, so as to provide for the new side which the *aedicula* was being given. The ornament on the cornice was extended, in a way that made it lop-sided; and though the narrow white edge of the old cornice was continued round the addition, it still seems possible to see a trace of the old left-hand edge under the left-hand corner of the pediment.

But to say that the left-hand edge is all a later addition is to simplify matters unduly; for there was a figure on the left-hand side, in the lower half of the panel, of which only the right arm and hand remain. The original design must surely have shown his head or at least his face. In this mosaic, as in No 18 discussed above, there were substantial losses in both lower corners replaced apparently in antiquity, and the curve of the arena was partly replaced, and partly extended, so as to reach from one side of the enlarged panel to the other. Until a more detailed photographic survey of these edges has been undertaken, it may not be possible to do more than state the probability that, in antiquity, many of the panels were enlarged. It also seems probable that, at that time as well as much later, mosaic infilling was added to patch sections already heavily damaged or corners from which the mosaic had entirely disappeared.

The shape and frames. In antiquity the mosaics were framed in small *aediculae* of plaster, the design of which is known from a drawing, published by Cecchelli, showing the nave before Cardinal Pinelli's restoration of the church was undertaken in the sixteenth century. The diagram here reproduced is made from that drawing, enlarged for ease of interpretation. Each mosaic had a triangular pediment of plaster to itself, with a frame made up of pillars on each side, with capitals above. These frames should perhaps be considered partly in the light of evidence that, in some of the panels at least, the upper parts of the right-hand and left-hand edges were bevelled so that the bounding line sloped inwards. At least three of Wilpert's plates, those showing Nos 5, 8 and 15 (top right-hand corner), have some indication of this bevelling of the edge. In the most recent restorations, as reproduced in Cecchelli's plates, it is shown much more often, and this presumably means that when the old plaster repairs were stripped down, indications were found of bevelling which had been concealed from Wilpert and his copyists.[70] It could be supposed that this bevelled shape was adopted by way of conformation with the capitals of the early plaster *aediculae*. If they had come from another church, however, their earlier settings might even so have been similar. The existence of bevelling in some of the mosaics and not in others, therefore, would not be conclusive evidence against (though certainly not conclusive evidence for) an early move from one church to another.

The sizes. The panels were by no means uniform in size and some of them were evidently placed somewhat askew. The aim of the eighteenth-century restoration was to impose upon the nave a regularity which it did not originally possess, but which eighteenth-century adherents of classical ideas thought it ought to have. The undertaking was gigantic. It involved taking down the columns, one by one, also reshaping some and making new bases, to ensure that they were precisely the same height and that the distances between them were identical. The existing fine plaster frames placed round the mosaics in this reconstruction are uniform. To achieve this, it was often necessary to provide the pictures with some sort of mount so as to fill out the frame. Only one, No 19, seems, as mentioned above, completely to fill its frame without any such addition. The mounts took various forms. Sometimes they included (and still appear to include) metal strips to retain the edge of the mosaic, these strips being sometimes painted. Sometimes there is a 'mount' of mosaic (cubes of some plain or mottled colour), and at least part of the payments made to eighteenth-century mosaicists presumably included this work.

It is likely that several of the problems discussed here can be explained by this intention of the eighteenth-century restoration to give uniformity of size and shape to the panels. But some of the mosaics (those in which what is manifestly early work extends beyond the 'edge' of the mosaic) obstinately resist accommodating themselves to this explanation. Only a new survey with a wealth of photographic detail would provide the answer. It seems as if the archaeological facts concerning the mosaics and their relationship to the masonry, as well as the deductions to be drawn from these facts, will remain in dispute until the walls are again opened up. Even then, it might prove that the evidence had been destroyed when the last work was done. For this reason the interpretation of the existing surface evidence seems specially important.

A suggested numbering of the mosaics of the nave

The orientation of the church being north-west (apsidal end) and south-east, the two sides of the nave are to the south-west and north-east. In the list which follows, mosaics Nos 1–12 are

84

on the south-west side, and Nos 13–27 on the north-east side (the numbers running from the apsidal end on both sides). Spaces where disintegrated mosaics have been replaced by a painted scheme (for example, the representation of Jacob's Ladder) have not been included in the numbering. The mosaics are set in frames, above the cornice which tops the pillars of the nave. Several panels have been completely destroyed in the course of architectural alterations.

In the following list the panels are numbered according to the scheme used in the preceding text. References are also given in the notes to the photographs taken by Alinari and Anderson before the most recent restoration (that ordered by Pius XI in 1928), and to Cecchelli's plates.

South-west side

1 Single panel. Abraham and Melchisidec (Gen. xiv. 18) bring an offering of loaves and wine; Abraham is mounted on a horse, and behind him is a group of mounted warriors with lances. The right-hand side of this panel and much of the edge all round it have been extensively restored in mosaic.[71]

2 Abraham and the angels (Gen. xviii. 2). In the upper half, Abraham encounters the angels near the Oak of Mambre. The central angel is in a glory. In the lower half, the three angels are at a table, where they are served with food; in front is a jar of wine. On the left, Abraham 24 is giving instructions to Sarah, who is serving the food. Abraham's right hand is held up, apparently in blessing. Much of the lower edge has been restored in plaster.[72]

3 The parting of Lot and Abraham (Gen. xviii. 8–11). The patriarchs in the centre turn away from one another. Behind each are their wives and followers; with each are their children, in one case a youth, in the other two girls. In the background, on the left is a house, on the 46 right a walled city. The lower half shows a pastoral scene, largely destroyed; parts of the shepherd and animals (sheep, a goat and a cow) remain.[73]

   Then followed three mosaics, now destroyed.

4 Isaac blesses Jacob (Gen. xxvii. 18–29). Isaac reclines on a couch in front of a building with a classical portico. In front of the couch is a table, to the left of which stands Jacob, being blessed by his father. To the right is Rebecca. Behind her is, perhaps, an attendant. On the left is a garden with (apparently) bird-cages on which doves are perching. Three edges have been restored in plaster; the fourth (the lower edge of the upper part) remains comparatively intact. In the lower half, the upper part of the buildings is visible, with the head and shoulders of Isaac again.[74]

   Then followed a mosaic, now destroyed.

5 In the upper half, Rachel announces the arrival of Jacob; following her are two shepherds, with a flock of sheep on the right. Some of the sheep have bells round their necks. There is a hilly background. In the lower half, two figures (to the left of the centre) represent Laban and 47 Jacob meeting (Gen. xxix. 13); another group of three in the same panel shows Jacob being brought into the house. Leah is on the left, Rachel on the right. Much of the lower part is restored work in plaster.[75]

6 In the upper half (Gen. xxix. 18–19), Jacob asks Laban if he may have Rachel; Leah and her brothers are on the right. The lower half showed a rural scene, now almost completely destroyed; the upper section also has suffered damage on both sides and in the centre.[76]

7 In the upper half (Gen. xxix. 25), Jacob reproaches Laban for his deceit. Behind are a companion and a flock of sheep. Laban stands with Rachel and Leah in front of his house. Below, on the left, Laban is inviting three friends to the wedding (according to Cecchelli);

the background, right, is a pillared colonnade like that in the illustration of Joseph with Potiphar's wife in the Vienna Genesis. The condition of the upper scene is good. The lower half of the lower panel has been largely restored in plaster.[77]

8 In the upper half (Gen. xxx. 32), Jacob claims more for his labour. He stands in the centre, confronting Laban. With each are two companions and flocks of sheep. In the background on the right is a house, on the left are two shepherds' cabins. Below, Jacob and Laban are in the centre in talk; attendants on the right and left divide the flocks. The condition of the upper panel is good. The lower part of the lower panel has been largely restored in plaster.[78]

9 The upper half is in two sections, divided vertically by a tree. On the left-hand side, three men with peeled rods are watching over the flock (Gen. xxx. 37–39). On the right-hand side, Jacob is with two companions; the Lord speaks to him, reaching out of the clouds and touching him. The object on the right may be a well. In the lower half, Jacob tells his wives of the impending journey (Gen. xxxi. 4); with them are three children. Behind Jacob is a flock of sheep and two men, perhaps sons of Laban, arguing (Gen. xxxi. 1). The lower part of the lower panel has been largely restored in plaster.[79]

Here, under the window, was a mosaic, now destroyed.

10 The upper half shows the meeting of Jacob and Esau (Gen. xxxiii. 1); Esau stands in royal garments in front of a walled city. In the centre are Jacob and a companion, separated by a tree from other members of his household, including his two wives. There is a patch of restoration in plaster in the centre of the lower edge of this upper half. The lower scene has almost entirely disappeared, but there was a band of warriors with spears, no doubt the four hundred men with Esau. Perhaps the scene was that of the arrival of Jacob's messengers (Gen. xxxii. 4–5).[80]

Here, under the window, was another mosaic, now destroyed.

11 In the upper half, Hamar and his son Shechem approach Jacob, who sits on the right (an elderly figure, with his sons behind him). On the left are Hivites; in the background is the city of Shechem (Gen. xxxiv. 6–12). The upper and right-hand edges have been restored in plaster. In the lower half, Jacob's sons are in discussion with him; they are grieved because of Dinah's folly (Gen. xxxiv. 7). As in some other panels in this series, the lower picture precedes the upper in chronological sequence. About half of the lower section has been restored in plaster.[81]

12 In the upper half, Jacob's sons put the offer to Shechem (Gen. xxxiv. 13). Jacob sits behind them, on the left. On the right are Shechem and others; the city is in the background. The upper edge has been restored in plaster. The lower half has been largely destroyed, but it evidently showed a meeting in Shechem at which Hamar and Shechem persuaded their people to accept the conditions laid down (Gen. xxxiv. 20). Two men are standing up, speaking to a crowd; on the left are the walls of the city.[82]

Here followed three mosaics, now destroyed.

North-east side

The series on this side originally began with a mosaic which has since been destroyed.

13 The upper half shows the young Moses before Pharaoh's daughter (Exod. ii. 1–9). Moses stands in the centre before the princess, who sits to the left on a throne with a canopy; with her are five of her women, one of whom holds (apparently) a casket of jewels, another a basket of fruit. Moses wears the mantle of a young prince; the princess is also regally clad.

86

Above, in the sky, can be seen what seems to be a flash of divine lightning towards Moses. The scene is no doubt that of the adoption of Moses by Pharaoh's daughter (Exod. ii. 10).[83] In the lower half can be seen a semicircular amphitheatre in which sit a number of Egyptian sages, arguing with the boy Moses, who stands in the centre. This is no doubt an apocryphal 'infancy' scene, considered as a parallel to the boy Christ disputing in the Temple with the doctors. The condition of the whole panel is good[84] except for a narrow strip along the lower edge of the lower half.[85]

14 The upper half shows Moses marrying Zipporah. In the centre stands her father Raguel, with Zipporah on the left, Moses on the right, Raguel's hands being on their shoulders. Behind Moses are four youths; behind Zipporah, four maidens. Above Raguel's head is a 48 canopy or tent. The lower half shows Moses as shepherd, with a flock of sheep and two other shepherds, one of whom is seated; the other is also leaning on his staff. The gleam of fire on the right in the sky ought to be the burning bush, but is probably not. The shepherds, indeed, have bare feet (compare Exod. iii. 5), but so normally has Jacob in the earlier series of panels when he appears as a shepherd. The condition of the whole panel is good, except for the lower edge.[86]

Here followed three mosaics, now destroyed.

15 Single panel. The Egyptians overwhelmed in the Red Sea (Exod. xiv. 15–29). On the right is a walled city from which Pharaoh's army is pouring forth, with their chariots. The Red 7, 49 Sea has 'returned to its strength'; many Egyptian warriors have been overwhelmed, and their shields are bobbing about in the water. On the left, the Israelites are on dry land; Moses is stretching his hand over the sea (verses 26–27). The condition is similar to that of No 14.[87]

16 In the upper half, the Israelites (on the left) complain to Moses (Exod. xvi. 2–3). On the right, Moses prays, and his prayer is answered (as in Exod. xvi. 4–5). The lower half shows the arrival of the quails (Exod. xvi. 13). The three figures on the right were heavily restored in 22 mosaic either in antiquity or, more probably, in the ninth century.[88] There should be only one, or possibly two (Moses and Aaron). It is possible that this half of the panel originally contained a different scene. If there were three figures here originally, they were no doubt closely similar to the three in the lower half of No 17.[89]

17 The upper half shows the scene of the Waters of Marah (Exod. xv. 22–25). On the left, a group of Israelites complain to Moses about the bitterness of the water. On the right, the Lord, who reaches down from Heaven, shows Moses a tree; Moses puts it in the water to make it sweet and the Israelites drink. The lower half shows preparations for battle with the Amalekites (Exod. xvii. 8). At the bottom, Amalekite warriors are issuing from a walled city. Behind them (apparently) is the Israelite army, with Joshua in front in a glory; to the right are Moses, Aaron and Hur; Moses is talking to Joshua (as in Exod. xvii. 9). The condition is similar to that of No 14.[90] In this panel the meaning of the 'glory' for Joshua, implicit in Nos 24 and 27, is made explicit.

18 Single panel. The battle with the Amalekites (Exod. xvii. 10–13). In the left-hand part of the centre, above, Moses on a hill holds up his hands; he looks up towards what is (apparently) a divine sign of lightning in the sky. With him are Aaron and Hur. On the left, the Amalekites 50 are issuing from a walled city. The Israelite army is on the right; one Israelite draws a bow. The condition is similar to that of No 14.[91]

19 The upper half appears to show the sending-out of the Israelite spies (Num. xiii. 2). Moses, and presumably Aaron, are on the left in front of the Tabernacle; in the centre is the group

51 of spies; on the right, in the background, is one of the Canaanite cities. The lower half shows the threatened stoning of Moses, Joshua and Caleb (Num. xiv. 10). They are protected by the 'glory' of the Lord, which 'appeared in the tent of meeting' (on the right). This seems to be a more likely explanation than that of **Wilpert**, who thinks that the scene of Korah, Dathan and Abiram (Num. xvi.) is the one depicted. The condition is similar to that of No 14.[92]

20 The upper half shows, on the left, Moses handing the Book of the Law to the Israelites (Deut. xxxi. 9), and, on the right, Moses dying on a terraced mountain (Pisgah in Moab: Deut. xxxiv. 1–5). Below, priests, now specially vested, stand in front of and behind the Ark, which is carried on the shoulders of four Levites. The condition is very similar to that of No 14, though damage to the lower edge is somewhat greater.[93]

II, 8   21 In the upper half, the Ark is shown about to cross the Jordan (Joshua iii. 11–17). On the right is a group of armed Israelites with Joshua; in the centre, the Ark approaches the river, which is drying up; on the left, men are carrying the stones of Joshua (Joshua iv. 3). The lower half shows Joshua's spies (Joshua ii. 1). On the left, Joshua, in front of armed Israelites, sends out two spies towards the city of Jericho on the right. The condition is similar to that of No 20.[94]

22 The upper half shows Joshua and the angel (Joshua v. 13–16). In the centre is Joshua in front of an armed group of Israelites. He leans forward in homage to the angel (on the right), who has a spear (not, as in the biblical text, a drawn sword) in his hand. The lower half shows

53, 54   two scenes. On the right, the two spies are being let down from the walls of Jericho by Rahab. On the left, they return to Joshua (who stands in front of a group of three armed Israelites) to make their report. Here the spies are armed (they are not in No 21). The condition is similar to that of No 20.[95]

23 The upper half shows Jericho, with one of its walls collapsing (Joshua vi. 20); on either side are the armies of the Israelites. The figure in the city is Rahab (verse 23). The lower half shows, in the centre, the Ark being carried round (verse 6). To the left and right are six men with trumpets of rams' horns; in the background is a group of armed Israelites. The condition is similar to that of No 20.[96]

24 The upper half shows the assault on Ai (Joshua. viii). On the right is the city, with men fighting from the walls. On the left, in the background, is the ambush (verse 4); in the foreground, Israelites are fleeing, as Joshua has bid them do. Here, as later (in No. 27), Joshua's shield seems to be intended in the design to create a 'glory' in which he appears. In the lower half, on the left, the Lord gives instructions to Joshua (verse 1); on the right there is a confused scene, which apparently represents the army taking up dispositions. The condition of the upper half is good, but there has been considerable damage along the lower edge of the lower half.[97]

25 The upper half shows the putting to flight of the Amorites (Joshua x.). Joshua is in the centre on horseback, with other Israelite warriors round him; the bodies of the enemy lie stripped and dying on the ground; to right and left the kings are seeking refuge in caves

52   (verse 16). The lower half shows, on the left, a group of Israelite warriors, with Joshua in front; in the centre are hailstones (verse 11); above, in the sky, is the hand of the Lord; below, on the right, Amorite warriors take to flight. The condition is similar to that of No 24.[98]

26 Single panel. Joshua bids the sun and moon stand still (Joshua x. 12–13). Joshua, larger than life-size, dressed as a warrior, stands on the hill of Gibeon; in his left hand is his spear,

and over his arm his cloak. He is full face to the spectator, his right hand held out towards the sun. The two armies (the Israelites on the left) confront each other. There has been considerable damage, restored in plaster, along the right-hand and lower edges.[99]

27 The upper half shows Joshua and the captive kings (Joshua x. 16–24). The whole panel is badly damaged; but the theme of the upper half is clear. Joshua, full face, stands holding up his right hand as he gives his orders to the captives. Behind his back hangs a huge round shield which is designed to create a 'glory' for him, as in No 24. On the left stand three kings, their hands bound behind their backs; behind them are the armed Israelite warriors. On the right is another group of three warriors. Some of the damaged areas (for example, the breast-plates of warriors on the right, above, and parts of the figures on the right, below) still exist as restored in Renaissance plaster, scored to imitate mosaic. The lower half shows, on the left, Joshua seated, apparently with a group of warriors. Nothing can be made of the confused detail on the right; the jugs and jars may simply have been inserted by a restorer who misunderstood the theme. This is one of the only sections in the nave series in which a substantial area of restoration in Renaissance plaster, scored to look like mosaic cubes, remains.[100]

STA SABINA: THE MOSAIC OF THE NAVE

This church, famous for its wooden doors with panels, some of which were carved in the early fifth century, once had mosaics comparable to those of the Ravenna basilicas, with which (for example, S. Apollinare Nuovo) it is itself comparable in plan. The arcade on either side of the nave was decorated with mosaics architecturally similar to those of S. Apollinare Nuovo, or to the great series which still decorates the nave of Sta Maria Maggiore. The greatest interest of the surviving mosaic is indeed that it provides an example of the way in which the Sta Maria scheme (a paradigm for the full decoration of a fifth- and sixth-century Italian basilica) was once completed. There is now no trace of the inscription which originally existed in Sta Maria at the other end of the church from the apse, and which thus linked the apsidal mosaics and the series on either side of the nave in one great mosaic whole. In Sta Sabina all that remains of the scheme is precisely that element which has disappeared from Sta Maria. (The wording of the Sta Maria inscription has fortunately been preserved, however.) What survives in Sta Sabina is the actual mosaic inscription which once served to dedicate a whole series of panels now lost, at the end of the church furthest from the altar. It is flanked on the right by a figure symbolizing the Gentile church, on the left by a figure representing the Jewish church (forerunners of the series of medieval representations of the Church and Synagogue).[101] This mosaic may actually have preceded the triumphal arch mosaic in Sta Maria by a decade or so.

74

The 'Peter' referred to in the inscription (see below) is Cardinal Peter of Illyria; if the mosaic was made during the papacy of Celestinus I, this would date it, with its two figures, within ten years (422–32). But the inscription does not state this explicitly—only that the church was founded in Celestinus' reign. The inscription, in good classical lettering, in gold on a background of 'powder blue' with deeper blue lines, is bordered with a gold ornament. Each of the flanking allegorical figures is shown clad in a rich purple dress with a gold medallion, and each bears the appropriate inscription: ECCLESIA EX CIRCVMCISIONE and ECCLESIA EX GENTIBVS. Both are dignified Roman matrons, their stance natural and graceful, the faces individual, the drapery in heavy, rich naturalistic folds, giving a sense of three dimensions. Each figure holds a book; the lettering on both books is only a decorative convention. The books are held in each case in the left hand; the right hands are held over the books with the gesture of blessing in its western form.

The verse inscription reads as follows:

CVLMEN APOSTOLICVM CVM CAELESTINVS HABERET

PRIMVS ET IN TOTO FVLGERET EPISCOPVS ORBE

HAEC QVAE MIRARIS FVNDAVIT PRESBYTER VRBIS

ILLYRICA DE GENTE PETRVS VIR NOMINE TANTO

DIGNVS AB EXORTV CHRISTI NVTRITVS IN AVLA

PAVPERIBVS LOCVPLES SIBI PAVPER QVI BONA VITAE

PRAESENTIS FVGIENS MERVIT SPERARE FVTVRVM.

'When Celestinus [Pope Celestinus I, 422–32] held the highest apostolic throne and shone forth gloriously as the foremost bishop of the whole world, a presbyter of this city, Illyrian by birth, named Peter and worthy of that great name, established this building at which you look in wonder. From his earliest years he was brought up in the hall of Christ—rich to the poor, poor to himself, one who shunned the good things of life on earth and deserved to hope for the life to come.'

SS. COSMA E DAMIANO

The mosaic in the apse was offered, as is recorded in the inscription (see below), by Pope Felix IV (526–30). In style, the mosaics might seem earlier. Their idiom is entirely different from, and far more classical than, that of either the S. Vitale mosaics in Ravenna, dating from the reign of Justinian in the mid-sixth century, or even the earlier Ravenna mosaics of S. Apollinare Nuovo. The comparison gives the impression that Rome was still the capital, and kept more closely than other cities to the great tradition of the past. In this mosaic, the figures in the apse balance one another, St Peter's outstretched right hand being matched by the outstretched left hand of St Paul on the other side of Christ, and the figures of St Cosmas and St Damian, each with his martyr's crown, also in a formal pattern. But the clothes, despite their similarity in colour, are individual in style, as are the faces and attitudes. The figures are grouped, not simply juxtaposed; they do not have the hieratic stance and stylized appearance which was to be characteristic in medieval mosaics. They do not form a mere pattern, such as one sees even in the great mosaics of S. Vitale, only a generation later. Historically, this mosaic was to be an important influence on the design of apsidal mosaics for the next three hundred years, though during that time the style was to change so greatly.[102]

The mosaic commemorates Felix's reconstruction of a pagan temple as a church, in honour of two martyrs, the physicians St Cosmas and St Damian. Before a background of clouds, vermilion and grey-blue against the mauveish-blue semi-dome of the apse, Christ appears in the sky, in a tunic and mantle (marked with a monogram, 'I') of gold, and with a gold halo edged with

XI   SS. Cosma e Damiano, mosaic of the apse (c. 530). The central figure: Christ appearing in the clouds. The condition is substantially original.

grey. In his left hand he holds a rolled book; his right is uplifted, the palm open towards the congregation. He is an awesome figure, and, indeed, the mosaic as a whole (in spite of being visually clipped at the edges by the arch, built in later to the original arch) dominates the church in a way that is true of no other in Rome. On his right and left are St Paul and St Peter, similarly clad, though their tunics, decorated with *clavi* (the vertical stripes), are white, as are their mantles. St Paul has a 'monogram' similar to that of Christ; he and St Peter each hold a hand towards Christ as they present the two martyrs, who are not named. One martyr, standing on the right with St Peter, wears a martyr's crown and has a red satchel hanging from his wrist. The other martyr, standing on the left with St Paul, carries a martyr's crown; it seems that the seventeenth-century restorer (who may have been mistaken on this point) intended to represent him, also, as carrying a satchel. On the extreme right, also wearing a martyr's crown, stands St Theodore, a saint from Asia Minor who served in the army of Maximilianus and was martyred for having set fire to a pagan temple; his tunic is of rose shot with gold, his mantle, which is particularly splendid, of gold patterned in red.

On the extreme left stands Felix himself, offering the church. His figure, like the three sheep below, dates, unfortunately, from the seventeenth century. They all stand on the grassy bank of a river (the Jordan) on which flowers are growing. The austerity of the river pattern, compared with those in St John Lateran and Sta Maria Maggiore, is significant; fanciful classical decoration of that earlier kind has now been rejected. On each side stands a palm tree; on the left-hand tree is perched the phoenix, the symbol of resurrection, with rays round its head. In the design, the hand of Christ is perhaps intended to lead the eye to this symbol. (The divine hand, outlined in red above the head of Christ, is a modern indication of what the original *motif*, in the crown of the apse, is likely to have been.) Even the animals forming the traditional flock of sheep (symbolizing the twelve apostles) are individualized in stance, poise of head, and so forth. In the centre, on a hillock, stands the Agnus Dei, with a silver halo;[103] from the hillock spring the four rivers of Paradise,[104] here named in the gold band below the mosaic: GION, PISON, TIGRIS, EVFRATA. Bethlehem is on the right of the row of sheep. Jerusalem, on the left, is part of the modern work. The remains of a fine classical border formed of crossed cornucopias, below the inscription, are notable and should be compared with the similar ornament on the outside of the apsidal arch at S. Vitale in Ravenna.

On the outside of the triumphal arch[105] is to be found an early example of a theme often copied in later work: the Agnus Dei on a throne (but here shown, exceptionally, lying on the throne, not standing), with the Cross above and the Gospel book below him.[106] On either side are candlesticks (the Seven Lamps of Revelation[107]) and an angel; on the left is the half-figure of a third angel, the symbol of the Evangelist Matthew, and, on the right, the Eagle, the symbol of St John. The angels' tunics, with a characteristic flaring-out at the ankles and mantles with the ends blown outwards, are thought by Matthiae to indicate a somewhat later period than that of the apsidal

XII   SS. Cosma e Damiano, mosaic of the apse (*c.* 530), left-hand side.
The two sheep on the left, most of the drapery on the figure above
(but not the head) and the drapery over the right knee of St Paul,
were restored in the seventeenth century.

mosaics. Below, on the left and right, can be seen the arms of the Elders carrying crowns; the interpretation is clear when later versions, which include the complete figures of the Elders, are compared with this.[108] The fragments surviving here are more naturalistic than the formalized imitations of later times. The fact that there are only two Evangelist symbols shows conclusively that this part of the mosaic has been cut down; there is no doubt that originally the figures of the Elders[109] also were complete and that the triumphal arch mosaic spread almost across the complete width of the original building. The background was gold, but it had not the richness of the gold used in the apse. The destructive architectural alterations were made during the reign of Urban VIII (1623-44). The theme involving the twenty-four Elders came originally from the Constantinian façade of old St Peter's.

The apsidal mosaic is one of the many of whose effect it is almost impossible, in a reproduction, to give more than a faint idea. In the original it is superbly impressive. The solid, 'three-dimensional' figures are without parallel (except, perhaps, in Sta Pudenziana, where the design has been much more drastically mutilated) in Roman ecclesiastical mosaics of the medieval period.

The inscription, which, in literary style as well as lettering, is probably the least unclassical of those with which we are concerned, reads as follows:

AVLA DI [Dei] CLARIS RADIAT SPECIOSA METALLIS

IN QVA PLVS FIDEI LVX PRETIOSA MICAT.

MARTYRIBVS MEDICIS POPVLO SPES CERTA SALVTIS

VENIT ET EX SACRO CREVIT HONORE LOCVS

OPTVLIT HOC DNO [Domino] FELIX ANTISTITE DIGNVM

MVNVS VT AETHERIA VIVAT IN ARCE POLI.

'This hall of God shines in its adornment with enamels, a hall where the precious light of faith gleams even more brightly. To the people a sure hope of salvation comes from the martyrs who heal their ills, and the temple before named as sacred[110] has increased in honour. Felix has made to the Lord this offering, worthy of the Lord's servant, that he may be granted life in the airy vault of heaven.' The word *medicis* alludes to the martyrs' profession, as well as to their cure of souls.

The mosaic was altered by Gregory XIII in the sixteenth century. He substituted a figure of Gregory the Great for that of Felix IV. Alexander VII had this replaced by the existing figure of Felix IV. There is reason to think that when the figure of Felix IV was restored, a copy of the original was available to the artist.[111]

THE FOURTH TO THE SIXTH CENTURIES: CLASSICAL ORNAMENT AND DECORATION

Figure ornament. In two mosaics of the early Renaissance, the apsidal mosaics of St John Lateran and Sta Maria Maggiore (to be discussed in more detail later), it seems clear that not only does the main mosaic follow the general lines of an antique predecessor, but that the lower border in each case is an almost exact transcription of what existed there before. In several Roman early medieval mosaics, the foreground shows the river Jordan. In the late classical versions of St John and Sta Maria, the foreground was similarly a river intended to represent the Jordan, and is so labelled. But it is represented differently: the whole landscape through which the river is flowing is peopled, and in particular the surface of the river is alive with small figures of *amoretti*, fishing, chasing animals, or navigating, which give the impression of originals of a most lively delicacy. The border is thus used, in these two mosaics, as a vivacious ornamental foil to the seriousness of the main theme.

XIV, 62-66

XIII   SS. Cosma e Damiano. Mosaic of the apse (*c.* 530), right-hand side.
St Peter with St Damian and St Theodore. The condition is substantially original.

The treatment differs slightly in the two examples. In the Lateran, *amoretti* in both lower corners of the mosaic are pouring out the river's waters from jars; in the Sta Maria mosaic, reclining river gods hold jars from which the water flows in the old classical fashion. (In Sta Maria, the river god on the right is a modern restoration, but there is no reason to suppose that the restoration does not follow the earlier scheme.) In the stream itself, many of the scenes are so similar in both mosaics that we are led to wonder whether, besides the Renaissance copies being by the same master, the originals may not also have been by the same hand: the *putto* who stands up on a raft, acting as a mast for the billowing sail, appears in almost identical form in both (the raft is, in fact, as in many antique versions,[112] a wine jar); another, who has harnessed a swan, similarly appears in both mosaics, as do the *putti* fishing from some kind of canoe. In both mosaics, water enclosures (areas of the stream fenced off from the rest) are a curious feature. The Sta Maria has excellent representations of a Roman merchant vessel; that towards the right-hand end is, like the river god at that end, a modern restoration, but the other is authentic, either thirteenth-century work following an antique original, or in fact the original itself. For it seems possible that Toriti was able to preserve large fragments of the actual classical material of this border, and to incorporate them bodily in his work. This would explain some of the obvious divisions which appear on the present surface. These are to be seen, for example, in Plate 66, showing the right-hand side of the mosaic. The horizontal line that divides the part of the mosaic with the large figures, above, from the smaller figures, below, is clear. Also discernible are some vertical lines (for example, through the tail of the fish in the swan's beak, or to the right of the foot farthest to the right) which seem to represent blocks in which the material was removed before being rebuilt into this scheme.

These borders give a good impression of the gay and amusing fancies developed in classical decoration, whether in a secular context or when mosaic was employed, as here, in the service of the Church. The cupola mosaics in Sta Constanza, destroyed early in the seventeenth century, are known to have contained fanciful detail in the lower register, as in these two examples. In the upper border of the early Renaissance mosaic by Filippo Rusuti on the façade of Sta Maria, the *motifs* are certainly derived from antique originals; but there is, in that case, no question of Rusuti having transcribed the border from an original pre-existing in the same position, as Toriti was doing in the two examples under discussion.

The acanthus scroll. Like the vine,[113] the acanthus scroll played a large part in the ecclesiastical decoration of the late antique period. Two types of scroll are to be seen. One is well illustrated by the apsidal decoration of the *atrium* in the bapistry of St John Lateran. That example is carried out in two colours of green, heightened with gold, and may date from the reconstruction of this part of the building by Sixtus III (432–40). The Lateran scroll is not 'inhabited' by animals of any kind (though there is a row of doves round the 'tabernacle' in the crown of the vault); but the elegant lamps (or perhaps flowers) in the centre of the volutes make bright flecks of orange, in contrast with the dark-blue background and the green and gold of the foliage.

Another type of classical scroll, more solid in appearance, is that displayed in the apsidal mosaic of St Maria Maggiore, a mosaic which is, it will be remembered, a Renaissance version of a much earlier work, which dates from classical antiquity. An example in stone, showing this same more fleshy type of volute, is on the porphyry sarcophagus of Sta Costanza, which once stood in the main niche of the mausoleum that is now the church of Sta Costanza. It is a widespread element in late antique design. Not only is the scroll in the sarcophagus similar in its forms to the Sta Maria scroll, but this one also is 'inhabited' by *amoretti* harvesting grapes, and also (as in Sta Maria) by

XIV Sta Maria Maggiore, main mosaic of the apse (a classical fragment
incorporated by Toriti into his mosaic; *c.* 1294). A river god (fifth century).
The drapery over the right leg is a later repair.

birds within the scroll itself. Associated with both scrolls are peacocks. These are a well-known early Christian decorative *motif*.

73, XXIV   The twelfth-century mosaic in S. Clemente, which has a magnificent scroll background, is believed (like the late-thirteenth-century mosaic in Sta Maria) to be a version of an antique original; and this original, from the look of the copy, must have been somewhat like the example 72   in St John Lateran in having delicate fronds typical of the Lateran scroll, and similar 'lamps'. Several small fragments of a scroll of this type, also with orange 'lamps' or flowers, are to be seen in the presbytery of S. Paolo fuori le Mura. It is impossible to judge whether these come from a classical scroll, or from a medieval version of such a scroll, and nothing seems to be known about the origin of those particular fragments. They are sometimes described as coming from the Cavallini mosaic on the façade. The form which that mosaic took, however, is sufficiently well known for it to be certain that this attribution is wrong.

152   The acanthus leaves at the foot of the S. Clemente scroll clearly derive from an antique type, one example of which is a well-known floor mosaic in Ostia.[114] In that, as in S. Clemente and also 199   in Sta Maria Maggiore, the leaves at the foot are quite unlike the elements that burgeon from them; and the vine in Sta Costanza also springs from an acanthus root.

71   *The 'tabernacle', or 'tent of Paradise', motif.* The mosaic in St John shows, in the crown of the apse, the first surviving example in Rome of the 'tabernacle' or 'tent of Paradise'. The *motif* derives ultimately from one that was frequently used within an arched recess by the mosaicists of the classical period. There is a good example in the National Museum at Naples. That the pattern was thought of originally as a tent is suggested by the representation of an actual tent or 48   canopy, above the head of the father-in-law of Moses, in the Sta Maria[115] panel showing his marriage. In mosaics of the Christian period this tent comes to symbolize the sky, and so apparently Paradise. In at least two mosaics (Sta Agnese and S. Stefano Rotondo), the design in the crown of the apse shows the stars against a black background of night. In the twelfth- and thirteenth-century examples, the scheme becomes increasingly elaborate and sometimes seems to incorporate xv   elements of a zodiac pattern. Examples of this are the three twelfth-century apses: S. Clemente, in which, in the roundel above the elaborate tabernacle, the 'day and night' *motif* is incorporated, 173, 174   Sta Francesca Romana and Sta Maria Maggiore. In the Lateran mosaic it is simple: the doves 71, 148   represent apostles as they do on the S. Clemente Cross.[116] Christ appears as the Agnus Dei. In 29   form, the *velarium* in the summit of the Lateran apse[117] differs from that in the old basilica of 181–182   St Peter's, which was closely followed in the thirteenth-century mosaic in the apse of S. Paolo.

The 'festoon' motif. This term is used here of the *motif* regularly deployed on the soffits of the arches, whether the arch stands free, as does the triumphal arch of Sta Maria Maggiore, or is actually part of the apse, as is more usually the case. It consists, in its developed form, of sheaves of flowers, leaves and fruit. The sheaf is generally beribboned, often inhabited with birds and 200   sometimes with other creatures, and is usually represented as growing out of a flower pot at the 61   base of the soffit on each side, the two sheaves meeting in the crown of the arch, in which a monogram or other *motif* is incorporated. Thus, the borders of the two apsidal mosaics in Sta 40, 41   Costanza, though they show the origins from which the series evolved, do not strictly belong to it, for they are not confined to the soffits, but line the lower edge of the mosaic also; moreover, they are continuous, and are not shown as growing in pots. These two borders have been extensively restored,[118] but enough remains to show the richness and three-dimensional solidity of the original work. They well convey the idea of paradisial plenty which was associated with both pagan and Christian notions of the after-life.

XV S. Clemente. Crown of the mosaic of the apse (*c.* 1125), showing the tabernacle. Above, the mosaic
of the triumphal arch; Christ is shown in a medallion against a background representing night and day

61　　The first example of the true festoon is on the soffits of the triumphal arch in Sta Maria Maggiore. It is puzzling because it is so highly conventionalized. Like so much else in this remarkable mosaic, it anticipates the medieval vision. The festoons consist of flowers in bands of blue and red, beribboned, but with no foliage to set them off, and each bloom almost identical with its neighbour. Nothing as conventional as this reappears till Paschal's mosaics of the ninth century, and

116　　in those, though the festoons are highly conventionalized, they bear no other resemblance to the Sta Maria example, but give a meagre impression in contrast with the latter's profusion.

　　It seems difficult, in fact, to relate the degree of stylization shown in the festoons to the date of the mosaic concerned, and nothing like a regular sequence of development is to be observed.[119]

75, 76　　In Sta Agnese and S. Lorenzo, for example, both much later (seventh-century) works, there is a considerable degree of delicate naturalism in the flowers and leaves. These two examples may be compared with the extremely fine vault mosaic in one of the chapels (that dedicated to St John the Evangelist) of the baptistry of St John Lateran, a mosaic executed in the reign of Hilarus[120] (461–68). The 'festoons' in this vault do not fall strictly within the definition used here, but are

68–70　　rather swags. Those on the ribs of the vault are shown as growing out of urns, not flower pots. Within the squared centre-piece, and surrounding the Agnus Dei, there is a wreath divided into four sections, each representing one of the four seasons with its various fruits and flowers; and on both sides of each rib are suspended, as it were, swags (semicircular in form, but with the upper segments blocked out by the corners of the central square) of leaves and flowers. It was perhaps the elegant naturalism of this work (which is of the greatest refinement) that inspired the festoons in Sta Agnese and in S. Lorenzo.

　　Later examples of the festoon incorporate medallion heads, and it is possible that this feature existed in antiquity also. The festoons of the apsidal mosaic in Sta Maria Maggiore were reworked, like the rest of the mosaic, by Toriti, who made considerable modifications to parts of the original

197　　design. But it is conceivable that the medallion heads there were an early feature, and echo something in the classical original on which the later work was based.

NOTES ON THE TEXT II

1 See pp. 96–97 for further discussion.

2 For later examples, see p. 16, where this technical point is further discussed.

3 For a summary description of the drum mosaics destroyed in 1620, see F. W. Deichmann, *Frühchristliche Kirchen in Rom*, Basle 1948, pp. 26–27. Stern, op. cit., pp. 169–185, gives a more detailed description in which he establishes not only the Christian character of the drum mosaics but their relevance to a mausoleum and their fourth-century date. The lower border was closely analogous to those in Sta Maria Maggiore and St John Lateran (see pp. 94–95 of this book).

4 The cast may be wrongly placed; the original was probably some yards in front of where it now stands. See H. Stern, 'Les Mosaiques de l'église de Sainte Constance à Rome', *Dumbarton Oaks Papers*, XII, 1958, pp. 157–218. Stern (p. 164)

quotes A. Prandi as his authority for this theory of the original position of the sarcophagus, and mentions the different opinions expressed by F. W. Deichmann (see Stern's note 31). But the sarcophagus is already shown in the recess in a sixteenth-century drawing reproduced by Stern.

5 For a drawing of this detail, as it was found by M. Armellini, see his *Le chiese di Roma del secolo IV al XIX*, Rome 1891, p. 1068.

6 See J. Wilpert, *Die römischen Mosaiken und Malereien der Kirchlichen Bauten vom IV bis XIII Jahrhundert*, 4 vols., Freiburg 1916, p. 286; also, for details, Plates 6 and 7. See also Stern, op. cit., p. 192.

7 Stern (op. cit., pp. 202–205; figs 38–46) gives some extraordinarily close pagan parallels to these 'Paradise' mosaics, and reserves judgment on the question whether the mosaics of the vault

of the colonnade have any Christian context. It is the sequence here that gives the strong impression that Christian symbolism was introduced, and in one detail at least Stern's interpretation seems to me mistaken. He considers the horns shown in the mosaic to be drinking vessels—another pagan symbol of the luxuries of the pagan after-life. In the mosaic which he illustrates for comparison the horns are indeed drinking vessels, mounted on stands (as horns used for this purpose were mounted, in classical as well as medieval times). In Sta Costanza they have no stands, but are equipped with straps for slinging over the shoulder. They should rather be compared with the hunter's horn in the S. Clemente mosaic, which, though it dates from the twelfth century, contains, as we shall see, many elements drawn from its antique predecessor.

8 This feature occurs also in the S. Clemente design; see pp. 98, 248. Note also Fig. 1 on p. 60.

9 See C. Leonardi, *Ampelos, Il simbolismo della vite nell'arte pagana e paleocristiana*, Rome 1947, pp. 68–69.

10 Successive numbers of *Römische Quartalschrift*, 54, 1959. The earlier article deals with the *traditio legis*, the subject of the second apse to be discussed here; the later article, 'Eine römische Apsis-komposition', relates the other apse (the first to be discussed here) to the apsidal decoration in the old basilica of St Peter's.

11 Loc. cit., pp. 8–14.

12 F. Gerke, *Das heilige Antlitz*, 1940, Plate 56.

13 See Stern (op. cit., pp. 166–185) for this conclusion.

14 They were probably made of mosaic; the inscription seems actually to have been incorporated in the mosaic, like those of many later works.

15 Adrian I (772–95) seems the most likely.

16 So Deichmann, op. cit., p. 54.

17 Compare the alterations made to the mosaic of SS. Cosma e Damiano by a pope particularly interested in Gregory the Great; see p. 94.

18 The architectural backgrounds on the left are largely original; on the right, mainly restorations.

19 In these two 'portraits' can be seen the beginnings of an approach to traditional iconography. For a discussion of the evolution of this iconography, see F. Gerke, op. cit., p. 39. On sarcophagi of Constantinian date it had not yet appeared. It is still absent from the St Paul shown in Plate III—

a powerful reason for dating that early. Also there is a St Peter, strikingly independent of the tradition, on a sarcophagus of about 340 (see Gerke, Plate 29).

20 For a reproduction of this fragment, see C. Cecchelli, *I mosaici della basilica di S. Maria Maggiore*, Turin 1956, Plate LXXXVI. In its style a classical naturalism still seems to survive.

21 There is a brilliant discussion of this mosaic in W. N. Schumacher, 'Eine römische Apsiskomposition', *Römische Quartalschrift*, 54, 1959, pp. 148 et seq.

22 Cod. Lat. 5408, fols 29 and 31; Cod. Barb. Lat. 4410, fol. 26.

23 For the whereabouts of these fragments see Schumacher, loc. cit., p. 149.

24 *Musaici Cristiania e saggi di pavimenti delle chiese di Roma anterion al secolo* XV, 'Mosaico della Bibliotheca Chigi', Rome 1873–99. Note not only the way the *tesserae* are shaped and set, and the organization of the colour (so far as this can be judged in reproductions of this kind), but also the use of flecks of vermilion as highlights on the cheek and lips. The corresponding feature can be see in Plate III.

25 As we should expect in work of the fourth century. See pp. 12–16 for a discussion of the introduction of the gold background. Work on the mosaic is recorded in the reign of Leo I. The date seems a likely one for this change. See *Liber Pontificalis*, ed. L. Duchesne, 2 vols, Paris 1886, 1892 (third volume of corrections, 1957), vol. 1, p. 329.

26 A word in praise of this preservation of fragments, in the first half of the seventeenth century, may not be out of place. We owe to it the superb Giotto fragment at Boville Ernica (Plate VI). Over the other fragment, in the Vatican, a new version of the Giotto was built in the eighteenth century. Also, we owe to the preservers the fragments from the oratory of John VII, in varying states of repair, but consolidated so that they give an excellent impression of the styles and techniques of the early eighth century. The one exception is the Virgin *orans*, now in Florence: a huge figure, the size of which must have made it very difficult to handle. And we do not know what happened to that after it had been taken to Florence; the damage may have been done there. For these John VII fragments, see pp. 155–156.

27 *Mosaik von der Antike bis zum Mittelalter*, German ed., trans. from Norwegian, Munich 1960, Plate 28.

28 Ibid., Plate 27.

29 See Gerke, loc. cit.,

30 Reproduced on the same plate as the swan in *Cenni storici della basilica Vaticana*, ed. G. B. de Toth, 1955, Plate 15.

31 See p. 296 for an account of this and another fragment which is certainly from the same mosaic, in this collection.

32 But see G. J. Hoogewerff, 'Il mosaico absidiale di S. Giovanni in Laterano ed altri mosaici romani', *Atti della Pont. Accad. Romana di Archeol. Rendiconti*, Series III, vol. XXVII, 1951–54, pp. 297–326. Hoogewerff, while regarding the 'miraculous head' (destroyed in 1884) as ancient, holds that the composition, with the Virgin and apostles, is thirteenth-century. For a discussion, see p. 312.

33 For an account of this technique of preparing a mosaic on an independent bed so that it could be moved *en bloc*, see p. 16.

34 'La decorazione Constantiniana della basilica Lateranense', *Riv. di Archeol. Crist.*, VI, 1929. For a different view see Hoogewerff, loc. cit. A bibliography of the most important articles is to be found in C. Cecchelli, 'A proposito del mosaico del abside Lateranense', *Misc. Biblioth. Hertzianae*, 1961, p. 13. In this article Cecchelli (rightly, I think) rejects Hoogewerff's opinion of the character of the original central feature in this mosaic.

35 Discussed on pp. 68–69.

36 See J. Ciampini's plate of 1690, reproduced by S. Weitzolat in *Misc. Biblioth. Hertzianae*, 1961, p. 19.

37 Munz's valuable account of this mosaic is quoted in full by Hoogewerff; loc. cit., p. 311.

38 In this respect, the original heads of the Sta Pudenziana mosaic form something of a contrast (see Plates 6, 42).

39 See pp. 94–95.

40 See p. 311 et seq.

41 *I mosaici della basilica di S. Maria Maggiore*, Turin 1956.

42 See pp. 16–17.

43 See also M. L. Thérel, 'Une Image de la Sibylle sur l'arc triomphal de Sta Maria Maggiore', *Cahiers archéol.*, 12, 1962, pp. 153–171.

44 *Early Churches of Rome*, Eng. trans. (1960) of French ed., pp. 63–66.

45 Wilpert mentioned some of them (op. cit., pp. 470–476); his selection forms an impressive list. A. W. Bryanck ('Das Problem der Mosaiken von Sta Maria Maggiore', *Festschrift Hans Hahnloser*, 1961, p. 24) expressed the suspicion that the artist of the first three (Abraham) nave panels (Nos 1–3 in the present book) was one of the artists of the triumphal arch—apparently the artist of the Presentation. Although these three (probably by the same hand, as Bryanck said) are more similar to the triumphal arch mosaics than are some others in the series, I cannot believe that they are by any of the artists who worked on the triumphal arch. And surely Bryanck is not justified in claiming the authority of G. Astorri ('Nuove osservazioni sulla tecnica dei mosaici romani della basilica di Sta Maria Maggiore', *Riv. di Archeol. Crist.*, XI, 1934), as he seems to do, for his view that the technique of the mosaics of the triumphal arch is the same as that of the nave panels.

46 Some of the figures have suffered too much damage, in this and other scenes, for one to draw final conclusions about the individual style. Incidentally, I cannot of course claim to be the first observer to have used the term *pointilliste* in this context; though I used it independently, it has occurred to others also.

47 The difference between the two hands could not be more strikingly illustrated than by the two colour plates, published facing one another, in G. Astorri, op. cit., p. 51. One shows three heads from the Presentation scene; the other, a group from the Massacre of the Innocents. The technique of the second, with its regularly placed *tesserae* and its even surface, is still classical. The technique of the other represents (as Astorri says of the whole arch) the beginning of a new age. And the contrast between them is almost as strongly marked as it could be.

48 See p. 14.

49 Cecchelli, op. cit., Plate XXXV (in colour), shows this.

50 L'Orange and Nordhagen's contention (op. cit., p. 65) that the band of sheep in the SS. Cosma e Damiano mosaic is the first in Rome with a gold background is technically correct. But in the triumphal arch mosaics of Sta Maria Maggiore gold had already been used to create the *mise en scène*.

51 For technical similarities, see Cecchelli, op. cit., p. 76, quoting other authorities.

52 Cecchelli, op. cit., Plate XXVII.

53 Cecchelli, op. cit., Plates XXXVII and XXXVIII.

54 A. Maiuri, *Roman Painting*, trans. S. Gilbert, Geneva 1953, p. 75.

55 Cecchelli's colour reproduction (op. cit., Plate XXXIII), though small, is invaluable.

56 C. Bertelli ('Un antico restauro nei mosaici di Sta Maria Maggiore', *Paragone*, March 1955, pp. 40–42) not only recognizes that these figures are a restoration, but dates this restoration (rightly, I have no doubt) to the ninth century.

57 Op. cit., Plates XXXVII and XXXVIII.

58 Cecchelli, op. cit., Plate XI, lowest picture, upper half.

59 A recent discussion of the likely origins of all these designs is in Bryanck, op. cit., pp. 21–26. In being reinterpreted they have certainly acquired some western features, such as the *toga contabulata* worn by Moses' father-in-law in No. 14.

60 See Cecchelli, op. cit., Plate XXIV, for a detail.

61 See p. 79.

62 Cecchelli, op. cit., Plate XXXV.

63 Cecchelli, op. cit., Plates XLIII and XLIV.

64 Cecchelli, op. cit., Plate XXVII.

65 See Cecchelli, op. cit., Plate XXI for a detail.

66 Reproduced, with revisions, by Cecchelli (op. cit., Plate XVI).

67 Cecchelli, op. cit., Plate XXXIV.

68 Cecchelli, op. cit., Plates XXXIV, XLII and XLIII respectively.

69 See Wilpert, op. cit., pp. 420, 421.

70 The original plaster, with its impressions of *tesserae*, if it had survived, would have shown this detail clearly.

71 Anderson 17510: Alinari 30151; Cecchelli, op. cit., Plate XIV. The engravings in J. Ciampini, *Vetera monumenta . . .*, Rome 1690, pp. 200–224, show in summary form the state of all the nave mosaics in the seventeenth century.

72 Anderson 17511; Alinari 30125; Cecchelli, op. cit., Plate XV.

73 Anderson 17512; Alinari 30126; Cecchelli, op. cit., Plate XVI (based on Wilpert).

74 Anderson 17489; Alinari 30127; Cecchelli, op. cit., Plate XVII (upper half).

75 Anderson 17488; Alinari 30135; Cecchelli, op. cit., Plate XVIII.

76 Anderson 17487; Alinari 30132; Cecchelli, op. cit., Plate XIX.

77 Anderson 17486; Alinari 30130; Cecchelli, op. cit., Plates XX and XXI (detail from upper half).

78 Anderson 17485; Alinari 30133; Cecchelli, op. cit., Plate XXII.

79 Anderson 17472; Alinari 30134; Cecchelli, op. cit., Plates XXIII and XXIV (detail from lower half).

80 Anderson 17484; Alinari 30131; Cecchelli, op. cit., Plate XXV.

81 Anderson 17483; Alinari 30128; Cecchelli, op. cit., Plate XXVII (detail from upper half).

82 Anderson 17473; Alinari 30129; Cecchelli, op. cit., Plate XXVIII.

83 For the use of gold in this panel, see p. 14.

84 But see pp. 82–83 for a discussion of the original extent of this panel along the left-hand edge.

85 Anderson 17508; Alinari 30137; Cecchelli, op. cit., Plate XXIX.

86 Anderson 17513; Alinari 30142; Cecchelli, op. cit., Plate XXX (based on Wilpert).

87 Anderson 17482; Alinari 30136; Cecchelli, op. cit., Plates XXXI and XXXII (detail).

88 See p. 79.

89 Anderson 17481; Alinari 30141; Cecchelli, op. cit., Plate XXXIII.

90 Anderson 17480; Alinari 30140; Cecchelli, op. cit., Plate XXXIV.

91 Anderson 17479; Alinari 30143; Cecchelli, op. cit., Plate XXXV (perhaps the only usable photograph of this difficult subject).

92 Anderson 17507; Alinari 30139; Cecchelli, op. cit., Plates XXXVI, XXXVII (detail, upper half) and XXXVIII (detail, lower half).

93 Anderson 17478; Alinari 30138; Cecchelli, op. cit., Plate XXXIX.

94 Anderson 17506; Alinari 30144; Cecchelli, op. cit., Plate XL.

95 Anderson 17477; Alinari 30148; Cecchelli, op. cit., Plate XLI.

96 Anderson 17476; Alinari 30149; Cecchelli, op. cit., Plate XLII.

97 Anderson 17475; Alinari 30145; Cecchelli, op. cit., Plate XLIII.

98 Anderson 17509; Alinari 30147; Cecchelli, op. cit., Plate XLIV.

99 Anderson 17514; Alinari 30150; Cecchelli, op. cit., Plate XLV.

100 Anderson 17474; Alinari 30146; Cecchelli, op. cit., Plate XLVI.

101 In J. Ciampini's account of this mosaic (op. cit., pp. 186–195), there figures an engraving (facing p. 188) of the destroyed triumphal arch mosaics and another (facing p. 191) which shows what was still remaining of the upper half of the existing mosaic inscription in the late seventeenth century. Two male figures, one on either side above the existing figures symbolizing the two churches, survived at that time, as did the Evangelist symbols above.

102 The view has been put forward by Hoogewerff (op. cit., pp. 297–326; see especially p. 316) that this mosaic was based on one already existing in St John Lateran which he assumes to have been destroyed in the thirteenth century. He thinks that the St John mosaic was the model for the mosaics of Sta Prassede and Sta Cecilia. But the precise copying of certain details from SS. Cosma e Damiano in the lower border (the tiny rocks and flowers) in Sta Prassede shows that the former mosaic, not the one in St John, was Paschal's model. The St John mosaic must always have had a 'classical' border like that of the Toriti version in its present form, and if Paschal's artist copied the SS. Cosma e Damiano border, that mosaic, not the St John, must have been his model. For the St John border, see p. 98.

103 The use of silver, comparatively common in Byzantine mosaics, is here unique, among surviving examples, in the Roman series before 800.

104 Gen. ii. 11–14.

105 This mosaic was dated by G. Matthiae to the late seventh century; for a discussion see his *Le chiese di Roma dal IV al X secolo*, vol. I of Roma Cristiana, Rome 1962, p. 212. To me the technique of the setting of the *tesserae* seems so similar to that of the main mosaic that I doubt this later date. See Notes on the Text, III, 16.

106 A photograph exists (Anderson 5131) of an earlier state of this mosaic, in which this roundel was apparently restored in paint; the book is represented with five of its seals. It is difficult to know whether the existing roundel shows the original mosaic with this paint removed or a new mosaic version—probably the latter.

107 Rev. iv. 5.

108 Compare, for example, the Elders on the apsidal arch in Sta Prassede (see p. 206). The example in S. Paolo is modern, though the original was earlier than the mosaic in SS. Cosma e Damiano.

109 In Sta Maria Maggiore a single fragment was discovered of the earlier and much more materialistic treatment of the twenty-four Elders; see the reproduction in Cecchelli, op. cit., Plate LXXXVI.

110 Perhaps this is an allusion to the name of one of the Roman temples formerly occupying the spot: the Templum Sacrae Urbis.

111 See C. R. Morey, *Lost Mosaics and Frescoes of Rome of the Middle Period*, Princeton 1915, pp. 2, 37.

112 For example, in the second-century mosaic reproduced in L'Orange and Nordhagen, op. cit., Plate 14A.

113 For some discussion of the vine see pp. 60 and 62.

114 See the diagram on p. 60.

115 No. 14.

116 See p. 250.

117 See Schumacher, loc. cit., p. 159.

118 The touches of gold in some of the fruits all seem to be restorations, and to be perhaps a misreading of a yellow, used similarly to heighten the effect, which appears in some original sections. The mention of gold in Matthiae, op. cit., p. 136, is, I think, a most unusual slip which seems to affect several of the colours mentioned in the same passage. The central background is of a dun colour. The halos are blue. Yellow was used for intensifying the highlights in the draperies of Christ's robes.

119 Unfortunately, the festoons which no doubt existed on both sides of the mosaic in SS. Cosma e Damiano were destroyed in the reconstruction; therefore we do not known their character.

120 This dating follows that of Matthiae, op. cit., p. 145.

28 Sta Costanza. The porphyry sarcophagus, now in the Vatican Museum (mid-fourth century).

29   St Peter's. Fresco representing the Constantinian apsidal mosaic in the old basilica (mid-fourth century).

30   St Peter's. St Paul, as represented in the apsidal mosaic of the old basilica (detail from Plate 29).

31   St Peter's. St Paul, a surviving fragment apparently from the original Constantinian apsidal mosaic in the old basilica (mid-fourth century). Now in the Vatican Grottoes.

32 St John Lateran. Engraving of the original 'miraculous' head in the main mosaic of the apse, made before its destruction in 1884.

33 Sta Maria Maggiore, detail from mosaic panel in the nave, No. 20 (early fifth century). Three priests.

36　Sta Costanza, mosaic in the vault (mid-fourth century). A section seen approximately from the original position of the sarcophagus.　37 *above right*　Detail of the Paradise pattern.

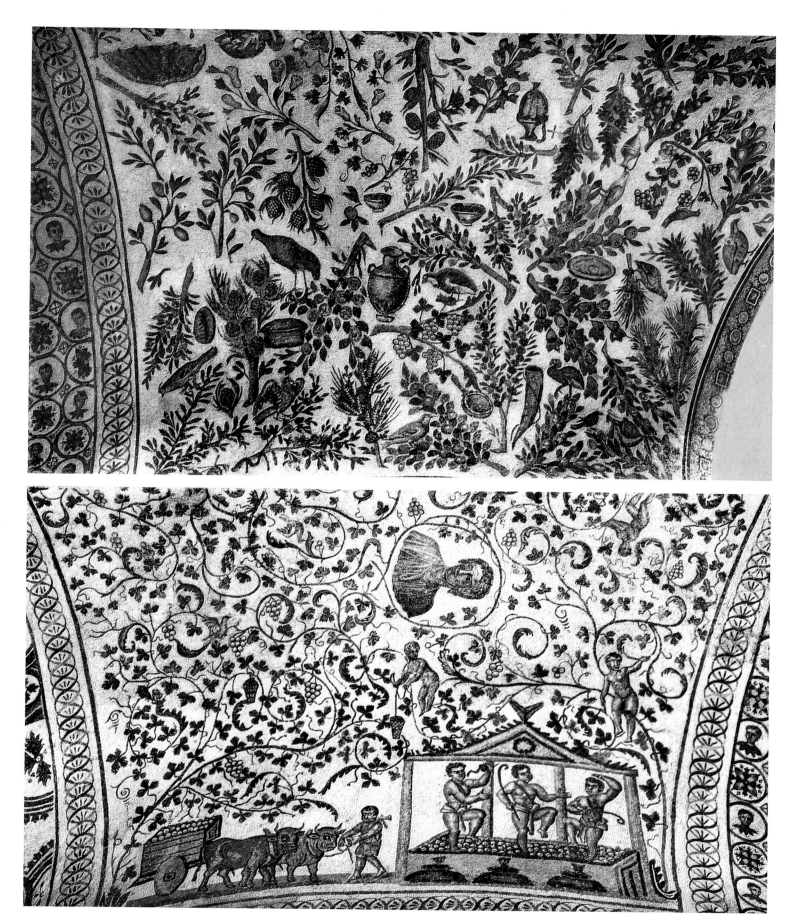

38 Sta Costanza, mosaic in the vault (mid-fourth century). One of the vine-scroll mosaics, representing the grape harvest; *putti* vintagers carting and pressing grapes.

39   Sta Costanza, mosaic in the vault (mid–fourth century). Detail from one of the vine-scroll mosaics; with portrait bust, perhaps of St Constantia's husband.

40, 41 Sta Costanza. Mosaics in two of the small apses (perhaps fourth century, third quarter).

42   Sta Pudenziana, detail from the mosaic of the apse (*c.* 400). St Paul.

43   Sta Pudenziana, detail from the mosaic of
the apse (*c.* 400). Three apostles.

44   Sta Pudenziana, detail from the mosaic of
the apse (*c.* 400). St Peter.

The mosaic inscription reads: DOMINVS ECCLESIAE / CONSER PVDENTI / VATOR ANAE

45   Sta Pudenziana, detail from the mosaic of the apse (*c.* 400). Christ.

46 Sta Maria Maggiore, mosaic panel in the nave, No. 3 (early fifth century).
Above, the parting of Lot and Abraham; below, a pastoral scene.

47 Sta Maria Maggiore, mosaic panel in the nave, No. 5 (early fifth century). Above, Rachel announces the arrival of Jacob; below, Jacob being brought into the house of Laban.

48   Sta Maria Maggiore, mosaic panel in the nave, No. 14 (early fifth century). Above, the marriage of Moses and Zipporah; below, Moses as shepherd.

49 Sta Maria Maggiore, mosaic panel in the nave, No. 15 (early fifth century). The Egyptians overwhelmed in the Red Sea.

50 Sta Maria Maggiore, mosaic panel in the nave, No. 18 (early fifth century). The battle with the Amalekites.

51 Sta Maria Maggiore, mosaic panel in the nave, No. 19 (early fifth century). Above, the sending-out of the Israelite spies; below, the threatened stoning of Moses, Joshua and Caleb.

52   Sta Maria Maggiore, mosaic panel in the nave, No. 25 (early fifth century). Above, the putting to flight of the Amorites; below, the hailstorm.

53 Sta Maria Maggiore, mosaic panel in the nave, No. 22 (early fifth century). Above, Joshua and the angel; below, the spies leave Jericho and return to Joshua.

54   Sta Maria Maggiore, detail from mosaic panel shown in Plate 53 (early fifth century).
Joshua doing homage to the angel.

55 Sta Maria Maggiore, mosaic of the triumphal arch (*c.* 435). Above, the Annunciation; Joseph's doubts.
Below, the Epiphany.

56   Sta Maria Maggiore, mosaic of the triumphal arch (*c.* 435). Above, Christ, during the flight into Egypt, is recognized by Aphrodisius; below, Herod and the Magi.

57 Sta Maria Maggiore, mosaic of the triumphal arch (*c.* 435). Angels from the Presentation scene.

58   Sta Maria Maggiore, mosaic of the triumphal arch (*c.* 435). Angels from the scene of the doubting Joseph.

59　Sta Maria Maggiore, mosaic of the triumphal arch (*c.* 435). Detail from the Epiphany scene.

60   Sta Maria Maggiore, mosaic of the triumphal arch (*c.* 435). Detail from the scene of the Massacre of the Innocents.

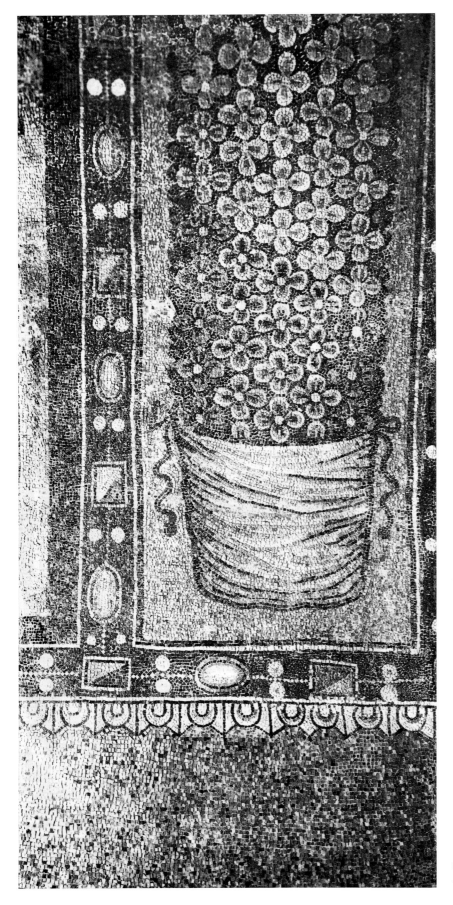

61 Sta Maria Maggiore, soffit of the
triumphal arch (*c.* 435). The base of the festoon.

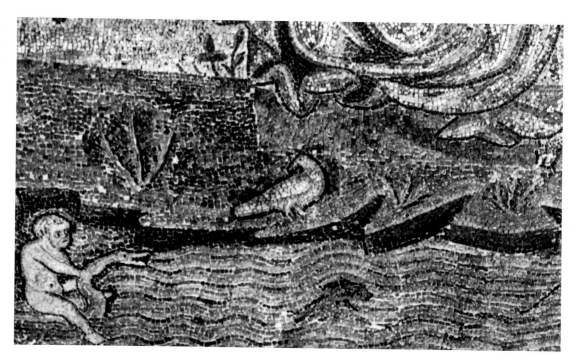

62 Sta Maria Maggiore,
main mosaic of the apse.
Part of the classical frieze;
apparently re-used by
Toriti, c. 1294.

63 Sta Maria Maggiore, main mosaic of the apse (by Toriti; c. 1294). A river god from the classical frieze; this figure is a modern restoration.

64 Sta Maria Maggiore, main mosaic of the apse. Part of the classical frieze; re-used by Toriti, *c.* 1294.

65 Sta Maria Maggiore, main mosaic of the apse. Detail from the classical frieze; re-used by Toriti, *c.* 1294. A *putto*, driving a swan in harness, rides on the back of a dolphin. The swan has a fish in its mouth.

66 Sta Maria Maggiore, main mosaic of the apse. Part of the classical frieze; re-used by Toriti, *c.* 1294.

67 St John Lateran, main mosaic of the apse. Detail from a version made in 1884 of Toriti's mosaic, itself based on a classical original.

68, 69   Baptistry of St John Lateran, chapel of St John the Evangelist, mosaic of the vault (fifth century). *above*   Central roundel. After Wilpert.

70 *right above*   Baptistry of St John Lateran, chapel of St John the Evangelist. Detail from the mosaic of the vault (fifth century).

71   Baptistry of St John Lateran, apsidal mosaic (*atrium*). Detail from the crown of the apse, showing the tabernacle and the pendent crosses (fifth century).

72   Baptistry of St John Lateran. Detail of the scroll pattern of the apsidal mosaic (*atrium*); fifth century.

73 S. Clemente, mosaic of the apse (*c.* 1125). Detail.

74   Sta Sabina, mosaic of the nave (probably *c.* 425). Detail. The figure represents the Jewish Church.

28 For the *putti* vintagers, compare the mosaic in Sta Costanza (Plate 38). The mosaics and the sarcophagus were clearly planned together.

31 The head is eccentric to the gold *tesserae* (which possibly date from the fifth century). A similar eccentricity in relation to the adjoining *tesserae* can be seen in Plate 33 (the head on the left) and in Plate 58 (the angel on the right), suggesting in the latter at least, as here, the glow of the face.

32 The work lines shown in the engraving suggest a technique similar to that of the head of St Paul shown in Plate 31. Note also what seems to have been the similar treatment of the strands of hair.

33 The head on the left is eccentric to the *tesserae*, as in Plate 31.

34 For the position of this roundel pattern in the series, see Plate 36.

35 The mosaics in the vault shown in this photograph, which was taken from the entrance, are the dolphin pattern (nearest the camera) and the Cupid and Psyche pattern.

36 This plate (the photograph was taken from the position of the sarcophagus) shows the Paradise pattern and, beyond, the roundel pattern of figures and heads.

38 Compare the design on the sarcophagus (Plate 28). The head in the centre of this example is largely, perhaps entirely, modern.

39 Here the head in the centre (probably that of Sta Constantia herself) is original. Compare the somewhat blotchy technique of the head shown in Plate 42, made a generation or so later.

40, 41 These mosaics have been heavily restored and, perhaps, substantially altered. That shown in Plate 40 seems, in its present form, to have been intended to represent a woman (possibly Sta Costanza herself) approaching the Almighty. The other mosaic, in its present form, shows the *largitio pacis*.

42 Almost all the lower part of what is shown in the photograph is modern, but the splendid head and the hand holding the wreath are original. Compare with this head the one shown in Plate 39.

43 The forehead and nearer eye of the apostle on the right have been somewhat restored. The join of the old and new work at the neck is very awkward. The other two heads are original, but by a different hand from the one that made the head of St Paul shown in Plate 42.

44 The head itself is original, but almost all the rest of the area of mosaic visible in the plate is modern.

45 This figure has been extensively restored in detail. But the startling highlights on the drapery seem to be original, as is the woman's cloak shown in Plate 6.

49 For a detail of this scene, see Plate 7.

55 Compare the preliminary sketch (Plate 1) of the angel at the top with the final version shown here. The design and position of the house was substantially modified in the later stages.

61 Compare the base ornament here with that shown in Plate 71.

62 The broken line, two-thirds of the way up the plate, may mark the join between classical work, preserved by Toriti, and his own mosaic above.

63 This is the modern version of the river god, at one end of the frieze. For the corresponding antique figure, see Plate XIV.

64 The vessel to which the *putto* has attached a sail is a wine jar, as often in classical work. The classical work here clearly includes the boy with the dog.

65 For the technique of representing the naked body by means of an outline with inner modelling, compare Plate 34.

66 The join between classical and medieval work seems to run below the feet of the large figures.

67 The frieze was strikingly similar to that in Sta Maria Maggiore; the original versions of the two mosaics may not only have been of about the same date but may also have been executed by the same classical artist.

68 The wreath round the Agnus Dei represents the four seasons. The very small *tesserae* of the halo give it a different texture.

69 The background is gold; for a detail, see Plate 70.

71 The Agnus Dei, and apostles symbolized by doves, can also be seen.

72 This scroll pattern is worked in two shades of green, heightened with gold, against a dark-blue background.

73 This mosaic was apparently based on a classical original, whose scroll was presumably similar to that shown in Plate 72. The twelfth-century version is harsher and more formal.

74 The date is established with a high degree of probability by the mosaic inscription *c.* 430.

III

THE 'BYZANTINE' WORKS OF THE SIXTH, SEVENTH AND EIGHTH CENTURIES

IT IS A MATTER OF DISCUSSION how far the fifth- and sixth- century mosaics of Ravenna are to be regarded as Byzantine, and how far Roman. One feature of later Byzantine work, as L'Orange and Nordhagen observe,[1] is the use of stone *tesserae* to represent the face and hands. There are two reasons for this: first, the wish to suggest a different texture; secondly, and perhaps more important, the fact that stone *tesserae* can be cut into much tinier and more accurately shaped chips than glass. (When glass is employed, the resulting sizes and shapes are to some extent haphazard, if very small chips are being made.) In the fine sixth-century portrait of St Ursicinus, in the 93 church of S. Apollinare in Classe in Ravenna, the use of stone for the face is apparent. To compare this with the twelfth-century portrait of St John Chrysostom in Palermo is to see where this road 19 was eventually to lead. But if we look back, instead of forwards, and compare the fifth-century portrait of the Virgin in Sta Maria Maggiore with that of Justinian himself in S. Vitale in Ravenna, 14, 13 it will be seen that, though in the latter (which dates from *c.* 530) the structural lines are more disciplined, yet in some ways the technique remains closer to that of the Sta Maria portrait than it is to that of St Ursicinus. Moreover, many of the *tesserae* in the Justinian portrait show tiny pits in the surface, like pin holes, where oxidization in the glass has taken place. Some of the materials may be natural stone. But glass is certainly used over most of the surface of this portrait head, whereas in that of St Ursicinus there appears to be none.

Two features, then, may be taken, in Rome, to indicate Byzantine influence in technical details: the disciplining of the structural lines of mosaic to emphasize the structural lines of the features, and the use of natural materials for the face. In the Justinian processions (and even earlier than this, in the mosaics of S. Apollinare Nuovo), smaller *tesserae* are already in regular use for the faces. This is something which had indeed been done long before by classical mosaicists, in order to 5 secure greater precision of detail. But in the Justinian–Theodora mosaics the process of disciplining the structural lines has only just begun, and the use, by preference, of natural materials to represent the flesh has not yet, perhaps, started. One may put this point in another way. Technically, the

Ravenna portrait of Justinian is still close to the Roman tradition. It forms a surprising contrast to

15, 16 two eastern Byzantine portrait heads from Hagios Georgios in Salonika, to be dated about the year 400. In these, the *tesserae* are already built into systematized patterns, and the structural lines are a significant feature of the work.

When the impact of Byzantine artistic ideas was felt in Rome in the fifth and sixth centuries, though the iconographic features of Byzantine mosaics were certainly imitated, technical details were often not copied. We shall see that in the famous example in the chapel of St Venantius, the resetting of the head of Christ unfortunately makes it impossible to determine the original technique. But the series of heads of saints which has survived in the apse of that chapel (even if they have been mainly reset), and which is of fine quality, seems technically to have been in the Roman rather than in the Byzantine tradition. The material is glass. There is some slight trace of responsiveness of the structural lines of the mosaic, in one or two of the heads, to the structure of the features; but this has not yet anything like the sophistication that it has in truly Byzantine examples. And the *tesserae* are often not noticeably smaller than those of the surrounding picture.

XVII In some ways, however, this fine mosaic shows powerful Byzantine influence. Its designers knew the S. Vitale mosaic and copied from it the stance; the heavy, sweeping cloaks, each decorated with its *tablion*; and the general arrangement of the figures in a row, in contrast with the rhythmic

XI, XII, XIII group of SS. Cosma e Damiano. Yet, technically, the craftsmen were working largely in a Roman
89–92 idiom. This is not true of the two superb portraits in S. Stefano Rotondo, of approximately the same date. Here the small *tesserae* of the flesh, and the regular structural arrangements of the *tesserae* in the draperies, betray either the strongest Byzantine influence on technique as well as design, or

93 perhaps the work of an actual Byzantine artist, conceivably a mosaicist who worked in S. Apollinare in Classe in Ravenna, as the comparison illustrated in our plates suggests.

The majestic spirituality of these two great figures is to some extent anticipated in the apsidal mosaic of Sta Agnese, if that is indeed a few years earlier, as seems probable. Here too the portraiture is of great refinement. But it is the wonderful proportioning of these three tall figures that make the mosaic so effective, and this is a quality which is certainly derived from Byzantine sources. In the SS. Cosma e Damiano mosaic, last (as we have reckoned it) of the classical series, it is the solid, overwhelming power of the theophany that is so impressive. With the mosaics of the next generation, Byzantine inspiration brings an other-worldly quality to the design, as well as at times a strong influence on the craftsmanship.

XVIII, 106–
109, 111,
113 In the mosaics of the oratory of John VII, so far as we can reconstruct them from remaining fragments, Byzantine workmanship is apparent in points of technique as well as of manner. The materials out of which face and flesh (in the Orte fragment, for instance) are constructed, are natural, not artificial. The central figure, on a far larger scale than any of the rest, dominating the whole design by sheer size, was the Virgin *orans*. So far as could be judged from the fragment that survives, she would not seem to have had that unearthly quality which St Agnes has in the Sta Agnese mosaic, though the whiteness of the face (with patches, rather than a suffusion, of colour) is strongly reminiscent of Sta Agnese. The *orans* position was certainly portrayed in several

99 Roman mosaics of about this time (such as that in the chapel of St Venantius) and had been portrayed not only in other media (examples being the carved wooden doors of Sta Sabina,
195 and several paintings in the catacombs), but probably at an early date in mosaic in St John Lateran, and is not in itself a certain sign of Byzantine influence. John VII was himself a Greek and the most recent work on these mosaics has shown the probability that many were actually made by Byzantine craftsmen.

The main mosaic is set, unusually, within the triumphal arch (which the bombardment of 1943 left more or less intact) and so cannot be seen from the nave but only from within the choir. The explanation lies in the complete remodelling of the church in the thirteenth century. Before that date, this was the triumphal arch of an apse which opened where the end of the nave is now. The work probably belongs to the episcopacy of Pelagius (Pope Pelagius II, 579–90), who is represented as offering the church and is shown without a halo of any kind. The view that it was reset (or that the central figure was reset) at a later date in the Middle Ages was no doubt based on the evident difference in technique between the central heads and the others, the faces of the central figures being worked in the smaller *tesserae* that we associate with Byzantine influence (contrast Plates 79, 81 with 82). The fine detail of photographs made by the Soprintendenza brings the point out clearly. I have no doubt that this difference is due to the original master-craftsmen rather than to any reworking of the mosaic later. One of those remarkable nineteenth-century scholars who did not have the advantages of photography but had visual memory and flair, M. Vitet, suggested in 1863[2] that the Christ was eastern but that the figures of saints, less austere and less tall, seemed to be in the Roman tradition.

The mosaic has been restored in modern times at both ends; but early peculiarities (for example И for N in the principal inscription, which is in square Roman capitals) remain. A sketch made in 1639[3] shows that the right-hand and left-hand edges of the mosaic were then missing, together with most of the representations of Jerusalem and Bethlehem. The drawing suggests that a large part of Pelagius's clothes, on the left, are a modern restoration, as are the lower part of those of St Hyppolitus, on the right, and most of the representations of the two cities.

The mosaic commemorates in particular St Lawrence (in golden clothing) and the building   77
of the church in his honour by Pelagius. It represents, in the centre, Christ, in purple-brown robes,   81
seated on the blue globe of the Firmament; in his left hand he holds a staff, and his right hand
is held up in blessing. On each side are St Peter and St Paul. With St Peter are St Lawrence   79, 18
(martyred in Rome in 258), who holds a book (which reads DISPERSIT . . . DEDIT PAVPERIBVS,
'He scattered and gave to the poor'), and Pelagius, in whose hands is a model of the church offered
to Christ. Pelagius is vested as an archbishop, in dalmatic, chasuble and pallium; the pallium is the
later form with three crosses, but these may be the work of a restorer. With St Paul are St Stephen   80
and St Hyppolitus, who holds a martyr's crown. The former is present because the church con-   82
tains relics of the saint; the latter is present because, according to legend, he was the gaoler of St
Lawrence. On the book held by St Stephen are the words A DE [sc. AD DEUM?] SIT ANIMA MEA,
'In the hand of God be my spirit', apparently a reference to Acts vii. 59. On the left, in the spandrel
of the arch, is Jerusalem; in the corresponding position on the right, Bethlehem. In form, these
are similar to the representations of Jerusalem and Bethlehem in the mosaic in the chapel of St
Venantius in the baptistry of St John Lateran (though the note in the previous paragraph about
restoration should be borne in mind). The ground of the main mosaic is green; the background
of sky is gold, into which St Lawrence's tunic merges almost indistinguishably. Under the arch
is a festoon of flowers, fruits and foliage, intertwined with a ribbon. Some of this (for example,   76
the lilies and bunches of grapes) is unusually naturalistic for the period, and the workmanship is
specially fine.

The drapery on the figures to the left and right of Christ is linear in treatment, no attempt
having been made to suggest light and shade on the folds. The figures are comparatively stiff and
formal, though a sense of composition has not yet been entirely lost. Matthiae,[4] whose opinion

of the extent to which the mosaic has been restored may be optimistic in view of the evidence of damage recorded in the drawing of 1639 mentioned above, distinguishes, nevertheless (convincingly, I think), between the work of three hands: the master, working in a broad, rather flat manner analogous to that of the Arian baptistry in Ravenna, and responsible for the figures of Christ, St Peter, St Paul and St Stephen; a second artist, who made the figure of St Hyppolitus and possibly the festoons of the soffit, working in the Roman classical manner of which he was one of the last representatives (the festoons seem to look back to the elegant work in the chapel of St John in the oratory of St John Lateran); and a third artist, responsible for the group of St Lawrence and Pelagius, who modelled his style on that of the Byzantine court but showed traces of his provincial upbringing. This characterizing of the style used for the figure of St Lawrence seems to me perhaps questionable, but the division of the work between the three hands is fully acceptable.

Matthiae rightly rejects the notion that differences of style in this mosaic are due to different phases of restoration. In the details of the portraits, these three styles are clearly differentiated. The artist of the Christ, St Peter, St Paul and St Stephen used very small *tesserae*, fairly uniform in size, for the faces, though for lines of shading he interspersed them with lines of larger units. The main texture is closely packed for the faces; for the drapery it is far looser. These heads are unlike anything that we have encountered so far in the Roman series, the head of St Agnes being the most similar. The St Hyppolitus, however (in which the material, to judge from the pitting that has occurred on the surface, is largely glass, as opposed to the stone used for the faces of the four heads worked by the master), would almost seem in place in Sta Maria Maggiore, the units being large, irregular and more loosely composed than in the Christ, St Peter, St Paul and St Stephen. But the penetrating glance of the eye is a lively feature, and gives this idiom a power which the St Peter and St Paul, for example, do not have. The St Lawrence, again, is (I think) in the Roman tradition; the *tesserae* are larger, the material is glass, and the structure is loosely knit. The hand, however, is surely different from that of the St Hyppolitus and conveys a sense of depth and mystery which is marvellously effective.

The series of figures was attributed to a later period by P. Baldass,[5] whose discussion of the styles of the drapery (though it reached a conclusion similar to that given above in distinguishing between the hands at work on the series) did not convince me that his later dating of the work is right. He succeeded, I think, in exposing the origin of eleventh- and twelfth-century styles in Rome, rather than in proving that any of the figures, in their present form, belong substantially to this later period. We can regard these drapery forms (in which the heavy, solid, naturalistic folds of the mosaics in SS. Cosma e Damiano are replaced by a flat pattern, mapped out on the surface) as the first signs in Rome of a medieval style of drapery, apparently derived from Ravenna, where the work in the Arian baptistry seems to have been its source. This style, with its completely linear folds, becomes the regular formula in work of the ninth century; and when in the twelfth, in some of the figures in Sta Francesca Romana, we notice a softer and more delicately modelled pattern (for example, in the St John there), we are led to suppose that the artist was deliberately seeking out earlier models. It is, in a way, a paradox that the first medieval mosaic in Rome should have been designed for a building which was constructed of fine classical materials, with magnificent carved details derived from antique sources. But it may be due to the strength of the Roman tradition in portraiture that, when so many other features became stereotyped, a noble series of portraits continued to appear in the mosaics of the next two hundred and fifty years. The finest heads in this S. Lorenzo mosaic are in quality the equal of any.

S. Teodoro

This mosaic, reproduced and discussed in detail (especially in the matter of its relationship to the mosaic of SS. Cosma e Damiano) by Matthiae,[6] is comparatively little known. But it is important, in spite of extensive restorations, since those parts that are original date from a period from which very little work in mosaic survives. The seventeenth-century restoration of the mosaic seems to have been done by an artist named J. B. Calandia.[7] The mosaic is in a shallow apse off the main rotunda of the church and shows, in the centre, Christ seated on the globe of the Firmament, his right hand held up (in the Latin manner)[8] in blessing, while in his left hand and on his left shoulder there rests a cross. Matthiae compares this treatment of the 'throne' of Christ with those in S. Lorenzo fuori le Mura (before 590)[9] and in one of the small apses in Sta Costanza. He regards this   77, 40 figure as probably earlier than that of S. Lorenzo. It is unfortunately impossible to know whether the original Christ was beardless, since the bearded head is completely new. On his right stands St Paul, introducing a figure with an elaborate patterned cloak (as in SS. Cosma e Damiano) who   85, XIII is holding in his hand a martyr's crown. On the left is St Peter, similarly introducing a figure   83 holding a martyr's crown.[10] Once again, as in SS. Cosma e Damiano, his cloak has a rich pattern. Above, the Divine Hand reaches down out of striated clouds. The unusual formal pattern in the border which ran all round the mosaic, and of which more than half remains in its original condition, is a notable departure from the main Roman tradition. Matthiae studied the question of the extent of the restorations, and gives a diagram which shows them. Original in his view are: the globe of the Firmament; the feet and lower outline of the draperies of Christ; the drapery on the right side of the upper part of his body; the left-hand side of the halo; the upper part of the Cross. On the left, much of the face of St Paul and the lower part of his drapery is original,   85 together with the adjoining fold of the martyr's cloak and the crown. On the right, the main part of the face of St Peter and of the martyr whom he presents, with the folds of the cloak   83, 86 hanging from St Peter's right arm, and his right foot, also represent original work. Fragments of the other figure, including the arm and a small section of the cloak, are also original. The pose of the two martyrs, as Matthiae pointed out, is similar to, and was derived from, that of the corresponding figures in SS. Cosma e Damiano. The figures still seem to have been composed in a group, unlike those in the mosaics of S. Lorenzo or in the chapel of St Venantius.   77, 99

Matthiae[11] sees in the mosaic a certain nervelessness in the design, indicating a comparatively degenerate original. There is no doubt that in its present condition the mosaic gives this impression; and in particular there is a weakness and poverty of expression in the much restored figure of Christ. The difficulty is to know how much of this is due to the restoration. Some of the details that are original (such as those illustrated in Plates 83, 85 and 86) seem to me of fine quality. These three illustrations incidentally show the brilliantly effective quality of the best restoration work done in Rome: the repairs are obvious, as they should be, but not obtrusive. The head of St Peter, which has points of similarity not only with the one in S. Lorenzo (Plate 79) but also with an early Vatican fragment (Plate 84) already mentioned, has been repaired on the lower right-hand side, where the point of the chin is new. The expression is, indeed, softer than in the S. Lorenzo head, but the result (here in the Roman tradition of craftsmanship, there in the Byzantine) may be thought more effective, as it is certainly more personal. There is a repair, in almost exactly the same place, in the head of the martyr whom Peter sponsors. The St Paul has suffered more   85 severely, and the domed forehead above the eyebrow is almost entirely restored. In all these portraits, however, there is a penetrating humanity which in no way permits us to decry the talents of the artist responsible. In the absence of evidence other than that of style, Matthiae suggests a date a little after the middle of the sixth century; the artist's work is closest to that of the artist who executed the figure of St Lawrence in S. Lorenzo fuori le Mura. But the hand is not the same.

STA AGNESE FUORI LE MURA

The mosaic commemorates St Agnes, martyred in Diocletian's reign (a commemorative inscription, set up by Pope Damasius less than a hundred years later, can be seen on the great stair near the entrance to the church), and also two popes, Symmachus (498–514) and Honorius (625–38), both active patrons of the church. The inscription implies that Honorius was the pope responsible for the mosaic; the practice of marking a patron still living with a square halo, which could have made the point explicit, is not found in Roman mosaics[12] till nearly a century later.[13] The mosaic itself is simple and splendidly effective. There are three figures against a dull gold background: St Agnes in the centre, with Pope Honorius and Pope Symmachus on each side. The simplicity of the design, with the tall, unearthly figures, the vivid portraits of the two men (in intentional contrast with the supernatural face between them), and the symbolic richness of the robes which St Agnes is wearing, make a composition which is as telling as that of almost any Roman mosaic. There is virtually no 'composition' to link the three figures, such as there still was in the mosaic of SS. Cosma e Damiano. They are independent (like the figures in a Byzantine frieze of saints), though widely spaced here. The central position of the saint is not paralleled in any other mosaic in our series. She stands on a small platform, and what seem to be the flames of her funeral pyre are shown on both sides of her feet. She wears a robe of dull purple or 'murrey-colour', decorated with a roundel of gold on which is a bird, the symbol of the spiritual life. Over her robe she wears jewelled vestments sometimes described as the robes of a Byzantine empress, though they are quite unlike those worn by the Empress Theodora in the Ravenna mosaic. Over her left arm she has a white scarf decorated with gold, and she holds in both hands a scroll sealed with a cross. On her head is a crown. The patches of colour on her cheeks anticipate a later Byzantine technique. On her right, Honorius, with a white dalmatic, chasuble of murrey colour and pallium, holds a model of the church which he is offering to her; on her left, Symmachus, similarly vested, holds a book. Both are tonsured. The ground is dark green, with an equally broad band of lighter green above.

The background of the main apsidal vault is gold, not so rich as in many other mosaics, perhaps because gold leaf in the 'sandwich' *tesserae*[14] was sparingly used, possibly because the *tesserae* themselves were reversed. In the crown of the vault there is a small segment of a circle of white sprinkled with red dolphin-shaped clouds; against this background the Divine Hand holds out a crown of martyrdom above the head of St Agnes. The white is bounded by bands of blue and black (representing probably the day and the night), both being scattered with stars. Lining the arch of the vault is the usual design of a sheaf of leaves, fruit and flowers (including grapes, lilies and pomegranates), growing out of a pot which is banded with stripes of colour, and which is shown as standing at the foot of the curve of the arch on both sides. The work has an elegance and naturalism that contrast charmingly with the unearthly character of the mosaic as a whole. At the crown of the arch is a cross in a roundel. There has been some restoration of the mosaic from time to time, especially in parts of St Agnes's dress and scarf and parts of the vestments of Symmachus. Two or three patches of restoration in the background are obvious. But the repairs generally affect comparatively unimportant sections of the mosaic, and the upper part, with the heads (the men's heads being specially fine), seems to be almost entirely original. The date of the mosaic is 625–38, as shown by the inscription.[15]

148

XVI   Sta Agnese fuori le Mura, mosaic of the apse (*c.* 625).
St Agnes, with Pope Honorius offering the church.

This chapel contains the most elaborate of the mosaics in the baptistry of St John Lateran. Made in the seventh century, some of the figures are strongly reminiscent of those in S. Vitale at Ravenna, with which the designer was surely familiar. The mosaics form the decoration of the apse and of the triumphal arch outside it. At the apex of the apse is Christ the Pantocrator (a bust), in a purple robe, with the right hand held across the chest, thumb to third finger, in the Greek style—an almost overwhelmingly large figure in the small scale of the apse as a whole. On each side are two half-length figures of angels, holding out their hands towards him in prayer. Matthiae well compares these angels with those on the triumphal arch of SS. Cosma e Damiano. He thinks the angels in that church are later in style than the mosaic of this apse; but to me the similarity of technique of the angels' faces there with those of the figures of the apse suggest that one must date them together.[16] The different form of the angel's wing (more linear in St Venantius) is also noticeable. The cloaks are blown outwards; each cloak has a monogram, in each instance H, for Johannes; here the allusion may be to the special honour accorded to the two Saint Johns in this church. The background is gold, with vivid patches of striped cloud around the divine figure. The colouring of the head is bold and vivacious.

Immediately below this group, on a smaller scale, is the Virgin in a robe of purple, holding up her hands (*orans*) and supported by four figures on either side, three on either side having each a halo. This range, or procession, of figures is continued most effectively on the walls outside the apsidal arch (again, there are four figures, this time each with a halo, on either side). Their variety is most unusual. They are not a stage army. Each is individualized in features, hair, clothes and stance, though the uniformity of heights, the equidistance of each figure from the next, and the repeated circles of the halos make the whole an effective pattern. The similarity of the Virgin in the centre to the figure in the Ascension picture of the Rabula Gospels has been noted and it has been suggested that the mosaic represents the Ascension. But the character of the figures, apart from the Virgin, makes the scene rather a theophany, though it is evidently based on the grouping of an Ascension. The element of composition in the apse lies only in the different stance of the figures to the right and the left of the Virgin.

Within the apse, the figures, except for the Virgin, are dressed either traditionally as apostles, or in ecclesiastical dress. They represent saints of major importance for this church: St Peter, St Paul, St John the Evangelist, St John the Baptist, and two others apparently associated with this chapel; one of these holds a model of the chapel, the other holds a casket. The saints who complete the series outside the recess of the apse are, so far as they can be identified, martyrs, perhaps all from Dalmatia. The ecclesiastics are vested like those in the Ravenna processions: archbishops, each with dalmatic, chasuble and, above it, the early pallium, with a single cross only; lesser ecclesiastics with dalmatic, like the two popes in the Sta Agnese mosaic. Those not vested as ecclesiastics wear the Byzantine cloak, or *chlamys*, decorated with the *tablion*. The patterns over the leg are thought of by the artist as being on the tunic below the cloak. This series of figures is one of the most notable achievements in the field of Roman mosaic.

Framing the triumphal arch is a simple pattern consisting of small crosses in roundels, separated by groups of quadripartite floral ornaments. On either side of the crown of this frame are two squares, each with two Evangelist symbols. Above the end figure on each side are rectangles with representations of cities, the usual Jerusalem and Bethlehem (though they are not named here). The form they take is comparable with that of those in the S. Lorenzo mosaic, not far distant from this mosaic in date. (The S. Lorenzo cities were no doubt adapted from these by a modern

XVII Baptistry of St John Lateran, chapel of St Venantius,
mosaic on the wall outside the apsidal arch (c. 640). Three saints.

restorer, but enough remained of the character of the original work to justify that being done.) All these features above the main design are brilliantly colourful.

The similarities with the Justinian mosaics at Ravenna might suggest Pope John III (561–75) as the John of the main inscription, but there is literary evidence that Pope John IV (640–42) from Dalmatia 'made a church for the blessed martyrs Venantius, Anastasius and Maurus, and many other martyrs, whose relics he caused to be brought from Dalmatia and Istria and to be buried in the aforesaid church by the Lateran fountain'. This is firm evidence for the date of the mosaics. They are a century later than the Justinian mosaics which inspired them.

A short article describing the most recent restoration[17] makes it clear that the mortar was becoming detached from the vault in many different places, and that there were many patches of poor repair which greatly prejudiced the effect of the original. The effect of the renewed mosaic is fine, though, probably inevitably, the character of the individual hands has been almost entirely lost. But the work in the present form gives, I have no doubt, a good 'composite' picture of the technique as well as the manner of the period.

It is worth while, since the mosaic is photographically well documented, to examine the records of the central group in the crown of the apse made before and after the latest work was done. In spite of the sequence of the serial numbers, photograph IV. 7. 10 of the Vatican Photographic Archive (Plate 100) is earlier than III. 2. 11 (Plate 98), one being taken before the most recent restoration, the other after. Some caution is needed because of the differing sensitivity to colours of photographic plates at the two periods. The Christ in this mosaic is in what seems to have been the gentle tradition of the 'miraculous head' in the apse of St John Lateran; the face has not the austere, terrifying power of the Christ in SS. Cosma e Damiano, though the recently restored version is perhaps more severe than the earlier. Relying only on the more recent version, one would conclude that the orderly work lines of the forehead suggested a Byzantine craftsman; and this may, in fact, be a justifiable view. But a comparison with the earlier version shows that the forehead has actually been entirely reset. The pattern of the *tesserae* is substantially new, though in some places it may have been possible for the restorer to trace the original lines from the remains of the original mortar. It is noticeable, however, that the regular lines running down the nose are similar in both versions. But a small section of one of the working drawings made during the most recent restoration shows that in all this part of the face (with the important exception of the mouth and chin) there had already been an extensive repair (indicated by vertical shading in the working drawing) at some much earlier period, long before the most recent work was done. We cannot, therefore, conclude that even the work lines of the nose are certainly original, though these could in the earlier restoration have preserved a still earlier pattern and so be good evidence.

In both recorded versions, however, what is immediately apparent is the difference in texture between the work on the head of Christ and that on the angels' heads. It may be that here, as in S. Lorenzo, the head of the Christ was by a Byzantine craftsman, or at least by one working in the Byzantine tradition. Further comparison between the two versions (when all allowances have been made for the effects of cleaning, and for differences due to the slightly different angles of the two photographs and the different degrees of sensitivity of the two photographic plates) raises questions whether the patches of colour on the angels' cheeks shown in the earlier photograph were in the original mosaic (as in some other examples of this period); whether the clumsier hands and broader fingers of both Christ and the angels in the more recent version represent the original; and whether the neck (more happily treated in the earlier version) has not been altered substantially in the more recent one. One sees also how, in the process of resetting, the drapery

152

has become reticulated with mortar lines. These too may conceivably give a more accurate impression of the original appearance than that given by the earlier photograph, since, as has been remarked earlier,[18] there is reason to think that Byzantine craftsmen sometimes planned the mortar lines to show on the surface of the mosaic.

The result of a detailed examination of the mosaic in the crown of the apse, then, is to raise doubts as to whether the details of setting, anywhere in this fine work, can be taken as certainly preserving the lines originally given by the seventh-century craftsmen. I should be ready, however, to accept some details in the notable series of portrait heads[19] as going back to the original   102, 104, 105 master: the white line down the ridge of the nose; the single dark *tessera* below the nose, above the mouth; the group of dark *tesserae* set with brilliant irregularity in the centre of the eye; the irregular shapes and sizes of the *tesserae* in general and the loose structure into which they are worked. In our colour plate showing the figures outside the apse, the dotted line of some of the   XVII drawing and the more obvious cloisons of mortar suggest a greater degree of Byzantinism here, in technique, than within the apse itself. And the design also, in this part of the work, is, as we have seen, more strongly Ravennate.

S. STEFANO ROTONDO
This church is believed to have been built during the reign of Pope Simplicius (468–83). There seems no doubt that its plan and its precise dimensions are derived from those of the church of the Holy Sepulchre in Jerusalem.[20] The discussion of S. Stefano and of its mosaic by Mâle is specially illuminating, and is followed here.[21]

The single remaining small mosaic is in an apsidal chapel. There is no indication of the date in the existing inscription. There are two figures, identified as SCS PRIMVS, SCS FELICIANVS, standing   91 on either side of a jewelled cross, above which, in a roundel, is the head of Christ (almost entirely a painted restoration); in the crown of the vault there is something difficult to identify which may have been the Divine Hand reaching down through a half roundel of white stars on a black ground, representing the Firmament. The background is gold; the ground is green, with red flowers. The beauty of this mosaic lies in the two highly individualized heads, which are marvellously fine. The heads and hands are worked (as in the figure of St Ursicinus from the church of   93 S. Apollinare in Classe at Ravenna) in a different material (stone) from that used for the main areas of the mosaic (glass). Similarity in the treatment of the hands as well as the heads suggests that the artist may be the same. Though the date (642–49, if Mâle's account, given below, is accepted) is almost exactly that of the St Venantius mosaic, these figures are the more powerful. Despite the presence of many ugly patches of plaster restoration in the background, the work on the heads is in the original condition and of superb quality. It is greatly to be hoped that when the time comes for restoring the mosaic, they will not have to be reset.

These two saints, Primus and Felicianus, were martyred in the reign of Diocletian. It is known that Pope Theodore (642–49) moved the relics of two martyrs from catacombs outside Rome to this church. The existing inscription reads:

ASPICIS AVRATVM CAELESTI CVLMINE TECTVM

ASTRIFERVMQVE MICANS PRAECLARO NVMINE VVLTVM

'Reader, thou lookest on a roof golden with heavenly apex and a face gleaming like a star and shining with a wondrously divine air'. The 'roof' is apparently the curved background of the mosaic, and the face that of Christ. In its present form this inscription is clearly incomplete, and Mâle links it with another recorded from the same church:

EXQVIRENS PIETAS TECTVM DECORARE SACRATVM
PASTORIS SVMMI THEODORIS CORDA DIREXIT
QVI STVDIO MAGNO SANCTORVM CORPORA CVLTV
HOC DEDICAVIT NON PATRIS NEGLECTA RELIQVIT

'Piety inspired the heart of Pope Theodore, who wished to decorate this sanctuary. He applied all his zeal to honouring the bodies of the saints by this fine decoration, nor did he forget the remains of his father'.

Mâle points out the particular association of Pope Theodore with the Holy Places, his father having been a native of Jerusalem and himself perhaps born there. He explains the unusual iconography of the medallion above the cross by reference to subjects on the *ampullae* which survive in the treasuries of Monza and Bobbio, the designs on which represent in miniature mosaics, and perhaps other works of art, to be seen in the Holy Places, from which pilgrims carried these mementoes back to Italy.[22] In Constantine's time, Mâle explains, 'the Cross did not celebrate Christ's sufferings, but his victory. If the Cross was represented at all, Christ was not yet shown upon it.' Thus one of the Monza *ampullae* shows the three crosses; the thieves hang on their crosses on either side of the central cross, which, though empty, is dominated by a bust of Christ. Mâle points out that the cross erected on Golgotha by Constantine, a tall cross of gold, may have been surmounted by some such dominating roundel; there was certainly some sort of mosaic above it. When Theodore planned this mosaic in S. Stefano, the true Cross had recently suffered many hazards. It was carried off by Chosroes, King of Persia, after the capture of Jerusalem in 614, was won back by the Emperor Heraclius in 628 and, because of the turbulent condition of Jerusalem, was eventually taken by him to Constantinople. The interest and anxieties generated by these events are, according to Mâle, the context of this representation of one of the earliest depictions of crosses in Jerusalem.

Though the mosaic has suffered damage, the individual quality of the 'portraits', and the precise dating (if Mâle is correct) to within the limits of Pope Theodore's reign, make it a most important monument.

S. PIETRO IN VINCOLI

There is a small mosaic in this church, the half-size figure of St Sebastian. He is identified by name, SCS SEBASTIANVS; otherwise he would be unrecognizable to those familiar with the Renaissance paintings of a naked youth bound to a tree, his body pierced by arrows. The mosaic has been framed and mounted as a formal altar-piece, and though it is set only a little above eye-level, the glass in front of it makes it difficult to study. The background, a dark-blue grey, is the dominating colour of the mosaic as a whole; against this the golden halo, lettering and edging of the cloak show up brightly. The cloak, of grey-blue, has the red-square patch (*tablion*) inset along the fringe; apparently, in this example, a similar patch is intended along the edge falling from the back of the shoulder. There is an armband of red and gold in a key pattern, and a roundel (represented as if embroidered) of red, gold and blue on the upper part of the right arm. The saint is middle-aged and bearded; he looks steadily through and beyond the beholder. In his right hand is a martyr's crown, which is supported by his left hand, veiled in the fold of his cloak. It is possible that the left hand originally held a cross.[23] The effect is austere, but surprisingly naturalistic. There is some modelling in the use of highlights and darker colour in the saint's cloak, but the flowers at his feet are entirely formal. It has been suggested[24] that the mosaic is associated with the special veneration of St Sebastian when an epidemic of plague in Rome was brought to an end by the carrying of his

96

relics in procession in the year 680. An inscription near the altar in the church gives that date, but is itself much later. General similarities between the cloak here and the cloaks in the frieze of the chapel of St Venantius suggest that this date may be right.

THE VATICAN GROTTOES AND ELSEWHERE: FRAGMENTS OF THE MOSAICS FROM THE ORATORY OF JOHN VII

The remarkable scheme of decoration that adorned this chapel is known both from sketches made before its destruction and from the frescoed ceiling[25] of the chapel of the *sudario* of John VII.

The decoration over the oratory door was divided into fourteen compartments, four of these at the top being subdivided each into two; on either side of a mosaic on a larger scale (which represented the Virgin with Pope John VII) were six smaller panels, and above the larger central mosaic was another smaller panel. Four of these smaller panels were subdivided to contain two scenes. The lowest on the left, for example, represented the Entry into Jerusalem, but it also included vignettes of the Raising of Lazarus and the Last Supper. Four of the seven were devoted to Marian themes: the Annunciation and Visitation; the Nativity, with the bathing of the Child and the Annunciation to the Shepherds; the Adoration of the Magi; and the Presentation (this scene including also the Baptism).

The portrait of Pope John VII was taken from the large panel. In his hands he carries a model 108 of the oratory in which the mosaic was originally set. He has a square halo, indicating that he was alive when the mosaic was made. The background is gold, broken with scattered *tesserae* of black, as, for example, in the mosaics of S. Apollinare Nuovo in Ravenna. There is an occasional red *tessera* where the upper glazing, and the gold-leaf or part of it, have been lost, revealing the red glass below.[26] It is difficult to believe that the highly individual face (with the beard, the slightly lop-sided tonsure, the wide-open eyes and the arched eyebrows) is not to some extent intended as a portrait. The use of much smaller *tesserae* (of stone, not glass) for the face and hands is, as we have seen, a Byzantine practice.[27] The background, unfortunately, may not be original, and since this photograph was taken the fragment has been reset.

A second fragment, from the lower left-hand panel, shows the head and shoulders of Christ, from the Entry into Jerusalem. He holds up his hand in blessing. This fragment is almost certainly 109 by the same hand as the head of John VII. A third fragment, from the Nativity, represents the nurse bathing the Child. In it the surface has suffered extensively. These three fragments, once kept 107 in the Lateran Museum, are now in the Vatican Grottoes, together with a fourth, representing the mourning Virgin from a Crucifixion. Of this only the upper half of the figure remains, but the style is unmistakably the same as that of the other three. The figure of 'Longinus' on the same panel is in such poor condition that it is impossible to say whether any of it belonged to the original or not. In the version in the chapel of the *sudario* Longinus does not appear. A fifth fragment, now in the church of Sta Maria in Cosmedin, is from the Adoration of the Magi. This has great charm 106 and what remains is enough to show that the whole was of outstanding quality.[28] Here the craftsmanship is manifestly Byzantine.

A sixth fragment is in the cathedral of Orte; an inscription on a tablet set into the lower left- XVIII hand corner of this fragment indicates that it was removed there from St Peter's in 1609. The inscription reads: IMAGO DEIPARAE VIRG. EX SACELLO JOHANNIS VII SVPRA PORTAM SANCTAM VETERIS BASIL S. PETRI ACCEPTA MDCIX, 'This representation of the Virgin, Mother of God, from the chapel of John VII above the sacred doorway in the old basilica of St Peter, was brought here in 1609'. Unlike the fragment from S. Marco in Florence, discussed below, this seems, apart from the main background of gold *tesserae* (which no doubt date from the seventeenth century), to be still largely in its original condition. The irregularities in the surface of the face, for example, seem here to be in the same state as they were left by the eighth-century craftsmen. The face, here again, is largely made up of stone *tesserae*, as are the hands, the *tesserae* being much smaller than those of the dress (in shades of blue) or of the gold within the halo; this, in contrast with the main background, may be original gold, broken by *tesserae* of a grey, faintly pinkish glass. (Possibly this pinkish-grey effect is due to the reversing of the *tesserae*, so that the thicker layer of glass is above the gold-leaf.) The rim of the halo consists of two rows of turquoise blue, within which is a single row of stone, and within that the gold. Apart from the dark blue-black chips used for the drawing, a brilliant orange is used in the face to light the cheeks: two or three *tesserae* as highlights, along with one or two for the lips. A small line of red is set beneath the chin, with a thin line of silver-green as a shadow below it. The effect of the whole is most charming: it has a grace and delicacy of touch which is outstanding. The artist of this sixth fragment seems to me to be the man who executed the portrait mosaic of John VII.

In the church of S. Marco in Florence there is another fragment from the same mosaic: a large (over life-size) figure of the Virgin in the *orans* position. This was the centre-piece in the original and so is different in scale. It is now set as an altar-piece. The Virgin wears a dress of deep blue and a jewelled crown. The inscription leaves no doubt that this is the remains of a figure which came from the oratory of John VII in the old basilica of St Peters'. It reads as follows:

VETVSTA HAEC DEI GENITRICIS IMAGO IN VATICANA BASILICA
SVPRA PORTAM SCAM ORATORIO OLIM A JOHANNE VII PONT
MAX SAL ANNO DCCIII CONSTRVCTO DIV SERVATA ATQ AD
HVNC DIEM RELIGIOSSISSIME CVLTA CVM IAM TEMPLVM
ILLVD IN AVGVSTIOREM FORMAM REDDENDVM DETVRBARETVR
E RVDERIBVS ERVTA EST: ET NEQVA AVT SALTEM MINIMA
IN EA DEVOTIONIS IACTVRA FIERET IN HANC ARAM ROMA
TRANSLATA MDCIX

'This ancient representation of the Mother of God once stood above the sacred doorway in the chapel built long ago by Pope John VII in the basilica of the Vatican. For long it was preserved there and has been regarded with veneration to this day; but when the building was being restored to a new splendour, this mosaic was moved and ruined in the process. This figure was rescued from the debris. So that there should be no, or the least possible, interruption in the ancient cult, the image was brought to this altar, from Rome, in the year 1609'.

Nordhagen, in his recent masterly analysis of this series of fragments,[29] has shown that, in this one, the face, the crown above it, the shoulders, and the bust down to the waist are original. So also is a large part of the skirt, but this has unfortunately been extended outward on either side, completely altering the proportions of the figure. In its present form, the impression this figure gives is unattractive. But Nordhagen's fine photograph of the head shows the splendid quality of the best work in this group of fragments.[30] His analysis has brought out the many Byzantine features in the technique of all these mosaics, and the view that some are actually the work of Byzantine artists must, I think, now be accepted.[31] Cecchelli attributed this figure, rightly, to the John VII series,[32] though Matthiae seems to doubt whether it comes from St Peter's. Here again, Nordhagen's analysis dispels any uncertainty which may have remained concerning this point.

XVIII Oratory of John VII in the old basilica of St Peter's. The Virgin,
from a panel representing the Nativity, now in the cathedral of Orte (*c. 705*).

Another fragment, representing the Child in his crib, the ox and ass, and the star above, was once in existence, but I have not been able to trace it.

Yet another fragment, in a somewhat different style, may come from the oratory of John VII. Its inscription attributes its rescue to the time of Paul V (1605–21). Unfortunately, unlike many other fragments rescued about this time, this has, I think, been entirely reset and is no use therefore for the purpose of throwing light on the technique of the period. It represents St Peter holding up his right hand in blessing (in the Latin manner); he is shown three-quarter face. The lines of the drawing are emphatic.[33] This fragment may have come from the left-hand inner wall of the oratory.[34] The artist is certainly not the same, however, as the man responsible for the portrait of John VII, but there are analogies in the draperies which seem to justify this date and provenance. Both these artists seem, in their use of broad blotches of colour in the draperies, to be looking back to the technique of the St Paul from the Constantinian apse.

III, 31

110 Also said to come from this oratory is Vatican Grottoes No 72. This mosaic is so set that it can only be seen at very close quarters, with the light catching it in patches that make it hard to form a general impression. The kneeling figures on either side have been said to represent the emperor Constantine and his mother St Helena. The inscription (1631) records it as having come from the ciborium in the oratory, though it is in fact quite unlike any of the series of mosaics considered here: VETVSTISSIMA HAEC VIRGINIS MVSIVA IMAGO ERAT AD CIBORIVM[35] IOHANNIS PAPAE VII HIC ANNO MDCXXXI EST POSITA. 'This ancient representation, in mosaic, of the Virgin was on the canopy of Pope John VII, and was placed here in 1631'. The gold *tesserae* are mostly in red glass, smallish and irregular in shape. The *tesserae* of the figures are comparatively tiny—not only those used for the flesh, but those used in the draperies also. The technique, with the long structural lines, seems to show Byzantine affinities. The rayed halo of the Virgin is of unusual form. Nordhagen thinks that a twelfth-century date for it is proved. To me, neither a twelfth-century nor an eighth-century date is, *prima facie*, convincing.[36]

THE 'CONFESSIONE' OF ST PETER'S: THE HEAD OF CHRIST

A fragment, set in a recess in the *confessione* and said to come from the oratory of Pope Anacletus,
111 shows a noble head of Christ, full face. This highly individualized portrait surely dates approximately from the time of John VII. It seems, though entirely reset, to be not only in the same style, but actually by the same hand, as the portrait of that pope. The arched broken line of the eyebrows, the double line of the nose, the line under each eye, with the suggestion of a second line—these are highly individual mannerisms common to both works. The comparison shows how badly the face of the *confessione* Christ has suffered; and, moreover, all the neck and most of the rest of the figure are later repairs. In my view, however, enough is left for us to accept the identity of the artist. The head of Christ in the Entry into Jerusalem (which, it is suggested above, is also by this artist) is seen three-quarter face, and accordingly the treatment is somewhat different. In it, more original work remains, and the neck shows how this was originally treated in the *confessione* figure, where the surface has been entirely remade. In his left hand Christ holds a book, open at St John's Gospel and bearing the inscription : EGO SVM VIA VERITAS ET VITA QVI CREDIT IN ME VIVET, 'I am the Way, the Truth and the Life; the man who believes in me will live'.

This mosaic was discussed by de Rossi,[37] who reproduced the sketch made by Jacopo Grimaldi early in the seventeenth century[38] and showed that since that time the mosaic had been drastically remodelled. In particular, the present form of the inscription dates from the reconstruction by Urban VIII; before this the lettering would have been partly uncial in form and there would have been alternate lines of red and black. He concluded that the mosaic had been so drastically altered that no certainty about its origin was possible, but that the balance of probability was in favour of it being the subject of a phrase in the *Life* of Leo III: 'et intro confessionem (basilicae beati Petri fecit) salvatorem stantem, dextra laevaque eius Petrus et Paulus habentes pariter coronas ex gemmis pretiosis', 'Furthermore, within the *confessione* of the basilica of St Peter, he caused to be made a representation of the Saviour, with Peter and Paul to his right and left, holding in their hands similar crowns of precious stones'. Architecturally, this is not easy to interpret in terms of the niche in the *confessione*; though St Peter and St Paul could presumably have been outside the niche (like the lesser saints outside the apse of the chapel of St Venantius), rather than inside (like the two saints on either side of the Virgin in the tiny apsidal altar-piece of S. Zenone). Moreover, the passage gives the impression of a figure seated rather than standing. I have, indeed, no doubt that, in spite of drastic reconstructions, the identification of the artist is certain and gives a date during the papacy of John VII or close to that time.

NOTES ON THE TEXT III

1 *Mosaik von der Antike bis zum Mittelalter*, German ed. trans. from the Norwegian, Munich 1960, p. 62.

2 In *J. des Savants*, June 1863, p. 351, quoted by G. B. de Rossi on S. Lorenzo fuori le Mura (*Musaici cristiani e saggi di pavimenti delle chiese di Roma anteriori al secolo XV*, 'S. Lorenzo fuori le Mura', fol. 2, verso, Rome 1873–99).

3 A. Muñoz, *La basilica di S. Lorenzo fuori le Mura*, Rome 1944, Plate 85. S. Waetzoldt, 'Die Kopien des 17 Jahrhunderts nach Mosaiken und Wandmalereien in Rom', *Römische Forschungen*, vol. VIII (*Misc. Biblioth. Herzianae*), Vienna 1964, Plates 227–230.

4 *Le chiese di Roma dal IV al X secolo*, vol. 1 of Roma Cristiana, Rome 1962, p. 205.

5 P. Baldass, 'The Mosaic of the Triumphal Arch of S. Lorenzo fuori le Mura', *Gaz. des Beaux Arts*, vol. 49, 1957, pp. 1–18.

6 *SS. Cosma e Damiano e S. Teodoro*, Rome 1948.

7 See C. R. Morey, *Lost Mosaics and Frescoes of Rome of the Middle Period*, Princeton 1915, p. 26.

8 But see Morey, op. cit., p. 30; there is reason to think that in the earlier version the manner was Greek.

9 See p. 145.

10 This head is closely related to a classical fragment now in the Vatican Grottoes but from an unknown source—another example of the strength of the early traditions. See Plate 84.

11 *Le chiese di Roma dal IV al X secolo*, vol. 1 of Roma Cristiana, Rome 1962, p. 205.

12 It appears in Greece at a date well before the seventh century, for example, in the church of St Demetrius at Salonika, though the significance of those 'halos' is disputed (see R. F. Hoddinott, *Early Byzantine Churches in Macedonia and Southern Serbia*, London 1963, p. 151). De Rossi, in discussing the mosaic of John VII, quotes literary evidence for the view that the square halo dates from the time of Gregory the Great (op. cit., 'Musaici dell'oratorio di Giovanni VII al Vaticano', fol. 5). On this point see J. Wilpert's account of the 'Rechteckige Nimbus' in *Die römischen Mosaiken und Malereien der Kirchlichen Bauten vom IV bis XIII Jahrhundert*, 4 vols, Freiburg 1916, pp. 107–113; here he discusses the so-called square nimbi at Salonika. See also W. N. Schumacher, *Römische Quartalschrift*, 54, 1919, p. 147.

13 Compare the mosaic of John VII (705–707) in the Vatican Grottoes; see p. 155.

14 See pp. 11, 14.

15 For an examination of the Byzantine character of this mosaic, see Matthiae, op. cit., pp. 209–210.

16 Compare the fine detail of the Angels' heads in Matthiae, op. cit., Plate 116, with the even finer detail in L'Orange and Nordhagen, op. cit., Plate 65, showing one of the main apsidal figures.

17 Anonymous article, 'Ristauro di mosaici fuori del Vaticano', in *Atti della Pont. Accad. Romana di Archeol. Rendiconti*, series III, vols XXII–XXIV,

1947–49, pp. 402–405 (with sketch on p. 401).

18 See p. 17.

19 The diagram printed with the account of the most recent restoration shows that in the restorers' view the work they were dealing with in all these heads was original, not later repair.

20 *Early Churches of Rome*, Eng. trans. (1960) of the French ed., pp. 69 et seq.

21 For a recent description of the church (with some allusions to its earlier mosaic decorations, long since lost), see Ritz, 'S. Stefano Rotondo sul Celio', *L'Urbe*, XXVII, No. 2, 1964. This article, however, contains no discussion of the oriental affinities of the church.

22 Compare the mosaic of the apse in St John Lateran, where the head of Christ appeared in a roundel above the cross; see p. 312.

23 So H. Chéramy in *Saint Sebastien hors les Murs*, Paris 1925, p. 18. Certainly there has been restoration and the mosaic as a whole may have been reset. But it is impossible (with the mosaic displayed under glass) to be confident of what is old and what is recent.

24 Chéramy, loc. cit.

25 Anderson 20321. In some ways, this photograph, despite the different medium of the original, gives a better impression of the iconography than the sketches of the mosaic. But see also S. Waetzoldt, op. cit., Plate 478.

26 For the use of red glass in the manufacture of gold *tesserae*, see p. 11.

27 Nordhagen, in *The Mosaics of John VII* (Acta Instituti Romani Norvegiae, vol. 2, 1965, pp. 121–166), has shown that the photograph used for our illustration shows this head in something like its original state. Most unfortunately, it has now been reset, and much of its quality has consequently been lost. For the clothes, see the note on Plate 108.

28 See also the note on Plate 106 for the present surface of this work.

29 Op. cit.

30 Nordhagen's plate (op. cit.) of this head shows its fine quality, and suggests at once the Sta Agnese head (our Plate 88). He reproduces an excellent photograph, also, of the upper part of the dress, which shows that, here too, much original work remains. Though restoration that is unnecessary is much to be deplored, it is greatly to be hoped that the modern work on either side of the dress, which has altered the proportions of the figure so much for the worse, will one day be removed.

31 This is definitely true of the Adoration fragment, and it is certain that all the hands represented were strongly influenced by Byzantine techniques; though I should still hesitate to say that these were all the work of a team of eastern craftsmen, since the S. Paolo mosaics were made so much later.

32 'Il Costume' (pts 12–16 of *I arte minori e il costume*, in the series Vita di Roma nel Medio Evo), Rome, n.d., p. 917.

33 This is in contrast with the mosaics of the Constantinian period, in which there is little drawing but in which the surfaces are modelled; or with the two medieval mosaics (Nos 22 and 23 in the Vatican Grottoes), in which, again, planes and surfaces are in general more noticeable than drawing, though the surfaces are often sharply contrasted, unlike the subtle modelling of, for example, the Constantinian cherub's forehead. But I am not entirely satisfied that the draperies of this St Peter and those at present associated with the portrait of John VII may not simply be the work of the same restorer.

34 There is a sketch in Wilpert, op. cit., p. 399.

35 'Ciborium' here probably means a simple *baldacchino* over the altar.

36 For a note on the state of the surface of this mosaic, see pp. 17–18.

37 Op. cit., 'Musiaco nella nicchia della confessione sotto l'altare maggiore della basilica Vaticana'.

38 Vat. Cod. Barb. Lat. 2733, fol. 250; reproduced in S. Waetzoldt, op. cit., Plate 492.

75, 76   S. Lorenzo fuori le Mura. Soffits of the triumphal arch; festoons (sixth century, last quarter).

77 S. Lorenzo fuori le Mura. Mosaic of the triumphal arch (sixth century, last quarter).

78   Dome of the Arian baptistry, Ravenna (fifth century, last quarter).

79   S. Lorenzo fuori le Mura, mosaic of the triumphal arch (sixth century, last quarter). St Peter.

80   S. Lorenzo fuori le Mura, mosaic of the triumphal arch (sixth century, last quarter). St Stephen.

81   S. Lorenzo fuori le Mura, mosaic of the triumphal arch (sixth century, last quarter). Christ.

82   S. Lorenzo fuori le Mura, mosaic of the triumphal arch (sixth century, last quarter). St Hippolytus.

83 S. Teodoro, mosaic of the apse (sixth century, last quarter). St Peter.

84   Vatican Grottoes, classical fragment (probably fifth century). St Peter.

85   S. Teodoro, mosaic of the apse. St Paul (dated by Matthiae shortly after 550).

86   S. Teodoro, mosaic of the apse. Head of a saint (dated by Matthiae shortly after 550).

87   Sta Agnese fuori le Mura. Mosaic of the apse (*c.* 625).

88   Sta Agnese fuori le Mura, mosaic of the apse (*c.* 625). St Agnes.

89   S. Stefano Rotondo, mosaic
in the apsidal chapel (*c*. 650). St Primus.

90   S. Stefano Rotondo, mosaic
in the apsidal chapel (*c*. 650). St Felicianus.

91   S. Stefano Rotondo. Mosaic in the apsidal chapel (c. 650).

92   S. Stefano Rotondo, mosaic in the apsidal chapel (*c.* 650). St Primus (detail of Plate 89).

93 S. Apollinare in Classe, Ravenna. St Ursicinus (*c.* 650).

94 S. Vitale, Ravenna. The 'procession'
of the emperor Justinian
(sixth century, second quarter).

95 Baptistry of St John Lateran,
chapel of St Venantius, arch outside
the apse. Procession of martyrs and
saints (seventh century, second quarter).

96   S. Pietro in Vincoli.
St Sebastian (probably 680).

97 Baptistry of St John Lateran, chapel of St Venantius, mosaic of the apse (seventh century, second quarter). Part of a working diagram used in the restorations carried out in 1946–47.

98 Baptistry of St John Lateran, chapel of St Venantius, mosaic of the apse (seventh century, second quarter). The central figure, before the restorations carried out in 1946–47.

99　Baptistry of St John Lateran, chapel of St Venantius. Mosaic of the apse (seventh century, second quarter), as restored in 1946–47.

100　Baptistry of St John Lateran, chapel of St Venantius, mosaic of the apse (seventh century, second quarter). The central figure, after the restorations carried out in 1946–47.

101   Baptistry of St John Lateran, chapel of St Venantius, mosaic of the apse (seventh century, second quarter). The Virgin, *orans*.

102　Baptistry of St John Lateran, chapel of St Venantius, mosaic of the apse (seventh century, second quarter).
Head of an ecclesiastic, labelled DOMNIO.

103 Baptistry of St John Lateran,
chapel of St Venantius
(seventh century, second quarter).
A young martyr; from the frieze
on the arch outside the apse.

105 Baptistry of St John Lateran,
chapel of St Venantius, mosaic of the
apse (seventh century, second quarter).
St John the Baptist.

104 Baptistry of St John Lateran,
chapel of St Venantius, mosaic
of the apse (seventh century, second
quarter). St John the Evangelist.

106   Oratory of John VII in the old basilica of St Peter's. Part of a panel representing the Adoration of the Magi, now in Sta Maria in Cosmedin (eighth century, first quarter).

107 Oratory of John VII in the old basilica of St Peter's. Fragment from a panel representing the Nativity, now in the Vatican Grottoes (eighth century, first quarter).

108 Oratory of John VII in the old basilica of St Peter's. Portrait of John VII, now in the Vatican Grottoes (eighth century, first quarter). Photographed before the mosaic was reset.

109　Oratory of John VII in the old basilica of St Peter's. Christ, from the panel representing the Entry into Jerusalem (eighth century, first quarter).

110   Mosaic fragment reputed to be from the ciborium of the oratory of John VII in the old basilica of St Peter's. The Virgin, with worshippers, sometimes described as Constantine and his mother Helena; now in the Vatican Grottoes (possibly eighth–ninth centuries).

112 The *Tribune of Benedict XIV*.
Eighteenth-century version, in the piazza
overlooked by St John Lateran, of the
mosaic originally set up in the Triclinium
of the Lateran palace (late eighth century).
The risen Christ, sending out the apostles
to preach and baptize.

113   Head of an apostle: a surviving fragment
from the mosaic originally set up in the
Triclinium of the Lateran palace (late eighth
century). Now in the Vatican Library.

75, 76 These festoons were executed by an artist still working in the classical manner. Compare Plates 68 and 70.

77 Christ is represented enthroned on the Globe of the Firmament, with saints on either side. Most of the cities (left and right), and the lower part of the draperies of the figures on the left, are modern restoration. The linear forms of the drapery seem to have been derived from Ravenna (see Plate 78).

79 This head has been worked in the Byzantine manner. The pale-grey *tesserae* in which the shadows have been rendered seem to be of glass, but the main material used for the flesh is stone.

80 The materials are the same as were used for the head of St Peter (Plate 79), and the manner is similarly Byzantine. Where the orderliness of the *tesserae* has been disturbed, this is evidence of slight repairs. Compare also Plate 18.

81 The materials used are various, as in the heads of St Peter and St Stephen (Plates 79 and 80), and the manner, again, is Byzantine. Contrast Plate 82. The patch of slightly larger *tesserae* to the right of the nose is a restoration.

82 This head has been worked in the Roman manner. The *tesserae* are of glass, and are irregular in shape, sizes and arrangement. For another head in the same manner, also from this mosaic, see Plate 17.

83 The lower right-hand corner of the chin, and the drapery on the left, are modern. This head was worked in the Roman manner, the *tesserae* being irregular and of glass, but there is perhaps some degree of Byzantine influence in the tendency to orderly work lines.

84 This head may have been the model for the St Peter in S. Teodoro (Plate 83). The *tesserae* are of glass.

85 All the forehead and some of the hair along it are modern. The *tesserae* are irregular and of glass, in the Roman manner, with some degree of Byzantine influence, as remarked on in the note to Plate 83.

86 This head, worked in the Roman manner, is almost in its original condition. The artist seems to be the same as the one whose work is shown in Plates 83 and 85, also illustrating this mosaic.

87 St Agnes, in the centre, holds a scroll; the flames of martyrdom are at her feet. On either side are Pope Symmachus and Pope Honorius, each wearing the pallium. Above is the canopy of Heaven, here representing day and night, and the Divine Hand.

88 This head was worked in the Byzantine manner, and the *tesserae* are of stone.

89 This figure is worked in the Byzantine manner, the material used for the flesh being stone. The cloak seems to be mainly original.

90 The fine head, like that of St Primus (Plate 89), is unrestored, but the rest has suffered heavy damage.

91 In the centre is a cross, and the bust of Christ in a roundel above it. Above is the canopy of Heaven, showing day and night (as in Sta Agnese), with (perhaps) the Divine Hand. On either side are St Primus and St Felicianus (Plates 89 and 90).

92 Compare Plate 93, and see the note on that plate.

93 The St Primus in S. Stefano Rotando (Plates 89 and 92) may be by the same hand as this figure. The similarities lie in the somewhat irregular setting (for a Byzantine mosaic) of the stone chips in the face; the semi-circular pattern of *tesserae* in the forehead; and the large, elaborately drawn ears. For this last detail, contrast, for example, Plate 96.

94 The emperor is in the centre. On his left are ecclesiastics; on his right, officials and soldiers.

95 Two saints are vested as ecclesiastics; two are dressed as courtiers. The work shows strong Ravennate influence.

96 This panel, executed in a somewhat provincial Byzantine manner, is said to have been extensively restored and altered. The different character of the lettering on the right from that on the left suggests a substantial alteration to the design on the right-hand side.

97 The vertical lines show the area judged, before the restorations carried out in 1946–47, to be an old repair.

98 Compare this plate with Plate 100.

100 The mortar lines appear far more strongly than before the restorations, and there are substantial modifications in detail (especially to the hands of Christ and of the angel on the right). But, owing to the different colour values of the emulsions used, the plates are no doubt not strictly comparable.

102 This head has been reset. But the material seems to be glass, and the technique followed by the restorer substantially Roman.

105 The technique used for this head (which has been reset) seems to have been substantially the Roman technique of the original, as for the head shown in Plate 102.

106 The work in this panel is manifestly that of a Byzantine craftsman; note the texture of the flesh, different from that of the rest, and the orderliness of the work lines in general.

107 The surface of this fragment has suffered more damage than the panel illustrated in Plate 106, and the craftsmanship is less fine. The hand does not seem to be the same as that of the panel shown in Plate 106.

108 Since this photograph was taken the head has been substantially altered by restoration. (For an account, see P. Nordhagen, 'The Mosaics of John VII', *Acta*, published by the Norwegian Institute, vol. II, 1965). The work on the drapery is entirely different from that to be seen in authentic work in the series (compare, for ex-

ample, the figures shown in Plate 109 or in Plate XVIII) and probably dates from a much later period.

109 In this panel the work is original, despite some patches of damage, such as that on the back of the raised hand.

110 Technically, the work in this fragment is quite different from that in the mosaics that were on the walls of the oratory. The lower section has been extensively consolidated, but the upper half seems to preserve original features. The pattern of the halo is not paralleled in any other Roman mosaics. The high degree of modelling might perhaps suggest an early ninth-century artist, though (with the possible exception of the fragment shown in Plate 113), no surviving example in Rome possesses this characteristic.

111 Virtually none of the setting of this figure seems to be original, but the reconstruction preserves enough of the style for the artist to be identified as the one who made the heads shown in Plates 108 and 109.

112 On the left, outside the arch, Christ gives the keys to St Peter (or possibly to St Sylvester), and the banner to Constantine. On the right, St Peter gives the pallium to Pope Leo III, and the banner to Charlemagne.

113 This fine fragment is probably the original head of the apostle seen second from the right in the eighteenth-century version of this mosaic (Plate 112). For another fragment from the same mosaic, see Plate 237.

IV

THE LATE EIGHTH AND
EARLY NINTH CENTURIES:
THE PASCHALIAN PERIOD

THE MOSAICS OF THE REIGNS of Leo III (795–816), Paschal I (817–24) and Gregory IV (828–44) belong to the period when that revival of the arts was taking place in western Europe which is associated with the patronage of Charlemagne and his successors. Artists of the period who were at the court of the emperor often sought out antique works as their models, and there were antique gems and ivories among the imperial possessions and in the treasuries of the monasteries which helped to provide their inspiration. In the eastern empire, on the other hand, the period largely coincided with the phase of bitter and often bloody struggle between a puritanical faction, which took as its aim the elimination of the worship of images, and the traditional conservative faction, which regarded the destruction of images achieved by the iconoclasts as impious. Owing to her geographical position, Rome could not altogether escape being involved in the iconoclast controversy, and was bound also to be affected by the artistic ideas of the Carolingian court artists. Roman mosaics of this period are not numerous, but one series at least, in the small chapel of S. Zenone in the church of Sta Prassede, has survived almost complete and comparatively unharmed by restoration. The mosaics in the chapel form, in their way, one of the most beautiful monuments anywhere in the medium.

This phase begins with the triumphal arch in SS. Nereo ed Achilleo, which, in the sixteenth century, still displayed the monogram of Leo III. The same monogram is also included in the mosaic that is built into what is now known as the *Tribune of Benedict XIV*, an eighteenth-century structure erected to display a version of the mosaic that originally decorated the banqueting hall of the old Lateran palace. The first stage, then, of the revival belongs to the papacy of Leo III, and the life-time of Charlemagne. From Paschal's reign (and so from a few years later) date the mosaics of the apse and triumphal arch in Sta Maria Domnica, a church with which Paschal   XX, 114–120 already had close links before he became Pope; the extensive series of mosaics in the church of Sta Prassede, including not only those of the apse and triumphal arch, but those of the arch   121–125, 127 outside the transept facing the nave (through which, as in Sta Maria Maggiore, the mosaics of the apse and the triumphal arch are seen, the three mosaics forming a single scheme of decoration)

—with the mosaics of the chapel of S. Zenone, already mentioned; and, finally, the apsidal mosaic of the church of Sta Cecilia in Trastevere. It seems likely that the Paschal mosaics were made in this order. To the patronage of Gregory IV, a decade or so later, are due the mosaics of the triumphal arch and apse in the church of S. Marco. This is put beyond doubt by the monogram of Gregory in the mosaic. With those the period ends.

A casual acquaintance with this group of mosaics may suggest that the style is purely linear, with no modelling; that the technique, as shown in the setting of the *tesserae*, is rough, even at times barbaric; and that the work too obviously lacks the extraordinary sophistication which marks those Byzantine mosaics (the series in Salonika, for example) which date from this period. This view would be superficial. The quality is indeed uneven, and the drawing sometimes trivial. And the impression remains that in some of the important mosaics the organization of the work was in some ways amateur. It seems that in the S. Zenone series (in certain respects the most significant), a change of plan led to the cutting off at waist-level of figures which had just been finished. In the mosaic in Sta Cecilia, Paschal, who was, as can be seen from a number of works due to his patronage, a devotee of the antique, was given by his leading mosaicist a classical vase out of which the mosaic festoons on the soffits were shown as growing. The vase, in the corresponding copy on the other side of the arch, seems almost meaningless, the base being shown as a sort of knob or ring. And it is true also that the borderline between, on the one hand, an extremely subtle arrangement of *tesserae*, in which the setting of each is an individual matter and relates to a particular effect of light at which the artist was aiming, and, on the other, a chaotic muddle with no plan in it at all, can be tenuous.

But the two superb angels' heads illustrated, from Sta Maria Domnica, show how subtle, at its best, this work is. The break in the drawing of the mouth; the single line used for drawing the nose of one (on the shadow side), this feature (in the other) being most delicately suggested simply by a subtle difference of light; the omission of the line under the eye; the strong, but by no means exaggerated, highlight in the eye itself; the charming difference between the two figures in the poise of the head, one looking upwards towards the Child, the other downwards towards the figure of Paschal at his feet—these are all masterly strokes. Technically, and in a wider sense also, these stylistic features seem to owe much to the *pointilliste* tradition of late antiquity, and in particular to the triumphal arch mosaic in Sta Maria Maggiore. As in that church, it is in the faces alone

XIX   Sta Prassede, wall mosaic in the chapel of S. Zenone (*c.* 820). Two women martyrs.

of the Sta Maria Domnica mosaic (and this was no doubt true of the *Tribune of Benedict XIV* also, as two surviving fragments show) that this quality is shown. This is the Roman tradition at its best. Most of the design, except in the faces, is severely linear. The sketching of the angels' wings, moreover, is not only linear but also perfunctory. There is already a wide difference between these and the coloured wings of the angels in the Adoration fragment from John VII's group in the old basilica of St Peter's, now in Sta Maria in Cosmedin, or the Vatican fragment from the same mosaic, in both of which the 'painted' colours of the wings are a noteworthy feature.

From the *Tribune of Benedict XIV* (the eighteenth-century mosaic version of which is stylistically a disastrous failure) two original heads survive, one of which is on permanent exhibition in the Vatican Museum galleries. But they are readily compared in Plates 237 and 238.[1] The irregularity of shape in the *tesserae*, and the calculated unevennesses of the setting, play a great part in the effects achieved. There is, however, so striking a difference in style between them that if one did not recall the differences between the work in different hands on the triumphal arch of S. Lorenzo, one could hardly believe that they came from the same mosaic. Both *Tribune* artists, however, seem to owe something to that classical revival which is so remarkably manifested in some of the ninth-century paintings in Sta Maria Antiqua. The work of one of them suggests that the ochreous complexions of many of the Paschal figures (remarked on particularly by Matthiae in the Sta Maria Domnica mosaic) may have been a feature of the *Tribune* mosaic also, and may be a consequence of the use of natural stone; whereas in others (perhaps, on the whole, the later) of Paschal's mosaics the heads, as we shall see, are of artificial materials. Technical considerations give no absolute lead as to whether the work of this period as a whole was eastern or western in its main affinities. But, contrary to what has sometimes been supposed, there seems to be some evidence of a growing reassertion of the Roman tradition in the Paschalian series. And the contemporary Byzantine work in Salonika is as different as it could be from this.

These late eighth- and early ninth-century mosaics in Rome seem to lose increasingly the sense of a large, rhythmic composition, the figures becoming, as in so many Byzantine mosaics, a stiffly formed row of creatures, each treated as an independent unit, unrelated to his neighbour. Thus, while the apsidal mosaic of Sta Prassede (like that of Sta Cecilia in Trastevere) is based, as Matthiae long ago showed,[2] on that of SS. Cosma e Damiano, it has almost entirely lost the rhythms of the original. The triumphal arch of Sta Prassede has some ambitious narrative scenes, including one that represents the approach of the saved souls to the Heavenly Jerusalem; in the chapel of S. Zenone there were also several narrative compositions; while the period starts with the not very successful Transfiguration of SS. Nereo ed Achilleo, a unique subject in Roman mosaics, the treatment of which is, incidentally, almost certainly Byzantine in character.[3] Some features of these narrative mosaics (like the representation of throngs of saints or angels by the multiplication of halos in the background; see Plate XX) are inventive and exciting; and it looks from the eighteenth-century copy as if the original of the *Tribune* mosaic represented the apostles with some sense of grouping, not simply as a row of individuals. But, in the apse of S. Marco, hardly any rhythmic relationship exists between one figure and the next. It is of some interest to look, in this context, at the tenth-century mosaic now on the tomb of Otto II, in which the left arm of Christ on St Peter's shoulder looks as if it had been added by way of an afterthought. The three figures in that work are virtually independent of one another. In the twelfth-century mosaic in Sta Francesca Romana, and in the apsidal mosaic of Sta Maria in Trastevere, the saints are in rows, not groups. It is a leap forward when at the end of the thirteenth century, with the work of Toriti, grouping reappears. The Sta Maria Domnica mosaic, regarded in this context, is an original composition. Most successful of all, though not so original, is the composition of the four angels supporting the roundel on the vault of S. Zenone. These may be derived from Ravenna, though the design is perhaps originally Roman.[4] In any event, perhaps from its extreme simplicity, this version is in some ways even more satisfying than that at Ravenna, and the symbol of the thoughts swept upwards to the Christ figure is most effective. XXIII, XXI, 127, 128

SS. NEREO ED ACHILLEO

The mosaic of the triumphal arch is the relic of a larger scheme which included the apse. There is no inscription, but the mosaic is certainly an earlier representative of the series which continues with those for which Paschal I was responsible. The attribution to Leo III (795–816)—Paschal became Pope less than a year after Leo's death, though he was not his immediate successor— seems well grounded; moreover, P. Ugonio, a Renaissance scholar,[5] noted on the arch the mono- gram of Leo III. It was Leo III who was responsible for the enlargement of the church, whose origins were at least three hundred years earlier.

The subject of the mosaic is unusual: in the centre, Christ, in a mandorla, holds up his hand in blessing (apparently the Latin form,[6] in contrast with the Sta Cecilia mosaic of Paschal's time). He is transfigured, with Moses and Elias on his right and left, Moses holding a closed scroll. Beyond are St Peter (on Christ's right), and St John and St James (on his left), worshipping him. The scheme is awkward, since the centre space, on account of the shape of the arch, is necessarily the smallest available for a figure, and yet has to accommodate the most important (that of Christ), while the three apostolic witnesses have to be grouped two and one in an uneasy balance. On the extreme left is the scene of the Annunciation; the Virgin, in a robe of brownish-red, is standing before (or, more probably, is thought of as seated on) a throne of gold. The angel is on the left (on the Virgin's right); his cloak may have been of gold. The corresponding group on the right-hand side of the mosaic is of the Virgin and Child; again, she has a throne of gold, and her robe is of brownish-red. The Child, who is seen frontally, is seated on her knee and holds in his hand an unopened scroll. Next to her, but on the inside, and so again not precisely balancing the other group, stands another angel.

As in many other instances, a photograph does scant justice to this mosaic, the bright and varying colours of which are its most striking feature. A gold scallop ornament edges the three straight sides, broken only by the mandorla of the transfigured Christ. The green grass is scattered with red flowers, and, corresponding to the scallop ornament along the straight sides, the curve of the arch has a narrow fillet of gold and red. Between this and the arch the colour is a vivid blue-green. In the upper part of the mosaic, the colour of the background becomes deep blue on the left and a medium blue on the right, before merging into the pale blue of the sky. On either side of the arch, the lower part of the work has been restored. The straggling ivy-frond ornament is an antique element which, though restored, is no doubt derived from the original.

The cloaks of St Peter and St John bear monograms. On the former's cloak (as in the chapel of St Venantius) the monogram seems to be actually the letter P. So far as can be judged, the mosaic has escaped drastic restoration (except, as noted above, in the lowest sections on either side). The drawing has a certain triviality of style which makes one consider the work to be less important than some of the Paschalian schemes created a few years later.

The subject of the decoration of the apse is known only from a Renaissance drawing, reproduced by de Rossi.[7] In the centre was a huge cross, reaching from the bottom of the mosaic almost to the top, against a draped background; on either side, confronting the cross, were three sheep. It is

Fig 4 A drawing, reproduced by de Rossi, which shows the apsidal mosaic, since destroyed, of SS. Nereo ed Achilleo. The design would seem to be iconoclastic in its sympathies, in contrast with the surviving mosaic (apparently of the same date) on the arch outside the apse.

hard not to link this design (which is most unusual in its simplicity) with the iconoclastic ideas which were during that period current in the eastern church. If we were to accept this link, we would have to suppose a change of plan (and, indeed, a change of allegiance) when the triumphal arch was decorated. A safer hypothesis might be that there were not yet artists available whom Leo was prepared to commission for a major work containing figures; since, if existing mosaics are sufficient evidence, there had been a period of several generations during which no major work in mosaic had been produced in Rome. The extreme simplicity of the apse mosaic may partly explain why no steps were taken to preserve the work later.

The restorations of the lower half of the triumphal arch, with their fresh colour, give the whole mosaic a somewhat spurious charm, though the bright colours in Sta Maria Domnica leave no doubt that this gaiety was intended in both mosaics. In Sta Maria it is brilliantly successful; here it is not, and the reason may be the triviality of the drawing, mentioned above. This is noticeable in other mosaics in the group also. On the nave arch in Sta Prassede, for example, where the design is of great interest, the execution of the figures is, in contrast with those of the apse, often similarly trivial. Even in the chapel of S. Zenone, where the workmanship is mostly excellent, there are lapses here and there, due perhaps to an assistant to the master craftsman. In SS. Nereo ed Achilleo, however, it is not a question of an occasional lapse. The standard of design and detail on the figures is simply of poor general quality. And the lack of competent artists may conceivably give a clue to the reasons for the original simple, 'iconoclastic' treatment of the apse itself.

THE TRIBUNE OF BENEDICT XIV (IN ITS ORIGINAL FORM)

This mosaic is well documented, and is an eighteenth-century version, made up in the reign of Benedict XIV, apparently partly with the help of manuscript sources, of the mosaic which originally decorated the Triclinium, or banqueting hall, of the old Lateran palace and which had been ordered for that room by Leo III (795–816). Benedict's inscription reads as follows:

BENEDICTVS XIV (1740–1759) PM ANTIQVISSIMVM EX VERMICVLATO

OPERE MONIMENTVM IN OCCIDENTALI APSIDE LATERANENSIS

COENACVLI A LEONE III (795–816) SACRO COGENDO SENATVI ALIISQVE

SOLEMNIBVS PERAGENDIS EXTRVCTI QVOD AD TEMPLI

LAXANDAM AREAM CLEMENS XII (1730–1740) INTEGRVM
LOCO MOVERI ET AD PROXIMVM S. LAVRENTII ORATORIVM
COLLOCARI IVSSERAT VEL ARTIFICVM IMPERITIA VEL REI
DIFFICVLTATE DIFFRACTVM ET PENITVS DISIECTVM NE
ILLVSTRE ADEO PONTIFICAE MAIESTATIS AVCTORITATISQVE
ARGVMENTVM LITERARIAE REIPVBLICAE DAMNO INTERIRET
AD FIDEM EXEMPLI IPSIVS CLEMENTIS PROVIDENTIA
STANTIBVS ADHVC PARIETIBVS ACCVRATE COLORIBVS
EXPRESSI ET SIMILLIMAE IN VATICANO CODICE VETERIS
PICTVRAE NOVA ABSIDE A FVNDAMENTIS EXCITATA
ERVDITORVM VIRORVM VOTIBVS OCCVRRENS VRBI AETERNAE
RESTITVIT ANNO CIICCXLIII PONT SVI III

'This is a copy of the ancient mosaic which once occupied the western apse of the refectory of the Lateran Palace, a room originally built by Pope Leo III (795–816) for meetings of the Holy Synod, and for the performance of other ceremonies. Because he wished to enlarge the area of the Lateran, Pope Clement XII (1730–40) ordered that the mosaic should be moved, and replaced undamaged in the adjacent chapel of St Lawrence. But whether by reason of the inexperience of the craftsmen, or from the inherent difficulties of the operation, it was broken up and completely destroyed. To prevent the disastrous loss to the world of letters of this notable piece of evidence of papal authority and power, Pope Benedict XIV (1740–59) ordered a new apse to be built up from the foundations, and a new mosaic to be made, faithfully reproduced from the accurate copy executed in colour, thanks to the foresight of Pope Clement, before the demolition of the building, and from a very similar representation in a manuscript in the Vatican library. So did Pope Benedict answer the prayers of scholars and restore to the Eternal City this mosaic in the year 1743, the third year of his papacy.'

A further inscription is a copy of an earlier record of restoration by Cardinal Francis Barberini in the Jubilee year 1625, a restoration which itself followed a much earlier restoration by Leo IV after which the mosaic had gradually fallen into decay. It may, then, be assumed that in its main lines the present mosaic follows the original, and as a historical document it is, indeed, as Benedict XIV realized, of great interest.

On the outside of the arch, on the left, Christ gives the keys to St Peter (or perhaps to St Sylvester, who baptized Constantine) and the banner, or *Labarum*, to Constantine. In the corresponding scene on the right, St Peter gives the Papal Stole to Leo III (shown with a square halo) and the banner of Christianity to Charlemagne (also with a square halo), inscribed DN CARVLO REGI, 'To our master, Charles the King'. In a cartouche is the inscription BEATE PETRE DONAS VITA [sic] LEONI PP [PAPAE] E [ET] VICTORIA CARVLI REGI DONAS, 'O blessed Peter, thou dost confer life on Pope Leo, and victory on Charles the King'.

In the semi-dome, the risen Christ is in the centre, holding an open book which reads PAX VOBIS; at his feet are, apparently, the Rivers of Paradise. He sends the eleven apostles out to teach with the words DOCETE OMNES GENTES VAPTIZANTES EOS IN NOMINE PATRIS ET FILII ET SPIRITVS SCVS [sic; sc. SANCTVS, for SANCTI] ECCE EGO VOBISCVM SVM OMNIBVS DIEBVS VSQVE AD CONSVMATIONEM SECVLI, 'Teach all nations, baptizing them in the name of the Father, the Son and the Holy Spirit. Lo, I am with you always, to the end of the world'. The flaring-out of the mantle of one of the apostles, St Peter, is reminiscent, in the eighteenth-century version, of some of the stylistic idiosyncracies of the Sta Maria Domnica mosaic, with its 'double cup' and 'lobster

112

114, 116

claw' folds. But of the existing fragments from the Triclinium, one at least does not look like

113, 237, 238 the work of that artist. Two survive.[8] One is perhaps the most 'painterly' work of any in the medieval series, with the subtlest gradations of light and shade, the result being a portrait of exceptional sensitivity. There is comparatively little difference in size between the *tesserae* of the face and those of the background. The other work (the traditional likeness of St Paul) is broader in treatment, and far less subtle; but the bearded, swarthy face is represented with great power. These fragments, however, seem, in style, to approach the classical tradition of the contemporary paintings in Sta Maria Antiqua. One of them is in some technical ways similar to work in Sta Maria Domnica.[9] But the contrast between them and the heads in SS. Nereo ed Achilleo is notable. The moral is one which has been mentioned before: it is dangerous to assume that a particular age is represented by only one style. The point (stressed by Malraux) that, in modern art, all fashions can co-exist, has a wider application.

In the fragment which is permanently exhibited in the Vatican Museum, the setting is in the form of an incrustation, and the materials used appear to be entirely natural stones. The sophistication of the style is in singular contrast with the rough materials and rough methods of using them.

Other noticeable details are that the clothes of the apostles were decorated with the elaborate patches fashionable in Paschal's mosaics and those in S. Marco a few years later; that on white draperies the lines of the drawing were in green, as in S. Nereo; that the sparse pattern of the festoons on either side makes it certain that the originals were like those in the Paschal mosaics also; and that at the crown of the arch Leo's monogram appears, not otherwise preserved. Thus, the revival which we are inclined to associate with Paschal (because several of his mosaics have survived) dates substantially from the time of Leo III (795–816).

Fig 5   Monogram of Pope Leo III.

This is one of Paschal's mosaics; and, if the central portrait is good evidence, this and the mosaic in Sta Cecilia in Trastevere might have been made at about the same date and that in Sta Prassede later. (But reasons will be given later for the view that the St Cecilia mosaic is, in fact, the last of the Paschalian works.) The design is original, and unlike anything else in Rome, while the colour is enchanting. The draperies, with their billowing forms, are certainly the work of a different artist (and, it would seem, emanate from a different workshop) from those of Sta Cecilia, though the linear character of both designs would set them firmly in the same period, even without the inscriptions and Paschal's monogram. A comparison of the drapery forms with those on the remaining copy of the Triclinium mosaic suggests that the designer of the Sta Maria Domnica mosaic may have worked for Leo III on the mosaic of the Triclinium.

xx
114
129

The restoration of the Sta Maria mosaic has been outstandingly successful.[10] The mosaic was cleaned in detail; a large section below the throne was replaced; and the iron ties of the 1841 restoration were replaced by non-corrosive metal. It is clear that the utmost care was taken, where possible, to avoid resetting, and that the restorers were intensely sensitive to the importance for the general effect of the original highly individual setting of each *tessera*. A photograph of one section of the mosaic taken before the restoration has been reproduced for comparison with the same detail after restoration. The two photographs at first give impressions that are remarkably different. In the earlier photograph, the mortar, apparently because of the dirt on it, tells much more, giving (with the dulled colour of the *tesserae*) a uniformly drab effect. In the other, the effect is due to the impression given by each individual *tessera*, clean and vivid. In comparing, then, the two photographs, it might even seem that we are here concerned with two methods of setting which had considerable difference between them. A closer examination, however, shows how mistaken this view would be. There has been no actual resetting at all. The same units are in the same positions, save for one or two tiny replacements.[11] But because they have all been cleaned each makes its separate effect, and in the result as a whole a transformation has been worked. This is restoration at its finest. Only lower down in the mosaic of the triumphal arch have there been some substantial areas of replacement. To judge from the photograph, the face of the prophet shown in Plate 119 is substantially new. But in the main mosaic, only the area below the throne represents new work.

117, 118

On the triumphal arch, in the centre, is Christ, in a mandorla, seated on the bow of the Firmament (the background being green), his right hand held out, palm outwards towards the congregation; in his left hand is a book, in the form of a roll; on either side is an angel with green halo and purple wings. The twelve apostles (each holding a book either in the normal form or a roll) are ranged, six on each side, St Peter, as usual, being on Christ's left, St Paul on his right. The ground is flowered. Below, on the left, is St John the Baptist, pointing towards the apse; on the right is St John the Evangelist, holding his right hand out in blessing. Each has a roll in his left hand. The folds of the cloaks in the upper frieze are blown out characteristically. Of the lower figures (only their hands are visible in Plate 114), St John the Evangelist has a tunic with double stripes of red. The Baptist is differently clad, with a gold tunic and purple cloak.

114

120

Within the apse, the Virgin is seated on a throne of gold, with a gold carpet spread out in front of her; on her knee is the Child, shown frontally, his right hand held up in blessing in front of his chest, his left hand holding a scroll. The Virgin is on a cushion of red and holds in her left hand a ceremonial towel with a fringe; her right hand is extended towards Paschal, who kneels before her and touches her shoe. His halo is square, to indicate that he was living at the time the mosaic was made. Her robe is deep blue, his vestment yellow. He wears the pallium. On either side of the throne is a throng of angels; three in front on each side have golden halos, the halos of the rest being bright blue, ringed with white. The suggestion of a multitude of angels is well conveyed by the many halos to be seen behind the front ranks of angels. The angels' tunics are white, with double red stripes down either leg. In this mosaic is to be seen at its finest the impressionistic treatment of the faces, discussed at greater length already[12] in relation to the detail in this mosaic. The ground, as in the triumphal arch mosaic, is flowered deeply. The usual band of sheep is missing; but the festoons of flowers in the soffits of the arch are there, in their Paschalian, somewhat spindly, form, with his monogram at the top in the usual manner. In earlier mosaics there is little doubt about the significance of these decorations. They symbolize the lavish plenty of the after-life. Here, though there is fruit and there are flowers, they are treated too schematically to be effective as symbolism.

A feature of this mosaic is the different bands of colour used in the background. For example, in the frieze of the triumphal arch the figures stand within an overall frame of gold, against a background of which the lowest band is green, sprinkled with white flowers; then there is a darker band of green, with red flowers, then a band of deep blue, then an upper band of green. Similarly, in the apse, behind the Virgin's head the background is deep blue; the lower part of the picture, however, has a background of green. It is the naïvety, coupled with the subtlety, of this work that gives it a special charm.

STA PRASSEDE

The mosaics in Sta Prassede form the most important ninth-century group in Rome. Those of the entrance arch to the choir (the triumphal arch), the apsidal arch and the apse itself commemorate Pope Paschal's building of the church, and his moving thither of the bones of Roman martyrs, in particular those of St Pudenziana and St Praxed, said to have been the daughters of Pudens, with whom, according to legend, St Peter had lodged in Rome. The two daughters of Pudens became martyrs for the faith, and Paschal, in the commemorative verse inscription, refers to their relics as the source of strength which may lift him to Heaven.

The little chapel of S. Zenone, off the north-east aisle, was built by Paschal in honour of Theodora, his mother, during her lifetime; she thus appears in it with the square halo. The chapel was designed to the glory of the Virgin, whom Paschal perhaps regarded as his special protectress,[13] and that of the women martyrs of Rome. Though at some period, probably just before it was finished, it was substantially altered, it remains a most charming ensemble, and used to be known as 'The Garden of Paradise'; with its mosaic of the Virgin and Child forming the altar-piece and the vault completely covered with mosaic, it is indeed one of the most notable monuments of its time. Here, incidentally, the setting of ninth-century *tesserae* can be studied at close quarters.

XX   Sta Maria Domnica, mosaic of the apse (*c.* 818).
The Virgin and Child, worshipped by Pope Paschal.

The mosaics of the choir arch (triumphal arch), apsidal arch and apse in the main church.
The alternation of colours in these mosaics, as seen from the nave, is a striking feature: the background of the mosaic on the upper half of the triumphal arch is dark blue; on the lower half, gold. The background of the apsidal arch mosaic is gold; of the apse mosaics, dark blue. The dark-blue colour, sprinkled with stars, of the painted vault between the triumphal arch and the apsidal arch, may represent an early colour scheme. There has been considerable restoration on the outside of the apsidal arch (for example, on the left lower side of the design, where the two lower rows of Elders are substantially restored); and the mosaic of the apse has apparently been completely reset, though the restorations have been finely done. But the mosaic pattern under the triumphal arch (flowers and fruits springing from a pot on either side, a repetition of the design under the apsidal arch) has been disastrously renewed, or imitated, and the yellow *tesserae* of the new work (laid in regular rows, as contrasted with the shimmering variety of the original version) are an object lesson in poor imitation. As is usual in the churches decorated by Paschal,[14] his monogram appears more than once, in the form shown here.

123, 124 *(margin)*

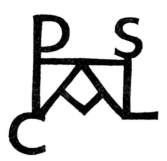

Fig 6   Monogram of Pope Paschal I.

As has been noted, and as Matthiae originally observed,[15] this apsidal mosaic and that of Sta Cecilia both derive from the mosaic of SS. Cosma e Damiano. It seems clear that the designer of the Sta Prassede apse was following that mosaic at first hand, whereas the Sta Cecilia design is copied from Sta Prassede. Thus, in Sta Prassede we see features, such as the river Jordan, repeated from SS. Cosma e Damiano that are absent from Sta Cecilia; while two small rocky lumps on the ground are faithfully imitated in Sta Prassede, but omitted in Sta Cecilia, and Christ is in the clouds, not virtually standing on the ground, as in Sta Cecilia. Another odd detail in Sta Prassede, taken from SS. Cosma e Damiano, is the plant at either end of the row of sheep. The outstretched right hand of Christ in Sta Prassede is modelled, as in SS. Cosma e Damiano—not simply marked with lines, as in Sta Cecilia. In work of this character it is inevitably difficult to discover precisely which artist did this and which did that. But to look at the row of sheep in Sta Prassede and to compare each (and the way its fleece is treated) with its neighbour is to become convinced that at least four different men were at work on this part (presumably one of the less important parts) of the mosaic. One of them, who adopted the simple solution of using straggly, roughly horizontal lines to represent the fleece, might be the man who worked on the same theme, in the same way, in Sta Cecilia. There are also signs that several men were engaged on the Sta Cecilia work (for example, the differing jars from which the two festoons spring, already mentioned).[16]

On the triumphal arch, the Heavenly Jerusalem is represented, the walls being of gold. In the centre, above, is Christ, standing in a robe of gold and red; on either side is an angel with a green halo and finely spreading wings (these have probably been largely renewed). Within the walls of the city are the twelve apostles, with St John the Baptist and the Virgin on the left, St Praxed in

124
XI, XII, XIII,
129 *(margin)*

a golden robe on the right. In the upper left-hand corner of the city is a youthful figure holding a scroll which bears the word 'lege' ('read'); the corresponding bearded figure on the right is probably St John the Baptist. In a wall-painting of approximately this period, two similar figures are the two St Johns; and in Sta Maria Domnica they also appear as here. St John the Divine might appear here as the supposed author of the Apocalypse,[17] and thus be associated with the theme of the New Jerusalem. Outside the walls, to right and left, are bands of martyrs waiting to be admitted. Each band is marshalled by three figures in rich vestments or lay clothes: one of green, one of red, one of blue (in the right-hand group all these seem to be ecclesiastics; the one in the centre has the pallium and may be a pope); the balancing group on the other side is garbed in gold, red and green (here the figure in green is a layman). Meeting the right-hand group is St Peter, with whom, actually in the city's gate, stands an archangel. The group on the left has women martyrs among it; the two leading figures among these wear robes of gold. Below both groups, to the left and to the right of the arch, are 'confessors', holding palm branches.[18] The main damage to this mosaic was done when architectural features and the gallery were added on both sides, breaking into the groups of 'confessors'.

On the inner arch of the apse, the design follows the pattern of SS. Cosma e Damiano, the Agnus Dei being represented, as there, lying on a throne, not standing. In the semi-dome of the apse Christ is in the centre. The other saints are, on the left: St Paul (the one figure in these mosaics   124 whose cloak carries a monogram, P in its Latin form), St Praxed and Paschal (with square halo), offering the church; on the right: St Peter, St Pudenziana and St Zeno. Flanking the figures, on both sides, are palm trees; that on the left has in its foliage a phoenix (compare both SS. Cosma e Damiano and Sta Cecilia). The figures here have not the supernatural tallness and waif-like slenderness of the Sta Cecilia mosaics. Paschal himself appears far more solid than in that church.   131 Draperies have patches of decoration in colour, as in Sta Cecilia and later in S. Marco. And the blown folds that flare out into a sort of double cup and are thus so conspicuous a feature of the Sta Maria Domnica mosaic appear in simpler form here, not only in the cloaks of the Elders on the apsidal arch but in the cloak of the angel just outside the gate of the heavenly city on the left. Below the river Jordan, in the apsidal mosaic, is the usual troup of lambs (against a gold background), with the Agnus Dei on a green platform from which the four rivers of Paradise flow.

The chapel of S. Zenone

Above the door leading into the chapel, but on the outside, is a double arching band of mosaic roundels. In the inner row, the Virgin is at the top in the centre, with, below her in the same roun-   125 del, her Child. Then there are tonsured male heads on either side (probably St Zeno—compare the representation in the apsidal mosaic—and his brother St Valentinus); otherwise this row consists of women, each wearing a crown (presumably women martyrs). The outer row consists of the heads of the twelve apostles, with St Paul on Christ's right and St Peter on his left at the head of the series; in the upper corners are two prophets. The faces are individualized, and the surface has that shimmering light that characterizes the mosaics of this chapel. Apart from the most unfortunate (and comparatively recent) additions of two heads in rectangles in the lower corners, this mosaic seems to be almost unrestored. These two added heads, of popes in tiaras, are said to have replaced an earlier pair in paint. They perhaps represent Paschal and some later pope.

The small mosaic altar-piece within this chapel is constructed in a niche of its own, and is   126 unfortunately very difficult to photograph. It represents a departure from the original design, since above it are the remains of a Transfiguration, the lower part of which has been cut away so that the mosaic could be accommodated in the recess. The architectural stonework might be contemporary with the rest of the chapel (here, as elsewhere, older materials being re-used), though the metal work must be a later addition. The mosaic is so different from the rest of the work in the chapel, belonging obviously to another school, that it has been dated as late as the thirteenth century. It represents the Virgin, as a young girl, with the Child seated on her knee frontally; he flings out both arms in a gesture of welcome. His right hand is held out in blessing, his left holds a scroll with the words EGO SVM LVX, 'I am the light'. On either side are saints, both holding martyr's crowns, presumably St Praxed and her sister St Pudenziana. The technique is entirely different from that of the other mosaics of the period. The gold leaf is on a red, not a green, glass base.[19] The *tesserae* are laid much more regularly, and there is a marked difference in size between those used for hands and face, and those used for the rest of the work. Certainly, then, it is the work of a different school, not simply of a different artist. To me a twelfth-century date, such as is often assigned to it, seems out of keeping with its delightful informality.[20] The mosaic above the door of the church of Sta Maria di Grottaferrata, about twelve miles outside Rome, yields some evidence to support the view that the mosaic in the chapel of S. Zenone was made in the eleventh century; see Appendix I and Plate 244. Some stylistic points seem to favour the possibility of an even earlier date, during the ninth century. The shadows of green in the faces appear already in the ninth-century Virgin 'Protectress of Constantinople' in Sta Sophia, a work of incomparably greater sophistication than this, but one which shares with it another stylistic device: the way the colours are 'drawn in' on the mosaic in long lines like strings of beads. But since this technique occurs also in the eleventh-century Grottaferrata mosaic, that argument is not conclusive, while the similarity of the treatment here and in Grottaferrata points to an eleventh-century date. The Greek form of the monogram for the Virgin, MP ΘY (which frequently appears in its Greek form in later Roman mosaics, and so would certainly not be a decisive indication of Greek workmanship), has apparently been altered to MR CH (but de Rossi read the letters as MateR EManuel). Above the Virgin's head is a 'tabernacle', as often in Roman mosaics in the crown of the apse. But it certainly does not conform to the traditional Roman pattern, and is more like a classical scallop shell.

To the left of the altar-piece, it is clear that the designs in the left-hand niche of the chapel were cut, like that immediately above the altar, when a change of plan was made. On the right-hand wall, Christ was shown in a mandorla, the subject probably being the Harrowing of Hell; only the upper half of the figure now remains. There are four quarter-length female figures in the small (north) arch: Theodora (Paschal's mother, with the square halo, the inscription being THEODORA EPISCOPA); St Praxed; the Virgin (the head here has been reset with great skill); and perhaps St Anne, mother of the Virgin. The three heads in this series which are in original condition are fine examples of the impressionistic technique at its best, and of the effect achieved by using each *tessera* as a point of colour, to be set at whatever angle it will tell most vividly. These four figures do not seem ever to have been full-length.

XXI Sta Prassede, mosaic of the vault in the chapel of S. Zenone (*c.* 820). Central roundel, with the head and shoulders of Christ.

Above these the Agnus Dei stands on a hill, from which flow the four rivers of Paradise; four deer, each pair a hind and an antlered stag, drink the water of the rivers. Above, on a gold background which gives character to all the upper part of the chapel, are, once more, three women martyrs. The inscriptions are nearly illegible, but the martyrs are St Agnes, St Pudenziana and St Praxed; all hold crowns of martyrdom. The purpose of the recesses here and on the other side corresponding to it is obscure. But the mosaic decorative lining of the sides of the recesses is original. They may have been intended for statues, or for some antique object like the marble vase used in the decoration of the 'façade' mosaic of this little chapel.

On the right of the altar, in the recess above a door, are three quarter-length figures, Christ in the centre and two saints, one (on Christ's right) tonsured, the other (who is not an ecclesiastic, since his cloak is decorated with a *tablion*) not tonsured. On the upper part of the wall are three full-length saints: St John the Evangelist, St Andrew and St James; above the main door entering the chapel from the church are two full-length saints, St Peter and St Paul, 'upholding' the throne of Christ. In the vaulted ceiling, against a gold background, four angels are supporters to the half figure of Christ in a roundel occupying the centre of the vault. Each stands on a globe. The motif here closely resembles that of the mosaic in the vault of the archiepiscopal chapel in Ravenna, and may be directly derived from it (though, as Wilpert points out,[21] the motif is originally Roman, not Ravennate). The arms (thin and formalized), the austere draperies, and the curve of the outer lines of the wings are all more effective than the corresponding features in the Ravenna mosaic, which might have been the model for this one. The plain vault isolates them, to their great advantage, whereas in Ravenna the vault, having the Evangelist symbols also, is, in effect, covered with a whole scheme of decoration. And the pictorial roundel in S. Zenone completes the design coherently in a way that the ☧ symbol at Ravenna does not. The faces of the angels in the chapel of S. Zenone show a high degree of most delicate modelling, which again belies the view sometimes put forward that the work of this group of artists is always entirely linear. The ornamental border used throughout, as opposed to the gemmed decoration used along the angles of the masonry structure, is not to be found elsewhere in Roman mosaics. On its tiny scale, this chapel gives the same impression of richness that the great Byzantine schemes of decoration in the eleventh and twelfth centuries give.

In several ways the mosaics of this chapel differ from other work of Paschal's reign. In particular, the ornament is different in character, the motif here used being made up of two elements (one in the shape of an hourglass, with a ring round the centre, and the other a cup) which compose together into a single pattern. It does not appear to be based on the antique. In this chapel only, however, among all the mosaics of the group, there is (in the vault above the altar) an inhabited scroll, springing on each side from a large central leaf with a fleshy rib. In the foliage are various animals. This is certainly an example of conscious classicism. The re-use of classical materials for the fine carved stone lintel of the door into the chapel, and for a number of details in the

XXII   Sta Prassede, mosaic of the vault in the chapel of S. Zenone
(*c.* 820). An angel supporting the central roundel.

immensely impressive. The design is unusual in its proportions, a broader band than usual being occupied by the sheep. This shifts the pattern of figures upwards towards the crown of the apse.

XXIII The main apsidal mosaic displays Christ against a background of gold. He wears a purple robe; his right hand is held up in blessing (in the Greek manner) and in his left hand he holds a book, the inscription in which reads EGO SVM LVX EGO SVM VITA EGO SVM RESVRRECTIO, 'I am the Light, I am the Life, I am the Resurrection'. It is to be noted that the texts are not from St Mark's Gospel, in spite of the dedication of the church. Like the other six figures of this frieze, Christ stands on a sort of mat or carpet, with an elaborate border round it. Theirs are inscribed with names, in a somewhat barbarous lettering, his with the letters A and W.[22] On the spectator's left is, first, Pope Gregory IV, with a square halo and wearing a gold chasuble and pallium; he holds a model of the church and is being presented by St Mark the Evangelist (who wears what may be a white dalmatic and a brownish mantle). Next to St Mark, on Christ's right, is St Felicissimus. The three on the spectator's right are (reading from left to right): Mark (pope in the year 336), who wears a chasuble of deep red, and pallium; St Agapetus (pope 535–36); and, on the extreme right, St Agnes in the traditional gold dress and holding a martyr's crown. In the apex of the apse, the Divine Hand holds a wreath.

The gold chasuble of Gregory on the left is balanced by the gold dress of St Agnes on the right. The balanced designs, here and in Sta Prassede, are in strong contrast to the composition of the mosaic in SS. Nereo ed Achilleo. The central figure is robed in purple. But one striking feature of the mosaic as a whole is the extensive use of white in the clothes of most of the figures, including St Peter and St Paul. The white *tesserae* look like marble and, as noted above, may be so.

Under Christ's feet, a dove with a halo perches on the edge of a fountain; farther below, overtopping the usual row of lambs representing the apostles, is the Agnus Dei. To the right and 135; cf IX, 168 left, as usual, are representations of Jerusalem and Bethlehem. Here the actual design is disintegrating. (This process had begun in the Sta Cecilia mosaic.) Bethlehem, on the right, is lettered as usual BETHLEHEM; Jerusalem is apparently not named. The frieze of lambs has, by contrast 136, 137 with those in the Paschalian mosaic, a certain solidity and three-dimensional quality which parallels what has been noted above as a new feature in the draperies of this mosaic. There are the usual festoons of flowers growing from pots on either side within the arch of the vault; where they meet there is the 'monogram' of Gregory (GREGORIVS PAPA) in the form shown here.

134 On the triumphal arch, against a background of gold in a roundel, is the bust of Christ. This beautiful detail is in a different manner from that of the main apsidal mosaic, and, as noted above, 133 is based on the Christ in Sta Cecilia of a few years earlier. It has not the ethereal charm of that head, but is in some ways so similar to it that one may think that both heads are the work of the same artist. On either side are roundels, bearing the symbols of the Evangelists. In the spandrel on the left is St Paul; on the right is St Peter. Each holds out his right hand towards Christ in the centre of the mosaic.

PGPRE
GORP
A

Fig 7   Monogram of Pope Gregory IV.

XXIII   S. Marco, mosaic of the apse (ninth century,
second quarter). Christ, with Pope Gregory IV and saints.

The artist whose work dominates the mosaic of S. Marco carried much further some of the artistic ideas which his predecessors, working for Paschal, had revived, and evolved a highly individual and original style. For reasons that are a matter of speculation, the Roman revival died with him; but its demise cannot be attributed to any lack of talent in his work. He might have found readier patrons in the eastern world, when the iconoclast movement came to an end, than in the west.

NOTES ON THE TEXT IV

1 In *Die römischen Mosaiken und Malereien der Kirchlichen Bauten vom IV bis XIII Jahrhundert*, 4 vols, Freiburg 1916, Plate 114, Wilpert gives the same comparison.

2 *SS. Cosma e Damiano e S. Teodoro*, Rome 1948.

3 There is a famous Byzantine example in the monastery of St Catherine on Mount Sinai.

4 In Ravenna there are two versions of it. Besides that illustrated in Plate 128, it is used also in S. Vitale with the Agnus Dei in the roundel; the design there is perhaps dependent in turn on one in St John Lateran (Plates 68, 69).

5 See G. B. de Rossi, *Musaici cristiani e saggi di pavimenti delle chiese di Roma anteriori al secolo XV*, 'Mosaico dell'arco della basilica urbana dei SS. Nereo ed Achilleo', fol. 1, Rome 1873-99.

6 But for the view that the scheme as a whole is Byzantine, see A. N. Grabar, *Byzantine Painting*, trans. S. Gilbert, Geneva 1953, p. 77. The attitude of the figures making obeisance is certainly Byzantine; compare the slightly later mosaic in Sta Sophia showing Leo VI receiving the investiture of Holy Wisdom. The case for strong Byzantine inspiration for the design as a whole—but not, I think, for the style—seems fully established.

7 Op. cit., 'Mosaico dell'arco della basilica urbana dei SS. Nereo ed Achilleo', fol. 1, verso.

8 Wilpert, op. cit., Plate 114, Nos 3 and 5; our Plates 237, 238.

9 In particular, in the ochre complexion (see p. 198). See also G. Matthiae on the different colours of the two faces surviving as fragments (*Le chiese di Roma dal IV al X secolo*, Rome 1962, p. 273, and, on Sta Maria Domnica, p. 276).

10 There is a short note on it by A. Terenzio ('Chiesa di Sta Maria Domnica, restauro dei mosaici', *Boll. d'Arte*, XXIX, 1935, Series III, Section II,

pp. 199-200).

11 In the hair of the angel on the right, for example, a tiny gap has been filled.

12 See p. 196.

13 Compare the theme of the mosaic in Sta Maria Domnica (see Plate XX).

14 Compare Sta Maria Domnica and Sta Cecilia in Trastevere.

15 The point, made by him in *Le Chiese di Roma* (p. 273), had already been established by him in *SS. Cosma e Damiano e S. Teodoro*.

16 See p. 196.

17 De Rossi (op. cit., caption to Plate 26) expressed the belief that the corresponding figure also once had a book in which was the word 'fide' ('fide' and 'lege' referring to the two ways in which a soul might be justified—by faith or by the law).

18 This theme is followed in a double-page drawing in a famous Anglo-Saxon manuscript: the *Liber Vitae* of the New Minster of Winchester, now in the British Museum (Stowe Ms No. 966). See Plate 122.

19 For green glass as a base for gold mosaic in this chapel, see p. 11.

20 E. Lavagnino (*Pietro Cavallini*, Milan 1959, p. 9) holds that it is early thirteenth-century; A. Venturi (*Musaici cristiani di Roma*, Rome 1925, p. 43) considers it to be twelfth-century. The eleventh-century painting in Sta Pudenziana (Wilpert, op. cit., Plate 234) is similar in composition but has none of the mosaic's charm. The gay gesture of the Child has some parallel in the Sta Maria Domnica mosaic. (Lavagnino seems to associate it—rightly, I think—with the Grottaferrata tympanum.)

21 Op. cit., p. 177.

22 Alpha and Omega; see Rev. xxi. 6

114   Sta Maria Domnica. Mosaics of the apse and the triumphal arch (*c.* 818).

115   Sta Maria Domnica, mosaic of the apse (*c.* 818). Two attendant angels.

116 *right*   Sta Maria Domnica, mosaic of the apse (*c.* 818).
The foot of one of the festoons, with detail of
the 'lobster claw' drapery folds.

119   Sta Maria Domnica, mosaic of the triumphal arch (ninth century, first quarter). St John the Baptist.

120 Sta Maria Domnica, mosaic of the triumphal arch (ninth century, first quarter). One of the apostles, from the frieze.

121 Sta Prassede. Mosaic of the triumphal arch (ninth century, first quarter). Left-hand side. Apostles and martyrs in the Heavenly Jerusalem. On the left, martyrs approach the City.

122 Detail from an Anglo-Saxon drawing from Winchester (*c.* 1025; British Museum, Stowe MS 966). Saints and confessors approach the Heavenly Jerusalem. The design was apparently adapted from the mosaic of the triumphal arch in Sta Prassede.

127 Sta Prassede. Mosaic of the vault in the chapel of S. Zenone (ninth century, first quarter).

128   Archiepiscopal chapel, Ravenna. Mosaic of the vault (sixth century).

129 Sta Cecilia in Trastevere. Mosaic of the apse (ninth century, first quarter).

130 Sta Cecilia in Trastevere, mosaic of the apse (ninth century, first quarter). Sta Cecilia.

131   Sta Cecilia in Trastevere, mosaic of the apse (ninth century, first quarter). St Peter and St Valerian.

132   S. Marco, mosaic of the apse (ninth century, second quarter). St Mark (left) and St Felicissimus.

133   Sta Cecilia in Trastevere, mosaic of the apse (ninth century, first quarter). Christ.

134   S. Marco, mosaic of the triumphal arch (ninth century, second quarter). Christ, in the central medallion.

135   S. Marco, mosaic of the apse (ninth century, second quarter). The city of Bethlehem, at the right-hand end of the frieze.

136   S. Marco, mosaic of the apse (ninth century, second quarter).
Detail from the frieze of sheep.

137   Sta Cecilia in Trastevere, mosaic of the apse (ninth century, first quarter).
Detail from the frieze of sheep symbolizing the apostles.

138   Mosaic, showing Christ flanked by St Peter and St Paul, which originally stood in the courtyard of the old basilica of St Peter's (said to date from *c.* 970–90). It has been cut down to form the altar mosaic for the tomb of Otto II in the Vatican Grottoes.

114 The mosaic shows the Virgin and Child, attended by the throngs of angels and worshipped by Pope Paschal. Above, in the centre, is Christ in a glory, and on either side a frieze of angels and apostles.

115 The brilliant impressionistic technique is characteristically Roman. For a larger detail of one of the angels in this group, see Plate 21.

116 The 'lobster-claw' folds on the left are characteristic of one of Pope Paschal's designers, who worked also on the apsidal arch in Sta Prassede.

118 A few missing *tesserae* have been replaced, but there has been virtually no resetting, and the work shows restoration at its finest.

119 The right side of the face (the spectator's left), including the cheek, eye and eyebrow, is modern.

120 There is a patch of restoration on the arm, just below the shoulder.

121 In the centre of the arch (on the right-hand side of the photograph, which shows only half of the arch) is Christ in the Heavenly Jerusalem. Within the city walls are the Virgin, St John the Baptist, St Paul (whose cloak bears his monogram, P), St John the Evangelist (whose monogram is H), apostles and St Praxed. Outside are archangels, and a group of martyrs, holding crowns, waiting to enter.

122 The artist has substituted confessors (shown in the mosaic original in the lower register—not included in the plate—holding palm branches as in the MS) for the martyrs with crowns. In the MS, the Heavenly Jerusalem (on the opposite page, not shown here) is relatively much smaller than in the mosaic.

123 Below, on the right, are twelve of the twenty-four Elders of the Apocalypse (Revelation iv), holding up their crowns. Above are two of the evangelists' symbols (the bull of St Luke and the eagle of St John), with two angels.

124 On the extreme left, Pope Paschal offers the church. Below are the Agnus Dei, and sheep symbolizing the apostles. The mosaic has been entirely reset; contrast Plate 129. The decorative patches on the draperies seem to represent embroidery, like the gold patches on Christ's garment shown in Plate XXIII.

125 The outer row of roundels shows Christ (in the centre) with the apostles. The inner row shows the Virgin and Child (in the centre), to the Virgin's right perhaps the young Pope Paschal, to her left St Zeno, and women martyrs. Of the heads in the four corners, the two at the top may represent the two saints John; the two at the bottom are modern, perhaps seventeenth-century. The condition is largely original.

126 The character and technique of this mosaic are Byzantine, and, like the mosaic shown in Plates 233 and 234, it was probably executed by a Byzantine craftsman. Its condition is largely original. See also p. 376.

127 The condition of this mosaic is largely original.

128 This mosaic was presumably the model for the mosaic of the vault in Sta Prassede (Plate 127). The long tapering wings, and some of the fold patterns in the hanging ends of the cloaks, seem to establish a direct relationship beyond doubt.

129 The mosaic shows Christ, with apostles and saints. Pope Paschal is on the extreme left. This mosaic, in contrast with that of the Sta Prassede apse, has not been extensively restored; in general, the setting is original.

130 This head was worked in the characteristic 'impressionist' Roman manner. Somewhat smaller *tesserae* are used for the face—and, in fact, for many other details when the artist feels inclined to use them. The material is apparently entirely of glass.

131 St Peter holds keys, St Valerian a martyr's crown. The hand of St Peter has apparently been reset.

132 The broad bands of colour—not intended to be stripes—used for the folds of the drapery give the work great solidity, and seem to have been inspired by a Byzantine original such as lies behind the similar technique used in the lunette of St Chrysostom (now described as ninth-century) in the church of Hagia Sophia, Istanbul. This Byzantine original may also have been responsible for the greater regularity of the *tesserae*. It looks as if marble was used extensively for the paler sections of the draperies.

134 This head was perhaps made by the artist of the head of Christ in the apsidal mosaic of Sta Cecilia in Trastevere (Plate 133). It is in quite a different style from the head of Christ in the apsidal mosaic of S. Marco (Plate XXIII).

135 Contrast the precision of the twelfth-century rendering of the same subject in the apsidal mosaic of Sta Maria in Trastevere (Plate 168).

136 This detail shows, as does Plate 132, the notable interest in plasticity displayed by the artist of this mosaic.

V

ROMANESQUE ART
IN ROMAN MOSAICS

FOLLOWING THE EPOCH which ends with the decoration of the S. Marco apse, there is a gap of approximately three centuries from which no major work in mosaic has survived. If any period had to be designated the dark age of Roman art, it might fall within this span. The restoration of churches is one possible criterion of continuity. There seem to be a few examples in the ninth century: Adrian III is said to have restored the baptistry of St John Lateran in 884, while the church itself, damaged by an earthquake in 896, was repaired a few years later. But from then onwards for a hundred and fifty years, records appear to be almost silent about any substantial scheme of restoration. There is one surviving mosaic, perhaps of the tenth century, made for a position in the courtyard of the old basilica of St Peter's, but adapted to adorn the tomb of Otto II   138
inside the church. It has been cut down in size, and a fair judgment of it is difficult. But to see a relationship between it and earlier, or later, Roman work is not easy. The hand of a craftsman from outside Rome, possibly from Germany, might almost be suspected. But I have no confidence in the tenth-century dating, though I have no alternative to suggest.

Desiderius, the Abbot of Monte Cassino, is said to have decided to re-establish the lost art of mosaic-making in Italy, in the second half of the eleventh century, and to have achieved this by introducing mosaic workers from Constantinople. The eleventh-century mosaic above the door of the church of Sta Maria di Grottaferrata, about twelve miles outside Rome, is of great importance in any discussion of the revival of the art in Rome during this period; it is illustrated in Plates 243–244. Mâle[1] suggests that it was 'these Byzantine masters who reinstructed the Roman artist in the technique of mosaic'. But he goes on to point out that the first surviving mosaic of the revival, that in S. Clemente, is, with the exception of one detail in the inscription (which was in fact almost as traditional as the ☧ sign), 'wholly Roman' in character. It has been suggested above that the mosaic of the small apse in S. Zenone is of eleventh-century Greek workmanship, like the tympanum at Grottaferrata. If so, it is the solitary surviving example, in Rome, of that revival. Vasari implied that the revival of the art of mosaic in Italy was due to Greek craftsmen.[2] But he was discussing thirteenth-century Florence, and the remains of the   XXIV, XV,
eleventh-century Roman revival are scanty indeed.   148–162,

The styles of the big twelfth-century mosaics in Rome—S. Clemente, which is the earliest;   175, XXV,
Sta Maria in Trastevere (including the main mosaic of the apse and the triumphal arch, and the   XXVI, 171,

139–143,
144–147,
178–180 mosaic of the façade, but excluding the thirteenth-century mosaics on the life of the Virgin), and Sta Francesca Romana—show few signs of influence such as one might expect, in the later of them at least, from the great Norman-Sicilian schemes of Byzantine mosaics in the south, or work in Venice and Torcello in the north. In this phase, in Rome, we seem to be concerned with stylistic development whose associations are primarily Ottonian. The lavishly decorated pages of certain Ottonian Bibles and gospel books seem the most likely claimants to be next-of-kin to the main apsidal mosaics in Sta Maria in Trastevere and Sta Francesca Romana. The artist's aim, in both fields, was to give an effect of extravagant richness. The gold background returns in its full splendour. The figures who in the Paschalian mosaics would have been simply vested are now robed (Plate XXVI, Sta Maria in Trastevere, apsidal mosaic) in the most gorgeous vestments the artist can depict. The simple, austere lines of some western European paintings of 139 the early twelfth century are found only in the central group of figures on the façade of Sta Maria in Trastevere.

XXIV
173, 174
148, 150, 151
156
170
171, 172 The apsidal mosaic of S. Clemente, which is in some ways as rich as the apsidal mosaics of Sta Maria in Trastevere and Sta Francesca, is different in style and in intention from them, and has no Ottonian relations. Its most striking effect lies in the contrast between the small suffering figure on the Cross (with the Virgin on his right and St John on his left) and the luxuriant Tree of Life which springs out, against the magnificent gold background, from the foot of the Cross, and which harbours within its branches the activities of the Church. The character of this Crucifixion makes it a harbinger of Gothic sentiment, in spite of its early date. The other two mosaics just mentioned have no such subtlety. Their concern is simply to display the heavenly splendour in a magnificent earthly form. And, unlike them, the S. Clemente mosaic has strong links with the past as well as the future: with the classical Roman tradition from which, as we shall see, considerable elements in the design, and some detail, are derived. Some of these classical elements passed into the fashion, and appeared on the triumphal arch designs, both here and in Sta Maria Trastevere. It is not difficult to see also, particularly in the figures of prophets which decorate these two triumphal arches (and similar figures once decorated that in Sta Francesca, but they have now disappeared), signs of the Byzantine inspiration that we should expect to be so much more powerful. But close Byzantine parallels are not easily found for these figures, and their attitudes, though not their facial types and draperies, are derived from figures on the ninth-century Roman triumphal arches. It is not till the next phase that the full tide of Byzantine inspiration floods into Rome.

STA MARIA IN TRASTEVERE: THE MOSAIC OF THE FAÇADE

The external mosaic of the façade of this church presents a problem both with regard to its subject and its date. The difficulty of determining the date is connected with the fact that several styles are represented in the series of figures. The latest were apparently made about a century after the earliest. There was a large-scale reconstruction of the church by Innocent I (1130–43); in 1140 the schism between Pope and Anti-pope was healed, partly through the work of St Bernard. The restoration of the church was, it has been suspected, a work of piety commemorating this triumph.[3] The main mosaic of the apse, to be discussed later, is no doubt of Innocent's time. The mosaic of the façade shows the Virgin and Child in the centre (with two donors), and on 139 either side five virgins. The central section of this mosaic, however (which shows the Virgin and Child, with the four central standing figures, two on either side), is very different in style from the apsidal mosaic. The stiff, formal lines of the earliest figures have their nearest parallels, perhaps, in some western manuscripts of the twelfth century. There is no other mosaic in Rome that has figures like them. A fairly firm date is provided for them, however, by some tricks of style that were clearly derived from Monreale, in particular the treatment of some highlights. This means that these figures are likely to have been made at some time during the last two decades of the twelfth century. 143, 144

As an exceptionally minute examination of this mosaic will be attempted here, it is important to assess precisely the main areas of restoration or renewal. One of these is the lower part of the central section. Here, the two tiny tonsured figures to the right and left of the Virgin's throne are late additions, and, whether because of damage caused when these were inserted, or for other reasons, there has been extensive renewal in this part of the mosaic. The lower part of the dress of the two figures on the left of the Virgin is identical, and perhaps entirely restored in both instances; for one of them, feet have been indicated, and this figure is shown standing awkwardly. No doubt the restorer was mistaken: her stance should be like that of the corresponding figures on the right, with the feet 'in profile'. The lower part of the Virgin's dress has suffered obvious damage also: much of this figure, together with that of the Child, has been reset by an artist who has followed precisely the original lines. 141

The second main area of restoration is the gold background to the left and right of the Virgin's head, which seems to have been extensively repaired (or, more probably, completely reset). 139

Thirdly, the gold background above the lamp held by the second figure on the right, patches of it by her left and by her right shoulder, and a patch below the hand of the third figure on the right—these have all been repaired. There is also a conspicuous repair adjacent to the right elbow of the third figure from the left. The cloak hanging over the right arm of the figure on the extreme left has been restored and also much of the upper part of the body and the face. Restorations are mentioned in G. Melchiorre's *Guide to Rome* (1840), as made by Nicholas V, Clement XI and Leo XII. But none need have been more than routine repairs. The marks on the gold background dividing the two last figures on the right do not seem to be associated with restoration, but might be finishing lines (where the moist plaster made ready for one day's work was used up and the next day's work was begun). There are extensive restorations of the ornament of the upper border. The ornament of the lower border is an entirely new, painted version.

It has been noted above that work of different periods can be distinguished in this mosaic. The three figures on the left are, quite obviously, in a different style from those of the central group, and date from the second half of the thirteenth century. In fact, however, not two, but three, phases are represented. 140

The first comprises the Virgin and Child, with the two standing figures on either side. The bodies and draperies are stiff and formal, and the bright highlights of white or gold, with which the draperies are enlivened, are a distinctive feature. They are particularly strongly marked on the clothes of the two who stand immediately on the Virgin's left (to the spectator's right). 139

142

The next phase is represented by the three figures at the right-hand end of the series. They have many marks also of this formal, Romanesque style: the bodies stiffly upright and thin, the draperies still with something of the austere formality of the earliest pattern. But the highlights are no longer conspicuous. The cloak of the figure standing third from the end, as compared with that next towards the centre, shows a roundness and solidity of form, the transitions from light to shade being subtly managed. The outside figure on the right represents a still greater degree of change than her two fellows. The draperies round the ankles of these two follow the same general pattern as in some of the earliest work, while, on the right, the treatment flows in less formal lines. 145, 147

242

242

245

The over-skirt, differently cut, falls in natural folds, unlike the flat panels of the other two, while the elaboration of the folds of the cloak also represents a further development of naturalism.

140   The three standing figures on the left of the panel belong to a third phase, a different stylistic world from the central group. Their draperies are almost exaggeratedly full, and hang in natural, strongly rounded folds; the hands droop, and are not held up with the palm outwards as in the
146 earlier work; the tilt of the heads is individual; the stance is much less rigid; the forms are solidly
147 embodied in the clothes. (As the figure on the extreme right shares some of these characteristics, she may be said to belong to a phase intermediate between the second and third, rather than strictly to the second, as do her two neighbours.)

    Once these differences are noted, other elements in the design are seen to confirm them. The
141, 142 bodies of the lamps held by the central group are circles, with other circles within them, rather than rounded spheres as are the lamps on the right. On the left, however, the figures hold lamps
146 of an elaborately fluted classical pattern. The crowns, too, in the left-hand group are of a classical pattern, contrasting markedly with the trefoil design of the rest. Here again, the figure on the
147 extreme right has a type of crown that is unique in this mosaic. She is associated, however, with the latest group, that on the left, in the veiling of the hand which holds the lamp.

    It is remarkable how clearly defined are the differences between the gold background as used in the three areas. The *tesserae* used for the gold in the central section (which may have been exten-
139 sively reset) are larger, and arranged with some regularity, often in roughly vertical lines. The
140, 146 background of the three latest figures, on the left, is made up of comparatively small *tesserae*, closely packed together; the work lines are generally horizontal rather than vertical. The dividing line between the two areas is unmistakable. On the right, the *tesserae*, which are of the larger pattern, are set altogether more loosely than those of the centre, and their work lines are more erratic. Here again there is no doubt as to where one area begins and the other ends; and this feature is a conclusive reason for supposing that there were only three main phases of work on the mosaic, not four (in spite of the individuality of the extreme right-hand figure).

139   When the centre group was made, the ground was at first marked by a straight band of colour, a few inches above the horizon. Below this, smaller *tesserae* were used. This band was destroyed between the three middle figures when the two small worshipping donors were inserted. These belong, as the loose folds of the draperies show, to the latest phase.

    Stylistically, then, the mosaic shows the development of a remarkable new series of conventions, the transition being from a highly stylized, linear representation of the human figure to one that is far freer, far more solid and far more naturalistic. Some of the details in the later style, like the lamps or the crowns, are obviously derived from classical sources. This is, in fact, the transition from Romanesque (in the form fully typical of much work done in western Europe in the first half of the twelfth century) to Renaissance. We shall have further opportunities for observing the later phases of this transition.

    Mâle[4] argued (in disagreement with earlier scholars, such as de Rossi, who regarded the mosaic as twelfth-century) that it belongs to the late thirteenth century, basing his view on an *obit* entry of the early fourteenth century which refers to a canon of the church 'who caused three images of virgins to be made in mosaic above the door'. He thought that the whole mosaic must have been made during the lifetime of this canon, being paid for, presumably, by several donors. There are, according to de Rossi, two such entries referring to additions or repairs to the mosaic; one donor 'fecit fieri tres ymagines musaycas virginum supra portas'; and another 'fecit reparari tres imagines musaicas'. Our examination of the mosaic has shown that the three figures on the right are an

246

addition to the original group, while those on the left show even greater differences in style from the earliest work, and might have been made a century later than it. These last three figures, though made to complete the series, belong, indeed, to a different stylistic world, and are no doubt the three virgins that were paid for last. De Rossi's two entries seem to be related to the second and third phases distinguished here. Vasari's statement that the façade mosaic was Cavallini's work[5] would be acceptable with regard to these three virgins, and the attribution may tentatively be accepted.[6] Certainly, both the donors next to the throne are thirteenth-century additions, one of them, no doubt, being the canon referred to by Mâle. The strongly classical quality of the later work bears out the attribution to Cavallini.

140

146

141, 142

We are here concerned, then, with one of those medieval works that was completed over a long period. The central group was already in existence by the late twelfth century. At that time, the supporting figures to the left and right may have been painted, as Vasari says; and this would explain the use of the word 'reparari' in the *obit* entry. The painted virgins were replaced by mosaic figures in two phases, during the first of which a serious attempt was made to match the style of the earlier work, while, in the second, something frankly new was substituted. For the execution of a design partly in mosaic, partly in the first instance in paint, there seems to be a precise parallel in the Grottaferrata Pentecost. But in that work the paint was never translated into mosaic, though no doubt this was the intention when money became available.

The subject of the panel has often been taken as representing the five Wise and five Foolish Virgins. The objection to this theory is that eight, not five, are represented with lamps lit.[7] It has been suggested that the flames in the three lighted lamps on the right-hand side are due to mistaken restoration.[8] This is an untenable view, for of the five figures on the right, two are represented with heads bowed in humility, not crowned (though they wear halos); the other three have crowned heads which they hold high. We should have, then, to imagine a total restoration, completely mistaken, of all three figures, not simply a mistake concerning the lamps. It seems strange enough to represent two Foolish Virgins with halos, let alone to represent three with crowns. Nevertheless, while I think it unlikely that the Wise and Foolish Virgins are the subject of the panel, I cannot suggest an alternative.

For parallels with the mosaic of the façade of Sta Maria in Trastevere in the mosaic of the triumphal arch in the church of Sta Maria di Grottaferrata, referred to above, see Appendix I.

S. CLEMENTE: THE MOSAIC OF THE APSE

The date of the apsidal mosaic in S. Clemente has given rise to considerable discussion.[9] The Cross, with the figure on it, and, on either side, the Virgin and St John, seem almost Gothic in sentiment. The size of the Christ figure is reduced, in order to emphasize the pathos of the group, which is vivid and heavily charged with emotion. If this is compared with the series of figures that form the main pattern in the twelfth-century apsidal mosaics in Sta Maria in Trastevere or Sta Francesca Romana, the difference of sentiment is striking. Those two mosaics can be dated with confidence to the mid-twelfth century. This, so much more Gothic in feeling, might be assumed to be considerably later.

XXIV

XXV

XXVI, 173

174

But the evidence is decisively against this. On the marble throne in the centre of the apse is the inscription ANASTASIVS PRESBITER CARDINALIS HVIVS TITVLI HOC OPVS CEPIT ET PERFECIT, 'Anastasius, priest and cardinal of this *titulus*,[10] undertook this work and brought it to completion'. If this inscription is intended to include, within the scope of the phrase HOC OPVS, the mosaic decoration of the apse and triumphal arch, the date would be *c.* 1127. Can this date be supported on stylistic grounds? The answer is 'yes'. Most important is the striking resemblance between the decoration of the exterior of the arch in Sta Maria in Trastevere and the same feature in S. Clemente. In both, the prophets Isaiah and Jeremiah fill the lower part of the triangular span on either side of the arch; their arms are outstretched, and scrolls are in their hands. There was a similar feature, which no longer survives, in Sta Francesca Romana. This was clearly the mid-twelfth-century fashion. Details like the symbol of the caged bird (explained in Sta Maria in Trastevere by the inscription CHRISTVS DOMINVS CAPTVS EST IN PECCATIS NOSTRIS, 'In our sins Christ the Lord is imprisoned', occur in both S. Clemente and Sta Maria. The same incipient classicism (still in some ways a cloak that fits awkwardly) occurs in Sta Maria in Trastevere, though in a more tentative form, and seems to be derived from S. Clemente. In the apsidal mosaics, there is a striking similarity, in the canopy in the apex of the vault, between the mosaics of all three churches, the similarities between S. Clemente and Sta Maria being even closer than those between either and Sta Francesca.[11] Yet both Sta Maria and Sta Francesca are dated securely in the mid-twelfth century. The features that seem to belong to a considerably later date in S. Clemente are, then, the achievement of an outstandingly imaginative artist, inspired by an unusual theme.

For the classical elements in the S. Clemente mosaic are, of course, as was seen long ago by de Rossi and by Wilpert, of cardinal importance, and provided the main theme for its designer. The new apse was built to replace an older, the history of which went back to late classical times. The magnificent scroll that covers the vault is derived directly from the decoration of that earlier vault. Its nearest relation is the fifth-century scroll which still survives in the baptistry of St John Lateran. The scroll is crowded with classical motifs or allusions: an *amoretto* climbing among the grapes in the festoons of the soffits of the arch; *amoretti* on dolphins, repeated within the great scroll on either side; *amoretti* blowing trumpets. In the context, these are much more likely to have been motifs drawn directly from the original mosaic of the apse, than allusions made by an artist whose mind was furnished with classical ideas (who would, indeed, be a remarkable phenomenon at this date). An almost conclusive proof in itself of Wilpert's view is to be found in a detail at the root of the central acanthus from which the great scroll develops. The small deer within this plant, with its head to the ground, is actually about to attack a snake, which the twelfth-century artist has mistakenly represented as a jewelled band. The symbol comes from the *Physiologus*.[12] The deer was said to eat the snake, shed its antlers, and grow new antlers, with a renewal of its youth. This misunderstanding of an earlier feature, which can nevertheless be recovered from the present design, is powerful evidence of its origin.

The theme of the mosaic symbolizes the life-giving treasure of the Cross of Christ. From the foot of the Cross here a great scroll or vine burgeons, which shelters the Church among its branches. The Church is represented by the small figures of the Fathers of the Latin Church and by other groups, sometimes symbolic, representing the laity. A great Cross was the focal point (far more dominating, in the original proportions of the apse, than it is now) in the mosaic in the

XXIV S. Clemente, mosaic of the apse (*c.* 1125).
The Crucifixion, with the scroll growing from the base of the Cross.

church of Sta Pudenziana. A Cross was the classical central theme in St John Lateran, the mosaic of which now exists only in a late version, but which goes back in its general design to the classical period. It is probable that the Cross was an element of the earlier mosaic in S. Clemente also, and the doves which represent the apostles (they are sharing the Cross, as the apostles are invited to do in Luke xiv. 27) are a feature of the iconography of the catacombs. Moreover, a fourth-century series, with each bird nimbed, has recently been discovered in Greece.[13] The birds probably belong also to the early design. They appear also in the *atrium* of the baptistry of St John Lateran, in the crown of the vault.

It has been suggested that the first and last lines of the difficult inscription are another element from the earlier mosaic:

ECCLESIAM CRISTI VITI SIMILABVMVS ISTI
DE LIGNO CRVCIS IACOBI DENS IGNATIIQVE
INSVPRA SCRIPTI REQVIESCVNT CORPORE CRISTI
QVAM LEX ARENTEM SET CRVS FACIT ESSE VIRENTEM

'We liken the Church of Christ to this vine, which the law causes to wither, but the Cross gives it life. A fragment of the true Cross, a tooth of St James, and a tooth of St Ignatius, rest in the body of Christ which is represented above this inscription.' The inscription is in two parts; the first and fourth lines are to be taken together, then the second and third, which refer to relics of St James and St Ignatius which have been built into the representation of the body of Christ in the mosaic above. But the first and fourth lines, taken together, give the theme of the mosaic as 'We liken the Church of Christ to this vine. Under the law it withered, but the Cross of Christ makes it flourish again with green.' They may thus belong to the original scheme. Mâle supposed[14] that the small figures in the volutes, and the crucified Christ, were medieval. On the view here put forward, the small figures probably had ancient predecessors, though Mâle is right about the figures on the Cross. In one group of small figures at least, an original in a technique familiar in the finest nave mosaics of Sta Maria Maggiore seems to lie behind the twelfth-century version.

But if there are early elements in the design, most of them have been transformed in the twelfth-century mosaic. The figures just mentioned, like the *amoretti* themselves, would hardly be recognizable, out of their context, as classically inspired. They have a vigour (an example is the princeling on the right of the group of three, near the left-hand side of the foot of the Cross, leaping to escape) which seems wholly medieval. And the superb effect gained by the setting of the gold on a rough surface of plaster, almost as though the background had been padded, gives this mosaic a marvellous quality of brightness that is almost unrivalled in the whole Roman series.

The mosaic of the apse as a whole, then, its wonderful central feature being medieval in conception, and its design and variety of incident being largely classical in derivation, was stylistically, owing to the fusion of elements just described, a unique phenomenon in its day. The designer in Sta Maria in Trastevere, who, a decade or so later perhaps, planned the *putti* holding out a sheet to be filled with plenty (a plenty which is symbolized in a classical idiom, with fruits, a vase, and doves at a bowl) may have been inspired by this mosaic. But in the main mosaic of the Sta Maria apse, his models were entirely different: a central theme drawn from French sources, and a style with the heavy richness of Ottonian work.

STA FRANCESCA ROMANA AND STA MARIA IN TRASTEVERE: THE MOSAICS OF THE APSES

These two mosaics, as has already been noted, are in some ways closely connected. In that of Sta Maria (Plate XXVI), Pope Innocent II is one of the three figures represented on the left of the

XXV   Sta Maria in Trastevere, mosaic of the apse (*c.* 1140). Christ enthroned with the Virgin.

seated pair (Christ enthroned with the Virgin) in the centre. Immediately on Christ's left (the spectator's right) is St Peter, distinguished from the rest because he alone does not wear ecclesiastical vestments. The other figures are saints and martyrs of the early Roman church (Laurentius, Pope Calixtus, Pope Cornelius, Pope Julius and Calepodius the Presbyter), and it seems likely that all of these were regarded as being connected in some way with the early history of the church. We can regard Innocent, therefore, who holds a model of the church in his hand, as the patron under whose auspices the mosaic was made; consequently we can date this mosaic to shortly before the mid-twelfth century.

The four figures on either side of the central group in the Sta Francesca mosaic are St Peter, St James, St John and St Andrew. Here we seem to notice a change from the traditional Roman choice of local worthies towards the fashion represented early in the next century in the mosaic of S. Paolo fuori le Mura, in which it is the apostles who are represented as a group. The apostles also form the main group in Toriti's mosaic in St John Lateran, though there they might be based on an earlier series.[15]

At first the two mosaics give widely different impressions. The central scene in Sta Maria is the Enthronement of the Virgin. Christ is in the centre (not, as in the mosaic which Toriti made for Sta Maria Maggiore at the end of the thirteenth century, one of two equal partners in the group, which is divided equally by the central line of the mosaic).[16] The background of the mosaic in Sta Maria in Trastevere is the sheer gold typical of Byzantine mosaics of the period. In Sta Francesca the figures are placed under an arcade of round arches, the pillars of which separate them as they do on many antique sarcophagi. Two of the pillars are twisted, as they often are also on such models. The other four are more fancifully decorated; and above the arcade is the representation of a brick structure, unique in Roman mosaics. The immediate derivation of this *motif* in Sta Francesca may have been an eleventh-century fresco in S. Clemente.[17] The figures of the Sta Maria mosaic give a more squat impression. But this is because of their heavy vestments. As remarked above, all except St Peter wear ecclesiastical vestments: five wear chasubles (four of these have the *pallium*, but not Calepodius), while St Lawrence seems to be wearing an elaborate dalmatic, with a rich cloak over it. It is these vestments that make the figures look solid. This can be seen if the representations of St Peter in the two mosaics are compared. The two figures are so similar, not only in most of the lines of the drapery, but also (for example) in the form of the book that St Peter carries (repeated with the figure of St James in the Sta Francesca mosaic, but otherwise unrepresented in the Roman series), that they clearly look back to the same original. We can identify this from an engraving published by Ciampini in the seventeenth century, though the mosaic itself has disappeared. It seems likely that the artist of the Sta Francesca mosaic was indulging in deliberate antiquarianism. The other figures in Sta Francesca come from different sources, except for St James, the type of whose draperies is based on those of St Peter. On the other hand, though St John also wears a toga above a tunic, the type seems there to belong to that of the series of apostles in St John Lateran and was perhaps consciously derived therefrom, since at the other end of the mosaic the resemblance between St Andrew and the Lateran series is strong. We seem thus to find in Sta Francesca a conscious intention to combine antique *motifs* in a new whole.

The small pierced, or arcaded, design that surrounds the foot of the throne in Sta Maria occurs also below the base of the twisted columns in Sta Francesca. The facial types, however, are in some ways curiously different. The face of the Virgin in the two works belongs to two different styles, that in Sta Maria being a striking anticipation of the later versions made under strong

XXVI   Sta Maria in Trastevere, mosaic of the apse (*c.* 1140). Three ecclesiastics, vested.

Fig 8 An engraving of the mosaic, since destroyed, in the church of S. Andrea in Barbara (468–83; the reign of Pope Simplicius). From J. Ciampini, Vetera Monumenta . . . (Rome, 1690). The figures on the right and left of Christ were taken as models by the artist of the mosaic in Sta Francesca Romana. Note not only the pose, and the general forms of the drapery, of the figures, but also the forms of the scrolls which they are holding.

174   Byzantine influence, that in Sta Francesca, represented precisely frontally, being awkward in treatment and provincial in manner. The figures of Christ and the Virgin in Sta Maria are perhaps by a different hand from the rest of that mosaic, the work in them being of great elegance. Some features in the thrones in the two mosaics, specially the unusual terminals at the foot of each side-piece, are so similar that some interdependence between the two designs can be assumed. It has been noted in another context[18] that the canopy in the apex of the vault is similar in these two churches and in S. Clemente (the correspondence being particularly close, however, between

XV, 173, 174   S. Clemente and Sta Maria).

In some details, however, there are notable differences between the two mosaics. The festoons in the soffits have only slight similarities. An elegant classical vase stands at the foot of each soffit in Sta Maria, and the roundels and inhabiting birds do not appear in Sta Francesca. The curious

178–180   mats on which the apostles are represented as standing in Sta Francesca may be derived from a
XXIII   similar feature in the ninth-century mosaic of S. Marco. These do not appear in Sta Maria. All
179   the apostles in the Sta Francesca series have haloes, which are often elaborate. None of the standing figures have them in Sta Maria. Unfortunately, the series of sheep which no doubt once existed

below the inscription in Sta Francesca has disappeared in one of the reconstructions, together with the representations of Jerusalem and Bethlehem. C. R. Morey thought that the date of the Sta Francesca mosaic was the time of the re-dedication of the church by Alexander III in 1161.[19] This seems a possible date, though to me one would be more acceptable which allowed for the influence of Sta Francesca on Sta Maria, and not the other way about.

The idiom of these mosaics, in relation to what preceded and what followed them, or to what was being done elsewhere in Europe to the east or the west, is not easily characterized. There is an interest in antique styles or *motifs*, as, for example, in the arcade of the Sta Francesca mosaic, with its twisted columns, or the *putti* holding a sheet loaded with symbols of plenty in Sta Maria. But this interest has no influence on the artists' individual styles, and is confined to the choice of *motifs*. So, if the artist of Sta Francesca copied figures from St John Lateran, those had no influence on the design of the figures adjacent to them. A few features, like the sheer gold background in the Sta Maria mosaic, seem to be Byzantine. But the main theme there, the Enthronement of the Virgin, is French and characteristically medieval.[20] It is of particular interest, since it reintroduces into the tradition the idea of a central group, an idea which, since the sixth-century apses, had disappeared, to be replaced (save in one ninth-century example, the original of the *Tribune of Benedict XIV*) by a simple detached series. The profusion of colour, and the concern, notably in Sta Francesca, to fill the background, recall, as suggested already, the elaboration of some Ottonian decorated manuscripts. We can do little more here than state doubts as to whether these two examples can be used, with any plausibility, to support the theory of a revival, as Mâle describes, 'brought about by the work of Byzantine craftsmen'.[21] It is true that this revival is said to have originated some hundred years before these mosaics were made. But if the first craftsmen of the revival were Byzantine, then that Byzantine character (at a time when magnificent mosaics in the Byzantine tradition were being made in the north, and in the south, of Italy) had been by now almost completely lost in Rome. What can be seen in both mosaics (more clearly, however, in Sta Maria) are some slight traces of that early 'classical' revival of which the S. Clemente apsidal mosaic is so noble an example. In neither case can I detect any traces of influence derived from the mosaics of Cefalu, or of the Palatine chapel in Palermo, which should, it seems, antedate them by a few years.

S. CLEMENTE AND STA MARIA IN TRASTEVERE: THE MOSAICS OF THE TRIUMPHAL ARCHES

As has been mentioned above, until the destruction of the mosaic of the Sta Francesca triumphal arch, there existed three triumphal arch mosaics of the twelfth century all designed to a similar pattern: in each case the two sides of the arch were occupied with figures of prophets holding scrolls, with palm trees behind them. The drawing which survives of the Sta Francesca mosaic shows that the words on Jeremiah's scroll were the same, except for a tiny detail (the omission of the word EST), as in S. Clemente. A different text from that in S. Clemente was chosen for the figure of Isaiah. It is the one used for Isaiah on the mosaic in Sta Maria in Trastevere. It is, of 171 course, not possible to say anything in detail about the style of the lost mosaic of Sta Francesca. A comparison of the two surviving triumphal arch mosaics suggests that, except for the fine bust of Christ in the central roundel of S. Clemente (which might, to judge from the treatment of the 158 hair, be by the artist of the central crucifixion), the rest of the work there is of less good quality than that in the Sta Maria mosaic. The figures are coarse and rather clumsy. The design in general 160, 162 is more elaborate in S. Clemente, with St Paul on one side and St Peter on the other, above the figures of the two prophets. St Lawrence, under whose feet is a gridiron, sits next to St Paul, and, on the other side of the arch, St Peter's attendant is St Clement, below whom is a ship, an allusion to his journeys to the west. The inscriptions accompanying these two are even more obscure than that of the main apsidal mosaic.[22] But the work on the figures of the prophets is, as we have seen, comparatively coarse. Some details, however (like the vertical line-shading on the v-fold hanging from the left arm of Isaiah in S. Clemente), occur in both mosaics, and also in the apsidal mosaics of Sta Maria and of Sta Francesca. These resemblances seem close enough to suggest that men from the same workshop were engaged on this whole group of mosaics. But the mosaic actually within the apse of S. Clemente (whose gold background, for example, is much looser in texture than that of the triumphal arch mosaic) suggests a different *atelier*. One may suspect that it was executed first, and the triumphal arch mosaic a little later, though certain details (for example, the two shades used for the hair in both mosaics) suggest strongly that the crucified Christ and the Christ of the triumphal arch roundel are in fact by the same hand. The pattern along the outside edge of the mosaic of the prophets in S. Clemente is an echo of one used by ninth-century Roman mosaicists. It is not repeated in Sta Maria Maggiore. There is a superficial 'Byzantinism' in the figures of the prophets. But this does not seem to imply any very profound influence,[23] and the general impression remains Ottonian rather than Byzantine, so that one must reckon that these mosaics too belong to a western rather than an eastern tradition.

158

LATE ROMANESQUE MOSAICS OR FRAGMENTS

One complete, small-scale mosaic and three fragments from a much larger scheme, all in what may be called a late Romanesque manner, survive from the early thirteenth century. Two fragments come from the apse of the old basilica of St Peter's. The scheme of this mosaic is known from two Vatican manuscripts,[24] and dates from the late fourth century. When the mosaic was repaired by Innocent III some time before 1216 (the year of his death), he inserted figures of himself and of the Ecclesia Romana, and it is the heads of these two figures, together with a dove, Innocent's badge, that survive.[25] In them is to be seen a new and far stronger Byzantine influence than has been encountered, in the mosaics discussed so far, in the twelfth-century work done in Rome. The use of fine *tesserae* for the face, the strongly marked patch of red on the cheek (as in the Virgins of Murano or Torcello),[26] the crown and pendants decorated with inset natural stones, and, above all, the work lines developed so as to suggest the structure of the face—these are derived from Byzantine sources.

176, 177

29

XXVII The most beautiful mosaic of the group is the small Virgin and Child in S. Paolo. Much of the border of this mosaic has been restored, but enough of the original border remains to show that the mosaic was made in this form, and is not a fragment, as might otherwise be supposed, of a large work. The Virgin is standing, with a charming inclination of the upper part of her body

XXVII S. Paolo fuori le Mura. Mosaic icon of the Virgin (*c.* 1210).

256

towards the left, and with her head leaning to the right. The Child, who holds a tiny scroll in his left hand and extends his right in blessing, sits on his mother's left arm, a curiously adult figure, as so many Byzantine artists imagined him. Her right hand is held open, the palm towards the breast, across her chest as in many eastern examples; and the Child's head, seen three-quarter face and with a high domed forehead, is also derived from an eastern original. Here are the same red patches on the cheeks, and the same fine *tesserae* used for the face and worked into structural lines, as have been noticed in the other examples in this group. The dark colours and highlights of flashing gold are wonderfully effective; but when compared with the Virgin of Murano, or of Torcello, there is a lack of sophistication which leaves this undeniably western work no less enchanting, though far less self-conscious, than the fine eastern work which influenced it so strongly.

1 *Early Churches of Rome*, Eng. trans. (1960) of French ed., p. 149.

2 *Lives of the Painters*, ed. W. Gaunt, 4 vols, London 1963, vol. 1, p. 54.

3 Mâle, op. cit., p. 133.

4 Op. cit., pp. 145–146.

5 Op. cit., vol. 1, p. 125.

6 The Cavallini mosaic worked for the façade of S. Paolo fuori le Mura, which only survives as a wretchedly poor nineteenth-century reconstruction in a different position, may have been, to judge from the reconstruction, related to this group.

7 In Vat. Cod. Barb. Lat. 4044 there is a series of pictures, made in the sixteenth century, of the façade mosaic. The artist has failed to capture the difference between the style in which the three figures on the left were executed and that of the rest. By what must surely be a mistake he shows the Virgin farthest but one on the right with lamp unlit, though she is crowned.

8 Mâle, op. cit., p. 146.

9 For an entirely different view from that taken in the following paragraph, see E. Scaccia Scarafoni, 'Il mosaico absidale di S. Clemente in Roma', *Boll. d'Arte*, XXIX, II, 1935, Series III, Section 1, pp. 49–68.

10 An ecclesiastical division.

11 When compared with the later canopy in Sta Maria Maggiore, for example, it will be seen that the three twelfth-century mosaics each have a closely similar outer band of decoration, unlike the late thirteenth-century mosaic.

12 See J. Wilpert, *Die römischen Mosaiken und Malereien der Kirchlichen Bauten vom IV bis XIII Iahrhundert*, 4 vols, Freiburg 1916, p. 518. For a slightly different pictorial version, see 'A Thirteenth-century Bestiary in the Library of Alnwick Castle', ed. E. Millar, presented to members of the Roxburghe Club, 1958.

13 Society for the Promotion of Hellenic Studies, *Archaeological Reports* (supplement to the *J. Hellen. Studies*), 1962–63, p. 24.

14 Op. cit., pp. 126–127.

15 See p. 312.

16 For a discussion of the relationship between the two designs, see M. Alpatoff-Moskau, 'Die Entstehung des Mosaiks von Iacobus Toriti in Sta Maria Maggiore in Rom', *Römisches Jahrb. für Kunstwiss.*, 1924–25, pp. 1–19.

17 V. Golzio and G. Zander, *Le chiese di Roma dall' XI al XVI secolo*, Roma Cristiana, vol. 4, Rome 1963, Fig. 96.

18 See p. 248.

19 C. R. Morey, *Lost Mosaics and Frescoes of Rome of the Middle Period*, Princeton 1915, p. 17. For the design of the destroyed triumphal arch mosaic, see S. Waetzoldt, 'Die Kopien des 17 Jahrhunderts nach Mosaiken und Wandmalereien in Rom', *Römische Forschungen*, vol. VIII (*Misc. Biblioth. Herzianae*), Vienna 1964, Plates 40 and 45.

20 See Mâle, op. cit., pp. 143–145. It is to be noted, however, that in Sta Maria in Trastevere the theme is the Enthronement, rather than the Coronation, of the Virgin.

21 Ibid., p. 139.

22 For Lawrence: DE CRVCE LAVRENTI PAVLO FAMVLARE DOCENTI. Perhaps, as with the other inscription, the verb is imperative: 'Do thou, Lawrence, serve Paul who teaches thee about the Cross.' Father Mulooley in 1869 transcribed the fifth word as FAMILIARE and gave this translation: 'Paul familiarly teaching Lawrence about the Cross.' The other inscription runs: RESPICE PROMISSVM CLEMENS A ME TIBI CHRISTVM (Peter is speaking), 'Behold, O Clement, Christ promised by me to thee.'

23 The prophets on the triumphal arch in S. Clemente are very similar to a prophet, in fresco, in one of the churches in Tivoli. For a reproduction, see P. Baldass, 'The Mosaic of the Triumphal Arch of S. Lorenzo fuori le Mura', *Gaz. des Beaux Arts*, vol. 49, 1957, pp. 1–18.

24 Cod. Lat. 5408, fols 29 and 31, and Cod. Barb. 4410, fol. 26.

25 A fine fragment of the fourth-century work is discussed elsewhere; see p. 68.

26 This is a return to an earlier Byzantinizing technique, as, for instance, in the face of St Agnes in the mosaic of Sta Agnese fuori le Mura. But it appears already in S. Clemente.

139 Sta Maria in Trastevere, mosaic of the façade. The central group. The date is *c.* 1190, except for the small figures of donors (thirteenth century).

140 Sta Maria in Trastevere, mosaic of the façade. Left-hand side of the frieze. The three figures on the left, probably by Cavallini, date from the last quarter of the thirteenth century; the figure on the right dates from *c.* 1190.

141 Sta Maria in Trastevere, mosaic of the façade. Detail from Plate 139. The figure on the
Virgin's left (*c.* 1190).

142 Sta Maria in Trastevere, mosaic of the façade. Detail from Plate 139. The figure on the Virgin's right (*c.* 1190).

145 Sta Maria in Trastevere, mosaic of the façade.
The fourth figure to the right of the Virgin
(mid-thirteenth century).

143   Sta Maria in Trastevere, mosaic of the façade.
The Virgin and Child (*c.* 1190).

144   Monreale, Sicily. St Anne: from a conch in the
cathedral (Sicilian-Byzantine; *c.* 1180).

146   Sta Maria in Trastevere, mosaic of the façade. One of the figures by Cavallini on the left-hand side of the frieze (thirteenth century, last quarter).

147 Sta Maria in Trastevere, mosaic of the façade. The figure on the extreme right (mid-thirteenth century).

148 S. Clemente, mosaic of the apse (c. 1125). Detail: the Crucifixion.

149 S. Clemente, mosaic of the apse (c. 1125). Detail from Plate 148.

150 S. Clemente, mosaic of the apse (*c.* 1125). The mourning Virgin (detail from Plate 148).

151 S. Clemente, mosaic of the apse (*c.* 1125). The mourning St John (detail from Plate 148).

153　S. Clemente, mosaic of the apse (*c.* 1125). Three figures from the scroll.

152　S. Clemente, mosaic of the apse (*c.* 1125). Acanthus root at the foot of the Cross.

154, 155   S. Clemente, mosaic of the apse (*c.* 1125). Details from the lower edge of the scroll.

156   S. Clemente, mosaic of the apse (*c.* 1125). Detail from the scroll. St Gregory; monk feeding a bird; and (above) *amoretti*.

157 S. Clemente, mosaic of the apse (*c.* 1125). Detail from the scroll. St Ambrose; the symbol of the caged bird; and (above) an *amoretto*.

158 S. Clemente, mosaic of the triumphal arch (twelfth century). Head of Christ in the central medallion.

159   S. Clemente, mosaics of the apse and the triumphal arch (twelfth century).

160 *right*   S. Clemente, mosaic of the triumphal arch (twelfth century). St Clement.

161 *left below*   S. Clemente, mosaic of the triumphal arch (twelfth century). St Lawrence.

162 *right below*   S. Clemente, mosaic of the triumphal arch (twelfth century). St Paul.

163　Sta Maria in Trastevere, mosaic of the apse (*c.* 1140). The Virgin.

164   Sta Maria in Trastevere, mosaic of the apse (*c.* 1140). Christ.

165 Sta Maria in Trastevere, mosaic of the triumphal arch (twelfth century). The prophet Isaiah.

166 Sta Maria in Trastevere, mosaic of the triumphal arch (twelfth century). Eagle in a medallion on the soffit.

167 Sta Maria in Trastevere, mosaic of the apse (*c.* 1140). St Peter.

169 Sta Maria in Trastevere, mosaic of the apse (*c.* 1140). Detail from the frieze showing the flock of sheep.

170   Sta Maria in Trastevere, mosaic of the triumphal arch (twelfth century). *Putto* holding a sheet, with symbols of plenty.

173 *right*   Sta Maria in Trastevere.
Mosaic of the apse (*c.* 1140).

174 *right below*   Sta Francesca Romana.
Mosaic of the apse (twelfth century).

171   Sta Maria in Trastevere, mosaic of
the triumphal arch (twelfth century).
The prophet Isaiah.

172   S. Clemente, mosaic of the triumphal arch (twelfth century).
The prophet Isaiah.

175   Sta Maria in Trastevere, mosaic of the triumphal arch (twelfth century). The angel
of Matthew, from the evangelist's symbols.

177 The head of the second of the two figures inserted by Pope Innocent III (1198–1216) into the Constantinian mosaic of the old basilica of St Peter's (early thirteenth century). This figure, which represents Ecclesia Romana, is now in the Barracco collection, Rome.

176 Fragment of one of the two figures inserted by Pope Innocent III (1198–1216) into the Constantinian mosaic of the old basilica of St Peter's (early thirteenth century). It represents the pope himself.

178   Sta Francesca Romana, mosaic of the apse (twelfth century). St James.

179   Sta Francesca Romana, mosaic of the apse (twelfth century). St Peter.

180   Sta Francesca Romana, mosaic of the apse (twelfth century). St John.

139 There is a frieze of five virgins on either side, carrying lamps, some of which are lit, some unlit. Some of this panel has probably been reset. This plate, Plate 140 and Plate 242 show the whole mosaic as it is now.

141 The lower part of the skirt is a modern re-construction. Contrast the skirt of the figure shown in Plate 142, which is original. For this particular detail (the lower part of the skirt) compare the similar 'ankle-folds' shown in Plate 240.

142 For the highlights in this figure, compare Plate 144.

143 Compare this central figure with that of St Anne in the cathedral of Monreale, Sicily (Plate 144). The technique of the highlights appears to have been directly derived from the work of the Monreale artist, though the Roman mosaic has none of the sophistication of the Sicilian.

145 This figure (like the one shown in Plate 147) represents a later stage in the mosaic's composition than that shown in Plates 141-143. The modelling in the face and in the bowl of the lamp is more developed, and the clothes are beginning to hang naturally. The lamp, represented as lit, is a puzzling feature on this side of the panel, if the Wise and Foolish Virgins are the subject of the mosaic. The figure in Plate 147 presents the same difficulty; there, as here, the Virgin holds her head high, in contrast with the Virgin shown in Plate 142, whose attitude is perhaps expressive of penitence or remorse and who yet is on this same side of the frieze. The dividing lines which are discernible between groups of gold *tesserae* in the background seem in some cases to mark the divisions between one day's work and the next, and not necessarily to betray later repairs.

146 Note the classicism of the stance, the classical form of the lamp and of the crown, the drooping hand and the plastic modelling of the draperies.

147 In the figure shown in Plate 145 (presumably the first to be executed of these two 'intermediate' figures), an attempt has been made to link the dress with the earlier design. Here the artist breaks away from the earlier design and the draperies and stance are altogether freer. The figure is linked, however, with that in Plate 145

by having the same gold background. (Contrast Plate 146, where, in Cavallini's background—the upper half is original—the *tesserae* are smaller and set in horizontal lines.) The harsh highlights on the right forearm and shoulder are modern.

148 The Cross is shared by the apostles, symbolized as doves, and is flanked by the Virgin *orans* and St John. The scroll springs symbolically from the Cross (see Plate 152), which is the source of all life.

149 The lower part of that section of the body which is shown in the plate has been restored.

152 In the classical original of this mosaic the ribbon-like object was doubtless a snake being devoured by a stag. Below are the four rivers of Paradise (and of the Four Gospels; the two ideas seem often to be conflated).

153 The scroll is intended, symbolically, to embrace all life. One figure is pointing to the Cross, another is escaping from its influence. The faces are strongly in the Roman tradition, the technique of the eyes, especially, recalling early fifth-century work in Sta Maria Maggiore, as seen, for example, in Plate 7.

154 This detail shows wild birds and huntsman's equipment—the latter, perhaps symbolically, stacked unused. It is possible that the symbolism (whatever it was) of the huntsman's horn in Sta Costanza (Plate I) was the same, the detail here being derived from the classical original.

155 The peacock was no doubt taken (like, perhaps, the details shown in Plate 154) from the classical original.

156 The *amoretti* were no doubt taken from the classical original.

157 The figure on the left, half-way down the plate, is St Ambrosius. The caged bird is symbolic ('Christ imprisoned in our sins'), as is explained in the triumphal arch mosaic in Sta Maria Trastevere, made a few years later. The trumpeting *amoretto* (above) is probably a classical *motif*, like, those already mentioned in the notes to Plates 154-156.

158 This powerful head is perhaps the last work in the

fully characteristic Roman tradition, with its loose structure and its effective use of erratically placed *tesserae*.

159 For the pattern of the tabernacle in the crown of the apse, compare the apsidal mosaics of Sta Maria in Trastevere (Plate 173) and Sta Francesca Romana (Plate 174). In Sta Maria the layout of the triumphal arch is similar to that in S. Clemente, as it was once in Sta Francesca also, before that part of the Sta Francesca mosaic was destroyed.

160 The work here has none of the greatness of the central medallion (Plate 158). It seems probable that that was executed by the artist responsible for the main apsidal mosaic.

163 The great refinement and regularity of the work in this head show Byzantine influence, in contrast with, for example, the head of Christ in the mosaic of the triumphal arch in S. Clemente (Plate 158), which is close to it in date.

168 Compare the ninth-century version shown in Plate 135.

169 The treatment of these sheep is solid and 'three-dimensional'. Contrast this plate with Plate 136 (the frieze of sheep in the apsidal mosaic of Sta Cecilia in Trastevere).

170 This *motif* is evidently a consciously classical one, like those to which attention has been drawn in the notes to Plates 154–157 (S. Clemente, the mosaic of the apse).

171 The greater elegance of treatment, compared with the handling of the same subject and of a design that is substantially the same shown in Plate 172, seems likely to have been due to Byzantine inspiration.

174 The figures of St Peter both here and in the apsidal mosaic of Sta Maria in Trastevere (Plate 173) are derived from the same original: a seventh-century mosaic, now destroyed, which was once in the church of S. Andrea in Barbara (see the sketch on p. 254).

176 For the design of the mosaic from which this fragment, and the head shown in Plate 177, come, see Plate 29.

177 The precision of the work lines, and their use to emphasize the structure of the face, shows the growth of Byzantine influence.

178 The drapery forms, like those of St Peter (Plate 179), were based on those in a seventh-century mosaic, now destroyed, which was once in the church of S. Andrea in Barbara (see the sketch on p. 254).

179 For a similar figure in the apsidal mosaic of Sta Maria in Trastevere, see Plate 173.

180 This plate has been made from a photograph which was taken in order to show areas of restoration, indicated by white lines. The draperies here may be consciously archaic, like those shown in Plates 178 and 179, but were probably derived from one of the figures in the apsidal mosaic of St John Lateran, of which now only the 1884 version exists.

VI

BYZANTINISM IN ROME
IN THE FIRST HALF OF
THE THIRTEENTH CENTURY

AT THE END OF THE TWELFTH, or the beginning of the thirteenth, century, Byzantine influence, as has been remarked in the previous section, was beginning to be felt in Rome. This phase, of which the apsidal mosaic in S. Paolo fuori le Mura, executed at the end of the first quarter of the   186 thirteenth century, is the first major work, is one in which the fashion is so strongly marked that, in one instance at least (that of S. Paolo), craftsmen trained in the Byzantine tradition were brought to Rome to plan and execute the work, while in another, the Capella Sancta Sanctorum, the style   192 is Byzantine to such an extent that one may suspect the workmen to have been immigrants from Constantinople itself, and not trained, as were the mosaicists of S. Paolo, in a provincial Byzantine school. The third example discussed in this section, a slighter work, is remarkably different from   193 the other two. Its style, though the flavour is eastern, is linked more closely with an earlier style represented in mosaic by the great mosaics of Chios, with their strong colours and powerful lines, rather than with the delicate, sensitive work which was typical of the eastern capital in the thirteenth century.

S. PAOLO FUORI LE MURA
The story of the S. Paolo mosaics is a melancholy one. The earliest, those of the triumphal arch, had they survived in their original form, would be among the earliest existing Christian mosaics in Rome, for the inscription probably declares their association with Galla Placidia (whose mauso-   185 leum at Ravenna contains one of the finest existing groups of mosaics in that city) and with St Leo the Great (Pope, 440–61). The mosaic of the apse, seen through the triumphal arch from the nave, includes a small figure making obeisance at the foot of Christ, and to this figure the name   186 of Honorius III (1216–27; not Honorius II, as sometimes stated) is attached. In January 1218 Honorius asked the Doge of Venice, Zaini, for craftsmen to execute the work. One was sent, and in due course there was a request for two more.[1] Constantinople had fallen to Venice only half a generation before, and after the sack of Constantinople many Byzantine works of art, and some

masterpieces of an earlier date from the Byzantine collections, were brought to Venice, where there was already a Byzantinizing school of mosaicists. While I have not been able to identify the hands that worked in S. Paolo in the mosaics of Venice or its neighbourhood, the few fragments that survive from this mosaic (discussed below) are undoubtedly Venetian in character, and in their way of notable quality.

But in 1823 a disastrous fire took place which destroyed the whole of the nave of the church. A drawing was made in the ruins shortly afterwards by Pinelli. This shows that the fire was checked before reaching the triumphal arch, which is shown substantially intact, with its mosaics, though it may have been seriously weakened. Through it, in the sketch, can be seen, as at present, the mosaic of the apse. What happened after the fire to the mosaic associated with Galla Placidia and Leo I is recorded in two inscriptions in marble, incorporated in the structure of the new triumphal arch on the nave side. It is there recorded that Leo XII (1823–29) in 1826, three years after the fire, ordered the removal from the ancient triumphal arch (which was unsafe, LABANTE) of the mosaics, and gave instructions that they should be preserved. The rebuilding of the arch began in 1829–30, and was completed (as a mosaic inscription at the apex of the soffits records) in 1840. Later, one of Leo's successors, Pius IX, in 1853 set up a new version of the old mosaic, and so completed, in the words of the commemorative inscription in the church, the 'splendid restoration of the mosaic which had been preserved and kept', on a new triumphal arch which had been constructed by Pius VIII.

Yet it is sadly apparent that the present mosaic is a travesty of the original, even though, as Pinelli's drawing shows, it certainly preserves the design which existed before the fire. The only specific difference between the old design, as sketched by Pinelli, and the new one is a change, or emendation, of a single letter in the inscription on the triumphal arch, CORPORI having been emended to CORPORE. But what we see now is, nevertheless, substantially a modern work; a complete reconstruction of the apsidal mosaic also had, apparently, been carried out before the fire. Four notable heads from Honorius III's mosaic (the later mosaic of the apse, which is at present our main concern) had been discarded, and now survive as fragments.[2] Three of these fragments are now kept in the anteroom to the sacristy, the fourth, also the head of a saint, is in the Vatican Grottoes, together with a fifth fragment representing a swan[3] attacking a snake.

It was not the fire, therefore, which brought disaster to the S. Paolo mosaics. Before the fire (probably only just before it, to judge from the style) some major restoration had been undertaken, restoration in which work still in excellent condition was discarded, and in which what was in effect a replacement of the apsidal mosaic was effected.

The details of the post-fire restoration of the apse are unfortunately not given in any such inscription as exists for the triumphal arch. The long marble inscription records the names of all the dignitaries who were present at the consecration of the basilica in 1854, and presumably the repaired version of the apsidal mosaic was by then in its place. In the modern version (executed, as we have seen, before the fire, though perhaps not long before), the old mosaic was almost entirely destroyed,[4] and the artists toned down the austere lines so much that, while the identification of the head of St Peter is beyond doubt, that of the two other fragments preserved in the anteroom to the sacristy is not so obvious. They are, however, almost certainly the two saints in the lower row (on a smaller scale than St Peter) on either side of the angels in the centre; that is to say, they are St James and St John. I have sometimes doubted the story of the restoration before the fire, so far as the apse is concerned, where the work looks typical of the first half of the nineteenth century at its best. But the evidence for the discarding of the four heads from the apsidal mosaic, before the fire, seems indisputable, and, accordingly, we must assume that the new mosaic there was made at any rate before 1823.

It seems likely that by 1800 the triumphal arch mosaic had already passed through many more stages of restoration than the apsidal mosaic, its early character being by then almost unrecognizable; whereas the new version of the apse is still comparatively close to Honorius's mosaic. The Cavallini mosaics originally made for the façade in the early fourteenth century have suffered still more disastrously. They now decorate the inner arches of the crossing. Here what now exists is a nineteenth-century version that is a ponderous travesty of the original on the façade.

Of the mosaic copies which (apart from the fragments and the fine panel of the Virgin and Child discussed earlier⁵) are all that the church still contains of what must once have been a superb scheme of mosaic decoration, the apsidal mosaic is the most satisfying. The formal dedicatory mosaic is not visible from the ground, but dates the mosaic to the papacy of Honorius III (1216–27). The tiny figure of Honorius (HONORIVS PP III), making obeisance at the right foot of Christ, is named; and the description is, indeed, repeated (in gold letters within the band of decoration, perhaps because of some change of plan when the work was in progress). The design (which, as mentioned above, is the work of Venetian craftsmen) is in fact a striking departure from the traditional Roman pattern. In the traditional Roman apsidal mosaic, the lowest band of decoration depicts a row of sheep, symbolizing the apostles. In S. Paolo there is a series of apostles, saints and archangels— fourteen figures in all. Each holds a scroll bearing words of a liturgical character, representing a song of praise and prayer for grace and in no way serving to identify the figures, who are identified by independent inscriptions on the background. Above this series, the main mosaic shows Christ enthroned in the centre, with Pope Honorius at his feet; on the left are St Paul and (on the far left) St Luke; on the right are St Peter and (far right) St Andrew. The figures are flanked by palm trees. The ground on which they stand is a pattern of flowers and birds. The cornice below the mosaic, presumably of nineteenth-century date, completely obscures the lower part of the central feature of the lower register of figures. This consists of the empty throne, with the Cross and other emblems of the Passion, flanked by angels, and it represents the Byzantine Hetimasia, or Preparation for the Last Judgment. Below the throne are five tiny figures of Innocents whose relics had been brought to Rome in 1204; on either side of them are the abbot and sacrist of S. Paolo.

186

In subject, then, this mosaic departs sharply from the Roman tradition. Even the names in the upper register are in Greek as well as Latin. The Hetimasia is a characteristically eastern theme. The angels flanking the Cross had not, so far, appeared in the main mosaic of any Roman apse —not, at least, in any that survives. Only the fragments can provide an impression of the style in detail, and, with the small exception of the swan, they are portrait heads only.

THE CAPELLA SANCTA SANCTORUM IN THE LATERAN

The inscription with which this chapel is signed, 'Magister Cosmatus fecit hoc opus', apparently refers to the building, though it has been interpreted (improbably, I think) as referring to the mosaic also. Since the Cosmati family were active throughout the thirteenth century, the inscription does not enable us to establish a more precise date within this period. But the reconstruction by the Cosmati is generally credited to Nicholas III, after an earthquake which had damaged the chapel in the time of Honorius III. It is equally possible, however, that the mosaic may date from the time of an earlier reconstruction of the chapel by Honorius himself.⁶

192 This mosaic is of great importance, but unfortunately is not generally accessible, since the public are not admitted to the chapel. It is on the vault, and was perhaps actually designed and executed by a master from Constantinople. It was made about the same time as the apsidal mosaic in S. Paolo fuori le Mura, to execute which, as mentioned above, Pope Honorius III asked the Doge of Venice to send him Veneto-Byzantine craftsmen. In this case no record is available, but the style (fastidious, mannered, and unlike that of anything else of its day made in Italy) suggests that the designer came not from Venice, but from Constantinople itself. Face and hands are worked with the tiny units adopted by Byzantine artists to make possible very detailed and subtle modelling. The result is highly individual, and did not commend itself to Wilpert, sensitive critic though he was. It is more likely to be appreciated now than it was in the second decade of this century. It is far more sophisticated than the fragments from S. Paolo, which are of approximately the same date, but have by comparison almost a provincial air.

The half-figure of Christ the Pantocrator is displayed in the centre of the vault, as in Greek churches of the eleventh and twelfth centuries, such as Daphni or Osios Loukas. The roundel is made up of lozenges of colour— a fine detail, copied at the end of the century by Cavallini in
XXX, XXXII Sta Maria in Trastevere and by Toriti in Sta Maria Maggiore.[7] The background is gold, extensively broken up by insertions of reddish-brown. The head has a halo with a jewelled cross, the face is bearded, the eyes are small and close-set and the cheekbones are preternaturally broad. The mouth droops slightly on one side. In his left hand Christ holds a book; with his right he gives a blessing. There are several details in which the Greek artist modified his design on the instructions of his western patron. The right hand held up in blessing (but turned towards the spectator), the manner in which the left hand clasps the book, and the jewels on the crossed halo—these features were out of fashion at this period in the east and would not have been seen in a contemporary mosaic in Constantinople. The artist seems to bow in deference to his western client, but he does so with a touch of bitter detachment, seen (as we may, if we allow rein to our fancy, imagine) in the facial expression that he has created. The tunic is slate-blue, the mantle murrey-colour. The roundel is supported by four flying angels with tunics of slate-grey; the figures have suffered considerable damage, but the design is superb. A splendid and well-known painting in Kariye Camii in Constantinople, part of which shows an angel unrolling the scroll of heaven, recalls the angels in this mosaic. That work is considerably later than this, but embodies basically the same Byzantine design.

In the main lunettes are busts of St Peter and St Paul, separated by a double cross ☩ , and of St Lawrence, St Agnes, St Stephen and St Nicholas. The four last-mentioned, named in the inscriptions in each lunette, are saints of whom there were relics in this chapel. These heads (though they show, technically, some eastern features) have none of them the fastidious aestheticism of the main mosaic, and are clearly not by the master.

S. TOMMASO IN FORMIS

193 This church no longer exists, but there is a mosaic roundel above the surviving entrance door into the hospice. Its date is 1218, and it is considerably earlier, therefore, than the two other Cosmati works with pictorial mosaics which will be considered later.[8] It is almost certainly also earlier than the mosaics of the Capella Sancta Sanctorum and of S. Paolo, though made within a few years of them. The inscription round the arch reads MAGISTER IACOBVS CVM FILIO SVO COSMATO FECIT OHC [HOC] OPVS, 'Master James, with his son Cosmati, executed this work'. The roundel of mosaic (now protected with an iron grille) is within a rounded canopy, surmounted by a cross

with equal arms. It shows Christ seated on a throne. He grasps with his right hand the right wrist of a white captive whose ankles are shackled and who holds in his left hand a cross; Christ with his left hand grasps the left arm of a black captive whose ankles are similarly shackled. The design has something of the character of a seal, and the inscription reads SIGNVM ORDINIS SANCTAE TRINITATIS ET CAPTIVORVM, 'The sign [or seal] of the Order of the Holy Trinity and of Captives'. (The charitable work of the Order was concerned with slaves.)

This little mosaic is remarkable not only for its subject (without parallel in Roman mosaics), but also for its style. The scheme seems to be derived from a seal. The Christ has undoubtedly an eastern prototype; the general impression is, nevertheless, wholly different from that given by either of the Roman mosaics contemporary with it. The Byzantine model was much earlier and was perhaps something like the swarthy figures in the powerful Chios mosaics made some two hundred years before. Small *tesserae* are not here confined to face, hands and bare flesh, but are also used in those part of the draperies (for example, over the right wrist) where more delicate modelling is sought.

It is most unlikely that an eastern craftsman was actually employed here. But whoever made the mosaic was affected by the current fashion for Byzantine idioms.

STA MARIA IN ARA CELI: THE CAPOCEI MOSAIC

The Capocei mosaic in Sta Maria in Ara Celi, if the mosaic is rightly associated with the senator of that name, dates from the mid-thirteenth century. The donor, under the aegis of St Francis, is shown worshipping the Virgin and Child. On the other side of the group, facing St Francis, is St John the Baptist. Originally, the mosaic may have been designed as part of an altar-piece in a peak-shaped frame; the traces of this shape are still clear in the upper part of the background. The upper right-hand and left-hand corners in this part have been restored, but this has not affected the figures. There has been damage to the Child's knee; the surface has been consolidated here, and missing *tesserae* have not been replaced.

The central group shows that, at least on a superficial level, Byzantine inspiration has been assimilated. This is apparent in the neat oval shape and delicate workmanship of the Virgin's face, also in the grave and sophisticated air of the Child, who has that strangely adult expression which 190 is a feature of Byzantine portraiture. But the small kneeling figure of the donor seems purely western and medieval. His face has none of that roundness which gives solidity as well as shape to the faces of the Virgin and the Child; shadows are hardly used, the drawing is sharp and uncompromising, and the expression, as in a western primitive, is one of childlike simplicity. I do not think that the mid-thirteenth-century date has been proved. The central figure has many superficial resemblances to work done a generation later. But I am aware of no parallels to the kneeling figure that would help to date it more precisely.

1 The letter is quoted by J. Wilpert (*Die römischen Mosaiken und Malereien der Kirchlichen Bauten vom IV bis XIII Jahrhundert*, 4 vols, Freiburg 1916, p. 550).

2 As exhibited now in the church, these fragments are described as being from Cavallini's mosaic on the façade, though the facts were pointed out long ago by Wilpert. The fifth fragment is assumed by G. B. de Toth (*Cenni storici della basilica Vaticana*, Plate 15) to belong (with two other fragments, both surely Constantinian) to Innocent III's reconstruction of the mosaic of the Constantinian apse. For the discarding of the fragments before the fire, see de Rossi (on S. Paolo). For Byzantine technique in these heads, see pp. 22–23. In the Vatican head, the halo is a restoration.

3 This is also reproduced in *Cenni storici della basilica Vaticana*, Plate 15. I doubt whether any of the three fragments illustrated on that plate are from the apse restored by Innocent III, though the other two magnificent pieces are certainly classical. One is shown in Plate 181 in this book.

4 Dr Bertelli tells me that, in his view, the mosaic may incorporate some original work. I should agree that, without examining the mosaic from scaffolding, it is almost impossible to be certain. But if any original work was to be incorporated, it is hard to see why four heads (including that of St Peter, and all apparently in good condition) were discarded. V. Golzio and G. Zander (*Le chiese di Roma dall' XI al XVI secolo*, Roma Cristiana, vol. 4, Rome 1963, p. 189) say that thirteenth-century work is recognizable in the lowest central section of the mosaic (the jewelled Cross and flanking angels,) and this view is derived from Wilpert's opinion (op. cit., p. 554) that the two apostles next to these angels were also comparatively untouched. It is certainly true that the apostles are in a more austere style, much closer to that of the original; also that the line of division between the two styles cuts unaccountably across the draperies of the figures. This could be explained if the new work had begun in the centre, and if the more austere style been rejected after the initial experiment with it. But see Wilpert, op. cit., pp. 549–554. From a distance, the work all looks to me 'modern'. De Rossi believed that the replacement was due to a major restoration which he found recorded in the reign of Benedict XIV. This date seems to me fifty years too early.

5 See pp. 256–257.

6 '. . . in superiori parti testudinis picturis pulcherrimis ornatam fundari jussit'; see M. Armellini, *Chiese di Roma*, Rome 1891, I, p. 144.

7 Probably also by Toriti, in paint, at Assisi, where he is believed to have worked in the vault of the upper church. The detail is originally Byzantine.

8 See pp. 334–335.

181 Vatican Grottoes.
Mosaic fragment representing
a dove (fourth or fifth
century).

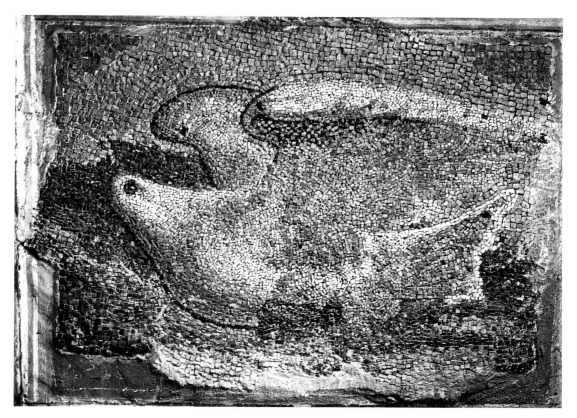

182 Vatican Grottoes, mosaic fragment, showing a swan (thirteenth century). Probably from the apsidal mosaic of
S. Paolo fuori le mura.

183   S. Paolo fuori le Mura.
Pinelli's drawing,
made immediately
after the fire of 1823.

184   S. Paolo fuori le Mura,
mosaic of the apse. Detail of
the modern version
(eighteenth or possibly early
nineteenth century).

185 *right above*   S. Paolo fuori le
Mura. The modern versions of the
mosaic of the triumphal arch and
(visible beyond it) the mosaic of
the apse.

186 *right below*   S. Paolo fuori le
Mura. The modern version of the
mosaic of the apse (eighteenth or
possibly early nineteenth century).
Christ with four apostles. Below,
the *hetimasia*.

TEODOSIVS CEPIT PERFECIT ONORIVS AVLAM ✠ DOCTORIS MVNDI SACRATAM CORPORE PAVLI

TV·ES·VAS·ELECTIONIS

189 S. Paolo fuori le Mura. St Peter – the only surviving head from the upper part of the original thirteenth-century Veneto-Byzantine mosaic of the apse; now in the sacristy of the church.

187, 188 S. Paolo fuori le Mura. Heads of apostles from the frieze in the lower register of the original thirteenth-century Veneto-Byzantine mosaic of the apse; now in the sacristy of the church.

190 Sta Maria in Ara Celi, the Capocei mosaic (probably mid-thirteenth century). Detail, showing the donor, a Roman senator of the period, worshipping the Virgin and Child.

191 Sta Maria in Ara Celi. The Capocei mosaic (probably mid-thirteenth century).

192   The Capella Sancta Sanctorum in the Lateran. Mosaic of the vault (*c.* 1220).

193   S. Tommaso in Formis. Mosaic roundel above the entrance door to the hospice.

181 This dove is probably from the same classical mosaic as the head of a cherub shown in Plate 5. There is a patch of restoration under the upper part of the near wing. Compare the swan illustrated in Plate 182, which is a medieval fragment.

182 This fragment is sometimes described as classical, but the technique seems Byzantine and it was surely taken from the original Veneto-Byzantine mosaic of the apse in S. Paolo fuori le Mura (Plates 187-189). See the lower border (shown at the foot of Plate 184) for its position in that mosaic.

183 The mosaics of the triumphal arch and apse can be seen still *in situ*, in spite of the damage by the fire.

184 Compare the head of St Peter (left) with the thirteenth-century Veneto-Byzantine original (Plate 189). The date of the modern version is not known, but it was made before the fire of 1823.

185 The original mosaic of the triumphal arch probably dated from the time of Galla Placidia (the middle of the fifth century). Restorations carried out from time to time in its long history have almost totally destroyed its character.

186 For the fragments of the Veneto-Byzantine original (1225) which survive, see Plates 20, 182,

187-189. The tabernacle in the crown of the apse was perhaps derived from that in the old basilica of St Peter's; see Plate 29.

191 This mosaic represents the Virgin and Child, with St John the Baptist (right) and St Francis (left), who presents the donor. Repairs are responsible for the conspicuous lines of mortar. The Byzantine fashion has strongly affected the design of the Virgin and Child, but the impression given by the mosaic as a whole is predominantly western.

192 This mosaic is perhaps the work of a Byzantine craftsman. Together with several others (Plates 193, 215-217), it was associated with work commissioned from the Cosmati, the extent of whose connection with the mosaics themselves is, however, uncertain. Members of the family were at work in Rome throughout the thirteenth century.

193 The main church has been destroyed. The Order to which it belonged worked for the freeing of slaves, white and black—hence the design of the mosaic, which was perhaps based on the Order's seal. Though there is an iconographic connection between the head of Christ here and that in the vault mosaic of the Capella Sancta Sanctorum (Plate 192), the extent of Byzantine influence in this work does not seem in other respects greater than in many western works of this period.

VII

THE ROMAN RENAISSANCE
AS EXPRESSED IN MOSAICS

THE APSE OF STA MARIA MAGGIORE contains, cheek by jowl, the greatest of Roman medieval mosaics (the Coronation of the Virgin) and the greatest surviving early Renaissance mosaic in Rome (the Dormition of the Virgin). They were designed by the same artist, Toriti, probably within two decades. Indeed, the mosaics of Sta Maria executed during the period 1290–1325, starting with the Coronation of the Virgin, continuing with a series concerned with the Life of the Virgin, with the fine façade mosaic by Rusuti, and with the elaborate scenes with which the decoration of the façade was completed, comprise, in fact, the bulk of the work discussed in this part of the book. Important work of this phase outside Sta Maria Maggiore, however, and which still survives, is the series by Cavallini in Sta Maria in Trastevere, which is closely comparable to the Toriti series on a similar theme, and offers some strange contrasts with it. The mosaic by Giotto known as the *Navicella*, destroyed in the seventeenth century, was also made during these years, and was undoubtedly the most famous mosaic ever produced. One or two precious fragments from it still exist, and it is possible to obtain from these some impression of the style in which it was created. Concentrated, then, in this single generation is a mass of work of high quality which shows the development of Renaissance ideas, in Rome, in the medium of mosaic: from the two-dimensional splendours of the Coronation of the Virgin in Sta Maria Maggiore to the 'three-dimensional' intricacies of the façade background; from the sweeping, other-worldly design of the Coronation, with its troop of angels crowded in a grandiose pattern of outspread wings, to the highly individual rhythms of the procession in the Dormition of the Virgin; from the conventional faces in the earlier mosaics to what seems to be a self-portrait of the artist in the latest. With this last-named work (apart from Giotto's *Navicella*, and a few minor mosaics), my survey ends. For, as will be shown later, when the technique of mosaic was used to convey the ideas and aspirations of Renaissance patrons, its essential qualities were fatally prejudiced. Mosaics became expensive, more permanent and more easily cleaned reproductions of paintings, and lost the aesthetic interest which throughout the Middle Ages they had retained.

ST JOHN LATERAN AND STA MARIA MAGGIORE: THE MAIN MOSAICS OF THE APSES
This latest series begins with two mosaics, each of which (characteristically for the time at which they were made) is largely a reconstruction of an earlier classical work, renewed and replaced

in the process of completing a large new architectural scheme. In St John Lateran, the medieval work was unfortunately subjected to still further reconstruction, when the apse was enlarged by Leo XIII in 1884. The scholar de Rossi saw this mosaic before and after this reconstruction. He vouches for the authenticity of the copy. But it acquired, regrettably, the slickness of a nineteenth-century work; and it lacks altogether the quality (derived largely from the roughness of the surface) which the original mosaic by the same artist, Toriti, shows in Sta Maria Maggiore.

The lower borders of both these mosaics have been discussed earlier,[1] since they are the only evidence still available (and good evidence, though in the one case some of it, at least, is second-hand, and in the other, third-hand) for this type of late antique fancy in Roman churches. These borders seem to have been closely copied from the originals (indeed, I have argued earlier that one of them incorporates sections of early work), and both borders illustrate the fascination that classical work exercised at this period on Toriti. It is less easy to say where the classical work begins and ends in the remaining parts of the two mosaics. The main theme has certainly been recast in both, if, indeed, it was not entirely new in the thirteenth century. We know that in the Lateran the head of Christ was a mosaic *emblema*, a classical centre-piece worked on its own independent bed, and incorporated complete by Toriti, in that form, from its predecessor. Whether the angels are part of the old design (they are certainly not part of the *emblema*) it is not easy to say; but the great Cross, for which there is an analogy in Sta Pudenziana, and probably in the original mosaic of S. Clemente also, is likely to have been a part of the early design. For the Cross surmounted by the head of Christ there is a sort of analogy also in S. Stefano Rotondo, which seems itself to be based on an earlier, in that instance an eastern, original. The vignette below the foot of the Cross is, again, probably early in its iconography. But there is no certain answer to the question how the ground on either side of the Cross was filled in the original apse. There may have been martyrs in the places now occupied by St Anthony and St Francis. The Virgin was no doubt represented *orans*, as the position of one hand still shows. The other has been moved, to associate her with one of the medieval figures inserted. The medieval intention (as we now understand it) was to emphasize the joy of the spiritual life: hence the inclusion of the founder of desert monasticism, St Anthony, and of St Francis; and the theme of the deer drinking from the rivers of Paradise—no doubt here conceived of, as usual, as also being the rivers of the four gospels. The mosaic was planned for the glorification of the two St Johns to whom the church was dedicated. Both the Evangelist and the Baptist are included in the main picture, with the Roman apostles St Paul and St Peter, and St Andrew. The work was also designed to commemorate St Francis (the founder of the order to which Nicholas IV, who takes his place with these apostles, belonged) and Pope Nicholas himself (who is shown, on a smaller scale, as a kneeling figure, under the special protection of the Virgin).

The Cross in the centre would be remarkable for bearing no crucified figure, unless it were the echo of a classical element, as suggested above. Above it is the Dove, shedding its influence by rays behind the Cross. The rivers of Paradise, flowing from the Cross, divide two and two, to show, in the delta thus formed, Paradise as a walled city. Outside the gate of Paradise stands the angel with the flaming sword. Above the walls appears a palm tree, in the fronds of which is a phoenix. At the feet of the mounds below the deer, on each side, is a group of three sheep. Immediately below is the Jordan, into which, however, the rivers of Paradise are not here represented as flowing. The Jordan is poured out by *putti* from two jars, one at each end of the design; the jar on the right is inscribed DAN (presumably part of the complete word JORDAN), that on the left has no inscription. The lower border thus falls into two sections, an upper and a lower. The upper

312

half (the ground on which the saints stand) is vivid green; the flowers are silver, with gold foliage. Among the flowers are more *putti*, and a number of creatures of which some at least are symbolic: peacocks (towards the end on either side); a cock, hen and chickens (as in S. Clemente; to the left of the centre); and, on the extreme left, a *putto* with a cage into which he is trying to entice small birds (again, as in S. Clemente).

In the crown of the apse is a wide semi-circle of blue. On either side of this are four winged angels: the wings have not the sweeping design that was to be a feature of Toriti's later work and which he may have derived from Cavallini (rather than *vice versa*); the explanation may be that the angels have been retained from the earlier design. In the centre is a seraph with six wings. Below the seraph appears the famous head of Christ—severe, anxious and staring.[2] On the blue   VIII ground are striated clouds of orange, gold and white in an early idiom, as in SS. Cosma e Damiano.

Below the main apsidal mosaic is a lower register of decoration, broken by four windows. In this register the nine remaining apostles are grouped: three at each end, one between each of the windows. On either side of each apostle grows a fruiting or flowering tree. The apostles wear tunics with full sleeves of wrist-length, and with *clavi* of blue; their mantles are silver-grey. Between St Simon and St James, on a much smaller scale, a Franciscan craftsman is shown kneeling at work, with a sheet of paper spread out in front of him, and dividers. Between the feet of St Bartholomew and St Matthew is a second Franciscan craftsman, next to whom there is an inscription.[3] The saints are not distinguished by emblems, though St James in the centre (unlike St Matthew) holds a book. St Matthew, and perhaps St Bartholomew, have on their cloaks the early ornament which was to develop later into the monogram. If this is not an antiquarian fancy on Toriti's part, it would indicate that the series of apostles belonged to the original late-classical scheme. But there survives no parallel among the early Roman mosaics for a series of apostles depicted like these; and, in this part of the design, Toriti could have been inspired by the thirteenth-century mosaic of S. Paolo. The ornament on the cloak, however, is an argument for an original of early date; and it may be tentatively conjectured that two of these saints in the earlier version were the models for the St John and another saint in Sta Francesca Romana. If so,   180 that would be conclusive evidence that they are of early date.

In Sta Maria Maggiore, the new element is the Coronation of the Virgin. The theme had been developed in France a century and a half before this mosaic was made, though the earlier centre-piece of the classical mosaic of the apse is likely to have been a representation of the Virgin in some form. This, at any rate, seems to be the implication of the inscription, which, set at the far end of the church, appears to have been related to the early mosaic decorations as a whole. The last four lines read:

ECCE TVI TESTES VTERI TIBI PRAEMIA PORTANT

SVB PEDIBVSQVE IACET PASSIO CVIQVE SVA

FERRVM FLAMMA FERAE FLVVIVS SAEVVMQVE VENENVM

TOT TAMEN HAS MORTES VNA CORONA MANET

'Lo, here thy witnesses bring gifts to honour thy motherhood, and below the feet of each lie the instruments of his martyrdom: the sword, fire, wild beasts, water and the bitter poison cup; yet for all these deaths a single crown remains.'

These verses probably refer to the original central group of the main mosaic. If so, there must have been martyrs on either side of the Virgin. The words do not seem to justify any conclusion as to whether she was represented with, or without, her Child. As has been observed early in this book, splendid arabesques or scrolls are a feature of classical mosaics, and probably the inhabiting animals, peacocks and other birds in the work discussed here derive from the classical period, as well as the scroll itself.

The recasting of the main theme in the thirteenth century was due partly to the emergence at that time of the Coronation of the Virgin *motif* as the most splendid tribute that could be paid her, and partly to the connections of Nicholas IV with the Franciscan order (connections which led to the inclusion in the design of St Francis and the hermit St Anthony). St Paul and St John the Baptist, on the other hand, may have been in the original design.

XXVIII In the centre of the apsidal mosaic, the Virgin sits at the right hand of Christ, who holds a crown over her head. The scene is set in a roundel, with a blue ground representing the Firmament, scattered with stars of gold and silver; the sun and the moon are below the footstool of Christ and of the Virgin respectively. The whole roundel is set against a gold background patterned

XXIX with the magnificent decorative arabesques, or scrolls, reproduced by Toriti from the fourth-century ruined apse. The arabesques are inhabited by birds and by some small animals: a rabbit and a basket of fruit; a rat at which a crane is striking; a snake in the talons of an eagle. The roundel is supported by groups of adoring angels. Characteristic of Toriti, as also of his contemporary Cavallini,[4] are the finely spreading angels' wings—so different, for example, from the wings of Giotto's angels in the almost contemporary Scrovegni chapel in Padua.

Gazing up at the roundel are, on the left, St Peter, St Paul, St Francis and, kneeling, Pope Nicholas IV (1285–94), fully vested with tiara and gloves. In the left-hand corner is the inscription IACOB; TORRITI PICTOR H [OC] OP [VS] MOSAIC [VM] FECIT, 'Iacobus Torriti, painter, made this mosaic'. Gazing up at the roundel, on the right, are the figures of St John the Baptist, St John the Evangelist, St Anthony and, kneeling, DNS [DOMINUS] IACOBVS DE COLVPNA [COLONNA] CARDINALIS, 'Lord Iacobus de Colonna, Cardinal'. He wears a bishop's vestments and mitre.

62, 64–66 Below lies the miniature band of decoration, similar to that in St John Lateran, but with richer
XIV detail, representing the four rivers of Paradise (Gen. ii. 11–14) flowing from the fountains in the centre; below this, at the gates of Paradise, stands the angel with the flaming sword. In the river are waterfowl, mythical monsters, ships, *putti* navigating rafts drawn by swans, and, at either end, a river god, one with a jar from which water is flowing. This section of the mosaic has already been discussed,[5] and the possibility was suggested that much of the classical material has actually been re-used here in its original form. These gods, with their jars (from which, in a purely classical representation, the rivers would spring, and not from the fountain in the centre), combine somewhat strangely with the *motif* of the four rivers of Paradise. But that *motif* also is characteristic of very early work and almost certainly belongs to the original classical design.

Immediately below the feet of the group of angels supporting the roundel on the right there is a
220 man fishing, a detail which (though it is known from a classical example and a mid-thirteenth century copy of it) may perhaps here be connected in some way with the similar detail in Giotto's *Navicella*,[6] though the precise nature of the association will probably never be established. The figure here is almost certainly an intrusion, inserted after the main work had been completed.
XIV Next to the feet of the river god on the left is a fine representation of an ancient sailing ship. It is thoroughly Roman, not medieval, in character. At the right end are the remains of an inscription, almost entirely destroyed, balancing that on the left, which gives the artist's name. At this end, the river god and ship are modern. In the crown of the apse there is an elaborate canopy of heaven.

This work has been described above as the finest of the Roman medieval mosaics. But it derives

XXVIII Sta Maria Maggiore. Main mosaic of the apse (by Toriti; *c.* 1294). Below, the Dormition of the Virgin (perhaps *c.* 1305), from the Life of the Virgin series (by Toriti; *c.* 1295-1305).

some of its quality from the fusion between classical and medieval *motifs* on which it is based. While Toriti's interest in antiquity is manifested again and again in the work, yet his own individual style is much less deeply affected by this than was that of his contemporary, Cavallini. (This point will be considered later when the series of mosaics by the two artists on the theme of the Life and Death of the Virgin are examined.) In the Sta Maria apse there is little trace of classical influence where one might expect it: for example, in the stance of the three tall figures on the right, and also on the left, of the central roundel. These figures may, on the other hand, show Byzantine influence; the type of St John the Baptist, for example, seems to depend on some Byzantine representations. But otherwise they are medieval. They are certainly not classical.

199

What is new in the mosaic is its magnificent composition. The twelfth-century apsidal mosaic of Sta Francesca Romana had consisted simply of a series of figures, like the façade mosaic (twelfth to thirteenth century) of Sta Maria in Trastevere. In the twelfth-century mosaic of the Enthronement of the Virgin in Sta Maria in Trastevere, the contrast with this later version of the same theme is remarkable. The two figures in the centre of that Enthronement mosaic are an uneasy pair because they are eccentrically placed. Christ had to occupy the central position, and so the Virgin was placed to one side. Here, however, the pattern is balanced, and composed in a roundel that is precisely central and is superbly supported by groups of angels, whose sweeping wings reach out into the field, the dark, spreading pinions forming a striking contrast with the gold. They press forward in eager worship, and the two groups, built up high on either side, give formal significance to the central roundel, as if they were holding it up as a mirror or window which made it possible to see into the depths of Heaven. Behind them, the standing figures, occupying what was probably the place of the martyrs in the original mosaic, are composed on a scale that blends well with the huge arabesque, leaving the predominance of the central figures unchallenged, and providing an excellent foil to the intricacies of the miniature classical detail.

174, 139–143,
145–147

XXV
XXVIII
179

The treatment of flesh and draperies has a new delicacy in which the use of smaller *tesserae* is exploited, though we do not see in the face of Christ or the Virgin the structural use of the work

XXIX Sta Maria Maggiore, main mosaic of the apse (by Toriti; *c.* 1294).
The scroll design, probably based on a classical original of *c.* 435.

lines that is characteristic of so much Byzantine work, while the *tesserae* themselves are never, in fact, as small as they are in the most delicate Byzantine examples. The artist (Toriti) signs himself 'pictor', and in one sense it might be said that in the portrait heads he had already begun to paint with mosaic.[7] Even the features of St Paul, traditionally so severe, are here softened. The naturalistic details of the birds within the arabseque are finely observed, but these may derive from the original, and not be Toriti's own contribution.

XXIX

STA MARIA MAGGIORE AND STA MARIA IN TRASTEVERE: THE MOSAICS ON THE LIFE OF THE VIRGIN

Toriti's full scheme for the apse in Sta Maria Maggiore[8] included seven scenes from the Life of the Virgin. For them he adopted a Byzantine iconography. At about the same time[9] Cavallini devised a similar series, below the main mosaic of the apse, also seven mosaics in all, but in this instance including a panel showing the donor of the mosaic, for the church of Sta Maria in Trastevere. Four of the panels in each series show the same subjects, and a comparison of them shows at once how precise these iconographic formulae could be, and how closely they were often followed. (It is in these formulae that eastern influence is most strongly apparent in both artists' work, though their mosaics never show a full-blooded Byzantine technique, as the comparison of any detail from Cavallini's series with true Byzantine work shows.) The comparison of the two series, that of Toriti and that of Cavallini, shows that though the Cavallini Annunciation has developed much further from the original type than the Toriti version, and has a dramatic rushing movement which contrasts with the hieratic solemnity of Toriti's picture, yet much the most advanced design in either series is the Toriti Dormition of the Virgin. The paradox is not easily explained.

XXXI, 203,
202
XXXII

While it is probable that the whole series in Sta Maria in Trastevere representing the Life of the Virgin was designed by Cavallini, the scenes which seem to show clearly the work of the master in craftsmanship as well as in design (in the softness of the draperies and in the delicacy with which the faces are individualized) are the Annunciation, the Presentation, and the dedicatory mosaic, together with several individual figures or details elsewhere. Unfortunately, there is a large area of restoration in the lower half of the Donor panel (seen in Plate XXX), and this affects not only the figures but also the inscription, though, by chance, the tiny monogram that can be associated with Cavallini is in a section of the mosaic which is original. The coarseness of the restorer's work (for example, in the draperies of the kneeling figure) brings out the amazing delicacy of the master's own mosaics. The suggestion has been made (see below) that Giotto played some part in the design and execution of this series. The reason for the suggestion is precisely the awareness that here Roman art enters on a new phase; our concern must be to examine and compare the individual works so as to bring out the main features of these developments.

210, 211,
XXXI,
XXXIII,
XXX

234

Toriti was certainly fascinated by classical antiquity, and many elements in his main apsidal mosaic in Sta Maria Maggiore are directly based, as has been noted, on classical models—if, indeed, he did not incorporate actual classical material. But Cavallini absorbed ideas similarly derived from antiquity in a way that makes them a deeper influence on his style as a whole. One scene common to both series is the Presentation in the Temple. Toriti's figures stand with the uncertain posture of figures in a medieval drawing, half falling or tottering forward. Cavallini's men and women have a natural poise. They are set in their places easily and serenely; and the environment itself is, in contrast with Toriti's version, acquiring a new depth through the illusion created by the artist's treatment of the architectural features. This might suggest a later date for

207, 209

XXX   Sta Maria in Trastevere, the Life of the Virgin series (by Cavallini; *c.* 1295). The Donor panel.

the Cavallini series. The answer to the question of date must, however, be far more complex. It is

202 difficult to believe that Toriti's mosaic of the Annunciation can have been executed after that of

203 Cavallini, since in so many ways it is in the earlier manner. But if we compare the two versions

224, 226 of the Dormition of the Virgin, we draw the opposite conclusion. Of this pair the Cavallini (which shows his studio in a comparatively uninspired moment) is surely the one which was finished first; the Toriti version reaches out far beyond it.[10] In the Cavallini the bier is too long for the space available, and the apostles are crowded together at either end. The two angels look like

214 one-winged creatures, and the attitude of Christ, turning his head away from the soul in his arms, is awkward. If Toriti learnt anything from this, it was that the space allotted to the subject, and

224, XXXII the shape of the design, must be different. His work, as a result, is one of the most noteworthy in the whole range of Roman mosaics for its originality, and to compare it with the Funeral

223 Procession in the Scrovegni chapel in Padua (a work which is, in its own way, a masterpiece, though certainly executed by a follower of Giotto, not by that master himself) is to see from what source the new influence has mainly come. We must not suppose that this particular Paduan work was completed before the Roman, and was the actual source of inspiration—only that many Giottesque ideas had been absorbed before the Sta Maria Maggiore Dormition was worked out in detail. This influence is not simply apparent in the perspective of the dwindling procession at both ends of the picture, where the rear of each line of figures is lost in the distance, striking though this feature is. More important is the individual rhythm, or counterpoint, of the draperies, the individual turn of each head, the individualizing of each face. These are unmistakable marks of the influence of Giotto, and they may, incidentally, give as likely a clue as we can hope to find of the character of his great *Navicella* mosaic in St Peter's, which is discussed later.

204, 206   Another subject represented in both series is the Nativity. There is little doubt, on stylistic grounds, that of this pair the Toriti is the earlier. The half-upright posture of the Virgin, borrowed

205 from earlier Byzantine examples, gives way in Cavallini's mosaic to an easy, reclining position. Also derived from the earlier model is the almost clumsy representation of Joseph, looking over his shoulder as if he were being bothered and wanted to be left alone. This has been transmuted by Cavallini into a meditative figure who has an air of solemnity, almost of tragedy—surely a far more sophisticated creation. In the Cavallini version, moreover, the Child lies fully in his cradle —not half in and half out of it, as in Toriti's panel. The Cavallini version has been expanded, partly to introduce a particular allusion to the traditions of the church for which he was working,[11] but also to include a pastoral addition of the shepherd and his flocks.

207, 209   If the two versions of the Presentation are compared with each other, and also with a third

208 version (Giotto's painting in the Scrovegni chapel), the Toriti would again seem to be the earliest, or the least advanced, of the three. Both Toriti and Cavallini provide a background of three *aediculae* as a stage set for the scene. But Cavallini used them (as does Giotto similar features in his paintings, such as that in the Scrovegni chapel) to give a three-dimensional quality to the whole. The perspective of the central feature in Cavallini's version is almost plausible, though it does not have the architectural reality which Giotto, architect as well as painter, gives to all such structures. In Toriti's mosaic, the *aediculae* form a pattern, but do not yield another dimension; and the central *aedicula* gives the impression of being out of drawing rather than of being a studied interpretation. The Toriti figures have an awkward stance, the two men appearing to be striding forward, though they are, in fact, standing still, and the Virgin and the aged Prophetess both standing stiffly upright. In the Cavallini, however, the figures stand easily and gracefully, and it is clear that in this panel the lessons of classical sculpture have been far more profoundly assimilated.

XXXI Sta Maria in Trastevere, the Life of the Virgin series (by Cavallini; *c.* 1295). The Annunciation.

My conclusion then, as to the stylistic relationship between the Cavallini and Toriti series, is that they were apparently being made at about the same time, in which case there must surely have been some element of rivalry between the two artists, since they were treating the same themes. But the creation of the Toriti series was spread over more years, so that not only was the first scene to be executed (presumably the Annunciation) earlier than any in the Cavallini series, but the latest (the Dormition) was later. The only possible explanation, indeed, of the inter-relationship seems to reside in mutual emulation, the climax being reached in the Toriti Dormition. And here it may be mentioned that the almost universal acceptance of 1291 as a firm date for the Cavallini series may, unfortunately, be unsoundly based. It originates, I think, in de Rossi, who stated it confidently. But the evidence he gives involves the hypothesis that an earlier observer, who saw an inscription which had already disappeared by de Rossi's day and who read the date in it as 1251, was mistaken, the true reading being 1291. This date may be right, but it seems far from being definitely established, as is sometimes assumed. A later date surely seems indicated in order to allow for the influence of Giotto's work (though probably not, by this time, of the *Navicella*), which is generally assumed to be evident in some parts of the series.

XXXII In his remarkable Dormition, not only did Toriti introduce conscious technical innovations, such as the dwindling perspective of the processions at either end of the picture; the rhythm and counterpoint of the draperies and postures, and the individuality of the faces, betoken a new epoch. It is always impossible to define a moment before which art was this, and after which it was that. In one sense, every great work is a decisive moment in, and decisively affects the future of, the history of art. In another, even the most original work is shown to be intimately linked with its past. But if any mosaic seems to represent the beginning of an era, it is this.

Apart from the differences of style, there are other features which differentiate Toriti's version of the Dormition from Cavallini's and other earlier versions. In addition to the angels in the sky, 226 seven heads appear, gazing down. These seem to be ancestors of the Magi, or of the Prophets who have foretold the birth of Christ, or of both. The nearest parallels to them (and fairly close to them in date) are the figures borne in on the clouds on either side in Giotto's *Navicella*. One, crowned, on the left, is King David, marked with the initial D. At the far left is the city of Sion (SYON); on the right, the Mount of Olives (MONS OLIVET). Of the three small figures in the fore-226, XXXII ground, below the bier on which the Virgin's body lies, the two Franciscans are no doubt Toriti's assistants. One of these might be the Brother James de Camerino who is represented as one of the craftsmen in the apsidal mosaic in St John Lateran; the other is also probably a craftsman. Alternatively, as Wilpert supposed, the pair may be Toriti himself and James de Camerino. The third 226 kneeling figure, however, is presumably a donor; he appears to be a layman, and his appearance and headgear are reminiscent of the Bertoldus shown in the dedicatory inscription of the Cavallini XXX mosaics in Sta Maria in Trastevere. It might be significant that here, as undoubtedly there, he is directly associated with St Peter in the design. What is clear is that this particular panel (possibly the whole series, but that would be a dangerous assumption in view of the difference in character between this panel and the others) was the gift of a different patron from that of the main apsidal mosaic (a mosaic connected, like those of the façade, with Cardinal Colonna), and that this lay patron was possibly Bertoldo Stefaneschi, whose association with Giotto's *Navicella* in St Peter's is well attested.

The last panel, then, in Toriti's series on the Life of the Virgin shows so remarkable a change in style that we are bound to assume the intervention of some powerful new influence. The most likely explanation is that Toriti became familiar at this stage with some of the work of Giotto.

XXXII   Sta Maria Maggiore, the Life of the Virgin series
(by Toriti; c. 1295–1305). A detail from the Dormition of the Virgin
(the last panel to be made; perhaps c. 1305).

Coupled with this change of style, there is in the mosaic itself evidence of a change of patron—a change which may also dissociate the Dormition mosaic from the earlier ones in the series. There is at least one detail which seems to be most readily explained as being derived from the *Navicella*: the presence in the Dormition of heavenly witnesses like those in Giotto's work. These points suggest a date early in the fourteenth century for the Dormition panel. But since the *Navicella* has been so variously dated, there are many unresolved difficulties; though if, as has often been suggested, Giotto's work dates from 1300, this would allow Toriti's to have been executed in the first decade of the fourteenth century.

Another small detail (already mentioned) in the main apsidal mosaic can perhaps be brought into relation with this complex problem: the figure, in the lower border of the main mosaic, of an angler. We know (for example, from Vasari's description of the mosaic) what a deep impression the vivid figure of the angler made. This antique *motif* is also present in the mosaic series with which the vault near the tomb of St Peter, under the old basilica of St Peter's, was decorated, though now only the preliminary sketch on the mortar remains, the *tesserae* having been completely lost. There is, moreover, at least one medieval example in Rome.[12] Giotto, it has recently been suggested,[13] was perhaps himself producing his own version of an antique *Navicella* which was disintegrating, as Toriti also was recreating an ancient mosaic; according to this theory there would be no intrinsic difficulty in supposing that the angler in the lower border of the main apsidal mosaic in Sta Maria was, there also, derived from a classical original. The unexplained feature, then, is that the figure seems to be almost certainly a later insertion in the border. Following the bank, or coastline, of the stream along its course, one discovers an obvious break in the line of this terraced bank, which otherwise runs along the whole border. Behind the angler's head, the line of the original border is clear. Unfortunately, an early break obscures any detail that there was immediately in front of the angler, where there is a strip of almost meaningless infilling. But at his back the border is plainly visible.

If this figure is an insertion, it is difficult to imagine its purpose—unless it is interpreted as an allusion to a detail in the *Navicella*, which was already famous. My suggestion is that Toriti himself may have made this insertion in his earlier work above, perhaps as a compliment to the master whose work had so powerfully influenced the Dormition panel. This insertion could have been made from the scaffolding erected for work on the Dormition panel immediately below. But the detail is puzzling, and the facts are not established beyond doubt.

To revert to the series in Sta Maria in Trastevere, an interesting theory was put forward by A. Prandi concerning the development of Cavallini's style. After the removal of the protective materials that had covered these mosaics during the second world war, Prandi studied them in detail, and wrote an article[14] based on the fine series of photographs that were taken after the mosaics were uncovered. He drew attention to important differences in technique, particularly in the size and handling of the *tesserae*, between some panels and others. He considered these differences to be evidence of the development of Cavallini's style. According to this view, the Donor panel would be the most advanced, and he suspected that this striking development might have been due to Giotto's influence (as I have suggested might also have been the case in the series by Toriti). I am not, however, entirely convinced by his argument. If, indeed, the Donor panel was excuted in 1291, Prandi's evidence would have to be very strong. That date was very early in Giotto's career. I think, moreover, that the technical differences mentioned above, which are certainly real and important, should more probably be attributed to the fact that different craftsmen worked on different panels. Unfortunately, Prandi only discussed three of the panels in detail:

220

XXXIII   Sta Maria in Trastevere, the Life of the Virgin series
(by Cavallini; *c.* 1295). The Presentation, set by the master himself.

the Nativity, the Dormition and the Donor panels. My belief is that, though Cavallini designed the whole series, the Annunciation, Presentation and Donor panels are the only ones which were executed either entirely or largely by him. I suspect, therefore, that the differences between the Nativity and Dormition panels on the one hand, and the Donor panel on the other, are due to the fact that in the two former Cavallini's design was executed not by himself, but by an assistant. But I certainly do not think that one can exclude the possibility of the master having been influenced by work of Giotto in the design or execution of the series as a whole.

STA MARIA MAGGIORE: THE MOSAICS OF THE FAÇADE

The series of mosaics on the façade of Sta Maria Maggiore was damaged, but not completely destroyed, when this front of the church was remodelled by order of Benedict XIV in the mid-eighteenth century. The series falls into two sections. The upper section, with an inscription carrying the name of the artist, Philippus Rusuti, has many links with the work of Toriti in the apse.

218 Its subject is traditional: Christ in a roundel, supported by angels, and with saints on either side. In the lower section, not only is the theme different, but it is treated in a wholly different manner. The subject here is the legend of the founding of the church of Sta Maria Maggiore.

The columns and mitres incorporated in the lower part of the design, above the window, are badges of the Colonna family, one of whom (Giacomo) was, as we have seen,[15] associated with the mosaic of the apse. De Rossi states that both cardinals of the Colonna family were represented originally on the façade.[16] Cecchelli links the façade mosaics also with Nicholas IV.[17] But this seems to suggest an impossibly early date for the lower half of the mosaic. Vasari relates a story[18] that the mosaic was completed by Gaddo Gaddi, and speaks with characteristic approval of the break with the Byzantine tradition which the later mosaics of this façade represent. The mention of Gaddi in this context has (probably rightly) been regarded with scepticism. In Cecchelli's view, the difference of subject is enough to explain the differences of style. To me, however, these differences seem so striking that I think there must have been a later artist, whatever his name, working (not necessarily at a much later date, but certainly in an entirely new idiom) on the lower part of the design. The two cardinals of the Colonna family were Giacomo and Pietro (died 1318 and 1326). We must assume that the lower half of the mosaic, which incorporates the Colonna badges, was planned, and probably also executed, by 1326.

218 The main mosaic is displayed under a magnificent border in the classical manner, with foliage scrolls which spring out of the upper half of the human body. The border—the lower edge of which is marked by an ornament that is a version of one repeatedly used in the Toriti mosaics, and also in the Cavallini mosaics in Sta Maria in Trastevere—suffered heavily in the eighteenth-century reconstruction,[19] which cuts the mosaics of this upper part into three arched sections. In the centre, in a circular roundel, against a background of blue scattered with stars, is the figure of the bearded Christ, seated on a broad and elaborately decorated throne. His right hand is held in front of his chest, in blessing; in the left hand he holds a book. The roundel is supported by four angels, the two lower angels each holding a candlestick, the two upper holding censers; it has a gold background, and a narrow green ground with small plants. Below the feet of Christ is the 'signature': 'Philippus Rusuti fecit hoc opus'. Before the restoration, there were, arrayed on either side, the Virgin, St Paul, St James, St John the Baptist, St Peter and two other saints; above them were the Evangelist symbols. The style is perhaps softer than that of Toriti, though it has less distinction, and it has not the delicacy of the finest Cavallini mosaics. The figures are somewhat squat.

The lower part of the mosaic is in four sections. On the left, above, is shown the appearance of the Virgin and Child, in a roundel supported by four youthful angels or cherubs (the heads and wings alone are seen), to Pope Liberius, who is sleeping below; an attendant is sitting near. The architectural setting represented, with its vaulted canopy and its elaborate upper structure with windows and a loggia, is characteristic of this later phase. There is one other scene (on the right, above) in which the Virgin and Child are again represented as appearing in a vision, also in a roundel. In both scenes, the roundels are of great charm. It is difficult to determine how much they have been restored, but it seems likely that in the right-hand scene, the left half—including most of the Virgin's face (contrast the texture in the surface of the Child's face, which is original), the shoulder, the lower half of the background of the roundel, and the hand—is restored work. It would appear, nevertheless, from a study of both the Child and also of the angels, that the treatment is far more 'advanced' than in the Rusuti mosaics above.[20] But I have the impression that the artist who worked on the version of a Giotto angel made for Pope Benedict XIV (see Plate 25) may have restored the Virgin's face in these roundels. The roundel on the other side of the mosaic, in the snowstorm scene, is more nearly in its original condition and provides a standard by which to assess this one. Faces are what attract eager restorers. Another panel shows the meeting between John the Patrician and the Pope, who sits holding up his hand in blessing. The Pope wears the tiara, and behind him stands a mitred bishop or cardinal—conceivably Cardinal Colonna. Below, on the left, kneels a figure who seems to be the artist.

These mosaics of the lower part of the façade series are thus concerned with a type of subject different from those previously treated in Roman mosaics: the legend of the founding of a church, by men who are viewed not as martyrs translated to heaven, but as human personalities; and the style is intended to emphasize the fact that the story is taken from life. The sense of the third dimension, already noticeable in some of Cavallini's mosaics, now becomes one of the principal features of the composition. Thus here the elaborate architectural canopies are far more developed than those included in the apsidal panels representing scenes from the Life of the Virgin—the canopied throne of Cavallini's Annunciation, for example, or the *aediculae* of his Presentation. There is an elaborate use of recession and 'perspective', well seen in the panel which shows the appearance of the Virgin to Pope Liberius, but characteristic of all the main designs. The effect of recession is not achieved through meeting lines of perspective (a technique which was still imperfectly understood), but is most notably created when the artist employs the device of a vaulted roof, or tricks of light and shade. The clothes are contemporary and the object is to create an impression of events happening in the everyday world—not in Heaven.

Some of the details in this lower series deserved Vasari's praise (he was contrasting them with what he called the 'Byzantine manner' of the work above). Moreover, they are not seen to advantage when viewed at their own level, as today they have to be viewed. Nevertheless, taken as a whole, this series has curiously little appeal to the modern eye. The fact surely is that, in this attempt to recreate imaginatively these realistic scenes, the artist was using the wrong medium. Mosaic was at its best when depicting Paradise, Hell or the glorification of martyrs, or when used to trace the huge symbolic patterns and arabesques which form the background of some of the finest works with which this book is concerned. The streets of the medieval city, on the other hand, were not good subject matter for the mosaicist, and, to do justice to their new themes, artists were to turn, rightly, to other media. The change of attitude is well shown by some of Vasari's incidental comments. For him, mosaic had value in that it gave a picture a lasting physical form. But he disliked the rough surface and variegated texture of mosaic which, developed from the

232

229

XXXI
XXXIII
328

fifth to the ninth century, survived in some late medieval work. 'Andrea Tafi', he says, 'deserves a high place among the old masters because, though he learned the principles of mosaic from the craftsmen he brought from Venice to Florence, yet he introduced great improvements into the art, uniting the pieces with great care and making his surfaces as smooth as a table (a most important thing in mosaics)'. The mosaicist attempted to meet this demand for mosaics which were simply durable substitutes for paintings, and in this manner ceased to make an independent contribution.

ST PETER'S: GIOTTO'S 'NAVICELLA'

The mosaic by Giotto known as the *Navicella*, which represents the story of Peter walking across the lake in the storm to meet Christ (Matt. xiv. 24–32), was from the first one of the most famous works of Christian art, and its destruction in the course of the rebuilding of St Peter's was the most grievous loss which that great achievement involved. The present version, in a lunette within the porch of the church, is not a thirteenth- or fourteenth-, but a seventeenth-century work, in execution and finish. Yet, because of the importance of the original, though that no longer survives, it is necessary here to give some account of it and of the part it played in the development of the art of mosaic in Rome.

From the time of the publication of an article by L. Venturi,[21] the view was long held that owing to restorations and reconstructions which had taken place before the seventeenth century, the design of the surviving version incorporated so many additions which were not based on Giotto's original that to discern anything but the broad outlines of this was impossible. In Venturi's view, these additions included the four half-figures being borne in on the clouds towards the sail of the boat (they are sometimes regarded as the Evangelists, but more probably represent Old Testament prophets; here they will be called the 'heavenly witnesses') and also the second figure (on the right-hand side of the sail) of the two representing storm winds. Venturi thought that the four 'Evangelists' had been introduced to emphasize that the scheme was an allegory (as distinct from other mosaics, originally placed near this, which represented popes), and also to introduce a further element of symmetry into the work. By the addition of these four figures, and of the second figure representing a storm wind, the design was now divisible into four parallel zones, each symmetrically balanced. The lowest zone, containing the famous figure of the angler, fishing with rod and line from the rock on the left, is balanced by the figure of the donor, Cardinal Stefaneschi, on the right. The zone above this contains the boat itself, and the disciples in it, with a castle on the left (the remains of which can be seen in the cartoon, but which is made clearer in earlier sketches) and the figures of Christ and St Peter on the right. The third zone is occupied by the storm winds (the two demonic figures on either side of the sail), the fourth by the sky and by the 'Evangelists' (or 'heavenly witnesses'). Venturi thought that this division into zones was imposed by later restorers on what had once been a much freer composition.

In the surviving version, one element which has disappeared from the scheme is the castle. But this appears already in a fourteenth-century sketch of the *Navicella*, and there is no doubt that such a feature was part of Giotto's original design. On the other hand, the earliest sketches do not show the heavenly witnesses, and they show only one (the left-hand one), or sometimes neither, of the storm demons. The earliest and most important, however, of these sketches on which Venturi relied, from the Pembroke collection at Wilton Park, is defective along the upper edge, and cannot be regarded as conclusive evidence of what the design did, or did not, originally contain in its upper part. Other sketches which he reproduced to support his hypothesis are very slight and certainly not intended to be comprehensive. They are interdependent and therefore useless as independent items of evidence for the nature of the original design. Moreover, in their treatment of the disposition and attitudes of the figures in the boat, some of these sketches lack certain elements (such as that of the disciple on the left, desperately hauling on the rope to stay the mast) which the original undoubtedly included. None of the early sketches, in fact, can be rightly described as a copy of the original. All seem to have been made from memory, and they give only a general impression, on a tiny scale, of the huge design.

While no attempt will be made here to give a detailed account of the vicissitudes through which the *Navicella* passed, the fine seventeenth-century cartoon of the mosaic in the Vatican is reproduced. This cartoon is full-scale, and was executed on linen. Also, further to the most perceptive analysis of the cartoon written by the German scholar Körte,[22] something will be said of the extent to which it can be regarded as a faithful reproduction of Giotto's work. It was commissioned from Cosimo Bartoli in 1628, the year in which it was decided that the mosaic would have to be destroyed. The cartoon was specifically intended therefore to be made as a record for posterity. *222*

First, however, a word must be said about the mosaic's original position and scale. It was in the forecourt of the old basilica of St Peter's, which it dominated. It was rectangular in shape. Körte calculates that the width of the present version, in the semicircular lunette, is nearly ten metres at the base, and that in its original rectangular form it was, with its border, approximately $13\frac{1}{2}$ metres wide and $9\frac{1}{2}$ metres high. A sketch made in 1629, which shows it in its architectural setting, proves that by then the first stage in the adaptation of the rectangle to a semicircular form had already been taken, but that three of the edges were then still straight lines, and that only the top was slightly arched. While Bernini was architect of St Peter's, the mosaic was not merely reconstructed: it was totally replanned so that it could be adapted to a semicircular setting. It had to be contracted in consequence. The heavenly witnesses were brought down to a lower level, so that the billowing clouds on which they were placed had to be lowered to a position half-way up the mast, thus becoming confused with the storm demons. The angler on the left and the half-figure of the donor on the right (originally, in Venturi's view, which is almost certainly right, a full-length or three-quarter-length figure) have suffered from the same process of compression. Thus, in the new version the angler's head is silhouetted against the boat. On the right, St Peter appears to have just stepped out of the boat, and his body masks its prow. Thus the entire disposition of the design was drastically modified. And though something of the contrapuntal movement of bodies and draperies in the boat was retained, the facial expressions of many of the figures (for example, the angler) have a disastrous inanity in the new version. These defects were inevitable, since the mosaic was replanned during a period when artistic ideals totally differed from those which flourished at the time the work was originally created. *221*

The cartoon of the *Navicella* was made when the rectangular design still existed. The mosaic had, indeed, already suffered, apart from certain medieval restorations about which more will be said later. Its border had been dispersed, and the two sides had evidently been cut away when the mosaic was moved. Thus, only a trace of the castle which was originally to be seen on the left of the mosaic appears in the cartoon. The cartoon itself was cut into sections at some time, undoubtedly in connection with the reconstruction of the design under Bernini's direction, since the upper half has been rounded off and the figures of the heavenly witnesses and the storm demons have been cut out to make it possible to move them to different positions. In recent years, the drawing has been reconstituted in rectangular form. *222*

Fortunately, it is the work of a fine artist. In some sections (for example, the pair of heavenly witnesses at the top on the right), nothing in his version would suggest that the original was Giottesque. These figures are prophets depicted by an artist of the early seventeenth, rather than the early fourteenth, century. But, as Körte has shown, the disposition of the figures in the boat, and in some instances the gestures and the actual features, must be echoes of the original, and can be very closely paralleled in other works by Giotto. Apart from the two disciples in the stern (one anxiously steering, the second hauling on a rope), the rest show amazement, bewilderment and terror; one is kneeling in prayer, at the apparition of Christ. Peter is sinking. On his face is an expression of pathetically helpless appeal which is no doubt derived from the original, as, presumably, is the magnificently statuesque, calm figure of Christ, who, with hardly a touch of his right hand, supports him. The storm demons no doubt embody sixteenth-century elements, though of the original design, the left-hand side (in which one of the demons and two of the heavenly witnesses appear) seems to have retained more of Giotto's work than the right-hand side. The figure of the angler derives in some way from antique originals. There is, in Rome, an antique sarcophagus picturing the story of Jonah, with a representation of an angler who is similarly detached from the scene into which he has been introduced. And the excavations carried out under St Peter's during the 1940s yielded the remains of what seems to be a mid-third-century mosaic, representing an angler, in a Christian context which gives the figure a definite symbolic meaning. Paesler suggested[23] accordingly that this and other details may have been derived from an antique original which Giotto's work was perhaps commissioned to replace. In the cartoon the figure of the angler shows, as Vasari observed, 'the extreme patience and intent concentration proper to his task'. It is difficult to believe that for Giotto this figure was only a symbol; it provided a dramatic contrast as well. Of the castle on the left only a trace remains in the cartoon, and apparently a strip of comparable size had disappeared from the right-hand edge. This indicates that the original design extended slightly, both to right and left, beyond the limits of the scene depicted in the cartoon.

The inscription (in a style which, as Paesler points out, might suggest that it was written for a far earlier work) ran thus: QVEM LIQVIDOS PELAGI GRADIENTEM STERNERE FLVCTVS IMPERITAS, FIDVMQVE REGIS, TREPIDVMQVE LABANTEM ERIGIS, ET CELEBREM REDDIS VIRTVTIBVS ALMVM HOC IVBEAS ROGITANTE DEVS CONTINGERE PORTVM, 'Lord, thou didst bid Peter walk over the watery waves of the sea; thou didst command him to have faith, and sustained him when in terror he began to sink. Thou didst restore him to fame, and to look kindly on goodness. As he prays to thee, Lord, on our behalf, grant that we too may reach our harbour'.

Giotto's mosaic was thus at once an intensely vivid piece of realism, and also, in general, splendidly symbolical. The appalled astonishment of the disciples, the rage of the storm, the grave calm of Christ, the infinite pity of the heavenly witnesses—these were all magnificently depicted. Something of this range of expression survives in the cartoon, which also contains an extraordinary foil to the tumultuous dynamism of the scene in the intense and unheeding concentration of the fisherman. The Church, almost submerged in stormy seas, needs succour as does Peter. Christ is there to give it succour; meanwhile, life continues, while the tremendous drama is played out unheeded.

While it is possible, with the guidance of the cartoon, to understand something of the significance of this masterpiece, to assess the style of the original is far more difficult. Vasari admired it partly for reasons which (as has been maintained earlier in this section of the book) seem to be at odds with the essential character of the medium; he admired it because, despite the fact that the artist was working in mosaic, he had achieved an exceptionally smooth surface and effects of chiaroscuro which would normally be expected only in a painting. 'It is a difficult task', he writes, 'to unite those pieces of glass to form the light and shade of so real a sail, which, even with the brush, could only be equalled with a great effort'. This is the sort of quality which is shown, for example, in the draperies of the Donor panel of Cavallini's mosaics in Sta Maria in Trastevere. XXX There can be no doubt that whatever else Giotto achieved in the *Navicella*, Renaissance critics thought that he had used the medium of mosaic for a purpose which might have been fulfilled by using paint, had the surface been smaller and not exposed to the weather; this was one of the main reasons why they praised the work so highly.

Even more puzzling, therefore, are the qualities of the two roundels of angels' heads, which are ascribed on good authority to Giotto and which undoubtedly formed part of this mosaic, whether the master himself, or one of his assistants, made them. One is in a church at Boville Ernica, some distance from Rome, the other is in the Vatican. Paesler's observation that the VI, 26 fragment in the Vatican still had attached to it a section of the original border of the *Navicella* was brilliantly developed from Körte's research.[24] Not only can the point be established, therefore, beyond doubt, that the head belongs to the border, but also something of the general character of the border can be established. The containing lines were of a geometrical pattern but these were entirely concealed when the head was 'restored' in 1727 by building over it a new mosaic head, bearing little relationship to the one underneath save in the general direction of its glance. The remains of the original head, together with what was, as Paesler pointed out, part of the border from which it came, were only discovered below this restoration, in comparatively recent times.

This head and the one at Boville Ernica, though they are from the same work, nevertheless differ remarkably. The head in the Vatican is austerely 'mosaicist' rather than painterly, and the *tesserae* of the face are much larger than those that Cavallini, Giotto's older contemporary (and, perhaps, for the *Navicella*, his assistant), would normally have used for the head or hands of a mosaic subject. It is a work of great integrity, but certainly does not conform to the impression which Vasari gives of the *Navicella*.

The head at Boville Ernica is softer in its modelling. The *tesserae* are somewhat smaller, but by no means tiny. A technical practice which links the two fragments, however, is the treatment of the shadows along the side of the face by a line, broken by the use of alternate cubes of light and dark colour, to soften the transition from light to shade—a broken line like that of the battlements of a city. This device may have been adapted from one of the Veneto-Byzantine mosaics of S. Paolo, a church in which Cavallini worked extensively in mosaic and sculpture (marble as well as wood). But it may possibly have been derived from antiquity; one of Paesler's most profound observations is that Giotto, to some extent at least, returned to the shimmering technique of earlier mosaicists, and was not content with treating the medium simply as a means of creating a more permanent 'painting'. It seems possible that Giotto deliberately devised a broader and more 'mosaicist' treatment for this border, in contrast with the more painterly naturalism of the narrative itself. Körte,[25] in pointing out some striking parallels between the two heads and work executed by Cavallini (who is said by Vasari[26] to have been associated with Giotto in work in mosaic in St Peter's), rightly drew attention to the difficulty, when assessing mosaics, of distinguishing between the work done by the master and that done by his assistants. In the series by Cavallini in Sta Maria in Trastevere, it seems as if at least two men worked on the actual setting of the *tesserae*, one of whom was more accomplished than the other, and might therefore have been the master himself. But it is, in fact, unlikely that there was a clear-cut division of labour even between one panel and another. The master was presumably responsible for the design, and he must often have wished to undertake himself the setting of areas that seemed to be specially important. In the case of these heads, then, it may be profitless to ask what precise part Giotto played over and above his responsibility for the design.

Something is known of the occasion of a number of the early (medieval) restorations of the *Navicella*. Venturi, aware that much work had been done on it, assumed[27] that it had been so much altered as to be only a shadow of its original self by the time the decision was taken to destroy it. It was so famous that it attracted too much attention, perhaps, from over-enthusiastic officials. But it is arguable that until the sixteenth century, when the process of Procrustean alteration began, the *Navicella* was regularly maintained, sections that had suffered in the course of time being replaced before damage was too extensive. This, in fact, would have been the proper way to preserve all medieval mosaics. On any reckoning, three hundred years elapsed between the date when the mosaic was finished and the date when the great cartoon was made. Drawings made somewhat earlier than this of the exterior mosaics made by Giotto's contemporary Cavallini for the façade of S. Paolo show that they had already suffered extensively, and even the mosaics executed by Cavallini for the interior of Sta Maria in Trastevere had been damaged by the end of the sixteenth century. At that time it was no longer possible, for example, to read the whole inscription on the Donor panel of that series. The maintenance work on the *Navicella* may have been very largely essential. Without it there would certainly have been considerable areas of disintegration. Whether or not the restorers incorporated new material is another matter. Bearing in mind that sixteenth-century authorities like Vasari had higher standards in this than in some other matters, one doubts whether this masterpiece, famous throughout Christendom, would have been subjected to the kind of alterations that Venturi suspected.

OTHER RENAISSANCE MOSAICS IN ROME

S. Crisogono. Vasari says that for this church Cavallini 'did many scenes in fresco'.[28] These have not survived, but framed and set in the centre of the apse (not built on its curve) is a large mosaic which has been attributed to Cavallini and must date from the last quarter of the thirteenth century. If it is by his hand (which is doubtful, and in view of the damage the mosaic has suffered agreement is hardly likely to be reached), it would be earlier than the well-known works that are certainly his, such as the Life of the Virgin series in Sta Maria in Trastevere. It is, however, noticeable that the folds of the headdress over the Virgin's forehead and on either side of her face are closely similar to those that seem characteristic of Cavallini. They are similar, for example, to the headdress in the Annunciation and Donor panels in Sta Maria in Trastevere, but dissimilar to the headdresses in the corresponding panels in Toriti's series in Sta Maria Maggiore. P. Toesca, however, does not regard this mosaic as Cavallini's work.[29]

The mosaic represents the Virgin enthroned, with the Christ Child on her left arm. He looks left, three-quarter face, and holds up his right hand in blessing. The throne has twisted pillars, represented as decorated in the Cosmatesque fashion. On the Virgin's left stands St James (not St Sebastian, as has sometimes been stated), holding a book. On her right is S. Crisogono, with a sword; he holds the scabbard in his left hand, the hilt in his right. The two saints are on a smaller scale than the Virgin. The fringe on the Virgin's cloak over her right shoulder is characteristic of this period, but is certainly not entirely confined to it; it appeared earlier in Venetian mosaics (for example, in the apse of Torcello).

The Virgin seems similar in pose as well as in feeling to the painted Virgin and Child on the tomb of Cardinal Matteo d'Aquasparta in Sta Maria in Ara Celi, which Toesca considers to be Cavallini's work. It is true that, on the tomb, the supporting figures are almost on the same scale as the Virgin. But a detail such as the slightly pouting mouth of the Virgin might be characteristic. It appears in several other mosaics by Cavallini and in the Matteo tomb picture; in the mosaic 211 in S. Crisogono, it is especially noticeable in photographs taken before the work was restored. Details of this kind might conceivably originate from a particular model who sat for Cavallini; the highly distinctive features of the nurse in the Birth of the Virgin panel, and the prophetess in the Presentation in the Temple, seem to be those of another individual model. The comparison suggests that Cavallini sometimes worked, contrary to what might be expected, from living models.

If Cavallini planned the work, the two supporting figures must have been executed by assistants. The Virgin's drapery has been modelled with considerable feeling (though, if it is Cavallini's work, it is certainly very different from his treatment, twenty years later, of a similar subject, the material being heavy and blanket-like, when compared with the light elegance he achieved later). It is, however, hazardous to assume the existence of only one style for Cavallini's draperies. Those of the apostles in his painting of the Last Judgment in Sta Cecilia are, in fact, much more similar to those in the S. Crisogono mosaic than they are, let us say, to those in the Donor panel in Sta Maria in Trastevere. These latter in some ways resemble a fragment on the wall at the left-hand end of the Sta Cecilia *Last Judgment* (the wall that is opposite that which bears the *Annunciation*, a 'school' picture).

Unfortunately, there has been damage, since repaired, to an area stretching across the Virgin's face, and extensive repairs have been carried out on the figure of S. Crisogono (for example, on his left hand, the scabbard held in it, and the background here). Metal crowns were at one time fixed over the heads of the Virgin and Child. These have now been removed. The *tesserae* in this mosaic seem more uniform in size than in the series by Cavallini in Sta Maria in Trastevere, in which smaller units were used fairly freely to portray faces and flesh. This may be a reason for dating it earlier, and may be thought to weigh against the attribution to Cavallini.

Sta Maria in Ara Celi: the lunette over the south door. This mosaic, which is of the school of Cavallini, shows the Virgin and Child in a roundel. The background is pale blue, with a mono- 233 gram and three stars. The Virgin's cloak is deep blue, with a fringe of gold. One of her hands is under the Child's left arm; the other supports him. He is wrapped in red and has a crossed halo. He looks up into his Mother's face, his right hand held up in blessing (not in the Greek manner); she gazes out towards the spectator. On either side of the roundel, in the corners of the lunette, is an angel holding a golden candlestick and candle; their drapery is buff, with shadows of grey and green. The only areas which appear to have been restored are part of the Virgin's halo and part of the halo of the angel on the right. The colours have to some extent lost their brilliant quality on account of exposure. The work is good (though not, perhaps, of the finest quality, as can be seen if the flowers and foliage are compared with those of the Donor panel by Cavallini in Sta Maria in Trastevere).

St Peter's: fragments in the Vatican Grottoes. There are two heads in the Vatican Grottoes which have survived from a mosaic apparently intended originally to decorate the small dome over the chapel of Sta Petronilla in the new basilica (as it was planned in the fifteenth century).[30] Both of them are by the same hand, and show a remarkable appreciation, on the part of an artist much later than Giotto, of the character of mosaic as a medium. One of them, a head of St Bernard of

27 Clairvaux, is a splendidly sensitive work in which the work lines are finely used to model the contours of the face. There is a patch of restoration on the top of the head, towards the forehead. The other head is that of a cherub. Most of the actual face seems to be original, though on the right-hand side there is a large patch of restoration on the neck which may extend as far as the left cheek.

84 There is also in the Grottoes a head of St Peter which has been attributed to Melozzo da Forli,[31] but which has surely been rightly described by L'Orange and Nordhagen[32] as antique. They date it to the fifth century. The loose texture is thoroughly characteristic of the antique period, and would not be present in fifteenth-century work. This mosaic seems to have been the model for

83 the St Peter in S. Teodoro.

Sta Maria Maggiore: the tomb of Bishop Gunsalves. Sta Maria Sopra Minerva: the tomb of Bishop Duranti. Sta Sabina: the tomb of Munoz de Zamora

215, 216 The Gunsalves tomb is in the north-west corner of Sta Maria Maggiore, near the apse. The mosaic, in a recess above the sarcophagus, represents Bishop Gunsalves, mitred, kneeling on the left, worshipping the Virgin and Child. On the gold background behind the Virgin's head is the monogram. On the left St Matthias is holding a scroll inscribed ME TENET ARA PRIOR, 'The altar in front holds me'. (This seems to be a reference to a relic of St Matthias.) On the right is St Jerome; he holds a scroll bearing the inscription RECVBO P̄SEPIS [PRAESEPIS] AD ANTRV̄ [ANTRVM], 'I lie near the manger cave'. The double reference here is to the bishop, whose tomb is near the famous relic of the crib of Christ in Sta Maria Maggiore, also known as Sta Maria del Presepe; and to St Jerome's burial at Bethlehem, the birthplace of Christ, at the 'stable cave'. The mosaic was presumably made after 1298, when the bishop died. The inscription concludes with the signature HOC OP FEC IOHES MAGRI COSME CIVIS ROMANVS, 'This work was executed by John, son of the master Cosmati, and a Roman citizen'. The inscription on the Duranti tomb (see below) suggests that there is a word missing here (FILIVS); if this word is included, the Gunsalves inscription would then read HOC OPVS FECIT IOHANNES FILIVS MAGISTRI COSMATE CIVIS ROMANVS, yielding the same meaning. But these words refer to the tomb in general, not to the mosaicist.[33] The two saints, Matthias and Jerome, are linked also as the subjects of mosaic pictures (much restored) on the outside of the arch of the apse, on either side. All the lower part of the tomb mosaic has been replaced in plaster.

The Duranti tomb is in Sta Maria Sopra Minerva and is closely similar in general design to the Gunsalves tomb. Here too the tomb is of a bishop, the mosaic is within the canopy, and the bishop is represented as a small kneeling figure, mitred, worshipping the Virgin and Child; here too the Child wears a garment shot with gold. On the Virgin's right stands a mitred saint; on her left stands St Dominic, the founder of the order to which Bishop Duranti belonged. A tall iron candlestick flanks the design on either side. The colours of the remaining upper half of the mosaic are particularly splendid. Unfortunately, here also the lower half of the mosaic has been entirely lost. (The tomb as a whole was restored, according to an inscription, in 1817.) The date of the bishop's burial is given, in a long inscription, as 1304. The work is signed IOHS FILIVS MAGRI COSMATI FEC HOC OP, 'John, son of the master, Cosmati, made this work'.

Though these tombs were designed by the same architect, the mosaics are by different hands. The draperies in the Gunsalves mosaic have an unusual flow; the head of the Virgin is held high,

334

but has a touching sadness. In the Duranti mosaic the fringed cloak on the Virgin's right shoulder is typical of the group of mosaics associated with Cavallini; but it does not seem plausible to attribute either of these mosaics definitely to his school.

Almost contemporary with the Gunsalves and Duranti tombs is that of Munoz de Zamora in Sta Sabina. Munoz was the Vicar-general of the Dominicans, to whom the church had been given. The inscription on the tomb gives the year of his death as 1300. It is not a wall tomb but is in the floor of the nave. Though it has sometimes been ascribed to Toriti nothing except the date seems to favour this attribution. We should certainly expect a floor mosaic to be treated differently from other types, but this work is medieval in spirit and contains no hint of Byzantium or of the Renaissance. The reclining figure is depicted in severe and noble terms, the quality of the design being very powerful. There is a skilful use of flat and highly glazed *tesserae* to emphasize the lines of the design, which are broad and strong. Apart from the face, in which some smaller units have been used, a considerable degree of uniformity in the working prevails throughout the mosaic.

NOTES ON THE TEXT VII

1 See pp. 94–96.

2 For details of the ancient predecessor of this work, see pp. 70–71.

3 J. Wilpert gives a version (*Die römischen Mosaiken und Malereien der Kirchlichen Bauten vom IV bis XIII Jahrhundert*, 4 vols, Freiburg 1916, p. 201).

4 For example, the angels in the Last Judgment fragment in the convent of Sta Cecilia.

5 See pp. 94–96.

6 See pp. 324, 330.

7 Jacopo da Camerino was the craftsman who executed the mosaic. See V. Golzio and G. Zander, *Chiese di Roma dall' XI al XVI secolo*, Roma Cristiana, vol. 4, Rome 1963, p. 197.

8 The probability that the Death of the Virgin was always intended to be placed below the Coronation of the Virgin here has been demonstrated by M. Alpatoff-Moskau ('Die Entstehung des Mosaiks von Jacobus Torriti in Sta Maria Maggiore in Rom', *Römisches Jahrb. für Kunstwiss.*, 1924–25, pp. 9 et seq. and Plate 3).

9 The date 1291 was given by de Rossi, but the evidence (which he gives) is surely by no means conclusive, though the date may be right. M. Barbet de Jouy thought he saw under the panel of the Nativity (which does not seem to offer much space for it) the date 1251; de Rossi (who said, perhaps rightly, that his observation must be taken seriously) concluded that he had misread

MCCXCI for MCCLCI, an unusual form of the date 1251. For details see G. B. de Rossi, *Musaici cristiani e saggi di pavimenti delle chiese di Roma anteriori al secolo XV*, 'Zona inferiore dell'abside di Sta Maria in Trastevere', fol. 3 (verso), Rome 1873–99.

10 Though Alpatoff-Moskau (see note 8 above) showed that Toriti, in conformity with a French model, probably planned the Dormition to be placed immediately below the Coronation, I strongly doubt his further contention that the whole of Toriti's series precedes that of Cavallini in Sta Maria in Trastevere.

11 This church was known as the Taberna Meritoria. According to a legend, a miraculous fountain of oil appeared on the site on the day of Christ's birth. The inscription and the building can be seen on Plate 206.

12 A painting, possibly of eleventh-century date, in S. Clemente.

13 W. Paesler, 'Giottos Navicella und ihr spätantikes Vorbild', *Römisches Jahrb. für Kunstgesch*, 5, 1941, pp. 49–162.

14 'Pietro Cavallini in Sta Maria in Trastevere', *Riv. del Ist. Naz. d'Archeol. e dell' Arte*, I, 1952, pp. 282–297.

15 See p. 314.

16 Op. cit., ('Facciata di Sta Maria Maggiore', fol. 1, verso). Here de Rossi quotes the description (1621) by P. de Angelis.

17 *I mosaici della basilica di S. Maria Maggiore*, Turin 1956, p. 16.

18 *Lives of the Painters*, ed. W. Gaunt, 4 vols, London 1963, vol. 1, p. 59.

19 De Rossi (op. cit., fol. 2) considered that this border was itself of eighteenth-century date, but this view seems to me untenable. See W. Paesler (op. cit., p. 91) for a comparison between the centrepiece of this border and one of the angels in the *Navicella*.

20 Such evidence as is available of eighteenth-century restorations or reconstructions of mosaics (the pseudo-Giotto head of 1727, for example, or the *Tribune of Benedict XIV*) sorely perplex anyone attempting to assess the style of these roundels. The Child must be basically the fourteenth-century original in both cases. De Rossi (op. cit.) mentions, however, a number of details that were at some time altered, both in these narrative pieces and in the mosaic above; and while it may be taken as certain that the elaborate architectural schemes in the background of the lower section are substantially original and convey the impression intended by the artist, to argue from the detail of any one individual figure may be dangerous.

21 'La Navicella di Giotto', *L'Arte*, 1922, pp. 49–69.

22 W. Körte, 'Die Navicella des Giotto', *Festschrift Wilhelm Pinder*, 1938, pp. 226 et seq.

23 Op. cit., pp. 49–162.

24 Körte, op. cit., p. 254.

25 Ibid., p. 255.

26 Op. cit., vol. 1, p. 125.

27 Loc. cit.

28 Loc. cit.

29 *Pietro Cavallini*, Milan 1959, p. 15.

30 See *Cenni Storici della basilica Vaticana*, 1955. The heads are shown on Plates 22 and 23 of that work.

31 Ibid., Plate 18.

32 *Mosaik von der Antike bis zum Mittelalter*, German ed. trans. from Norwegian, Munich 1960, Plates 50 and 51.

33 Other mosaics associated with work by the Cosmati in the thirteenth century in Rome are the frieze in the portico of S. Lorenzo fuori le Mura, the porch mosaic of S. Tommaso in Formis (see pp. 298–299) and a panel once in Sta Maria Maggiore and illustrated by Cecchelli (op. cit., Plate LXXXVI). The mosaic in the Capella Sancta Sanctorum should probably be added.

CHRVSGNS · ΜΡ ΘV · S IACOBVS

194   S. Crisogono. Mosaic panel in the apse (thirteenth century, last quarter).

195 St John Lateran. Main mosaic of the apse (by Toriti; reconstructed in 1884).

196 St John Lateran, main mosaic of the apse (by Toriti; reconstructed in 1884). St John the Evangelist, with St Anthony.

197 Sta Maria Maggiore. Main mosaic of the apse (by Toriti; *c.* 1294), with (below) some scenes from the Life of the Virgin series (also by Toriti; *c.* 1295–1305).

198 Sta Maria Maggiore, main mosaic of the apse (by Toriti; *c.* 1294). Angels supporting the central roundel.

199   Sta Maria Maggiore, main mosaic of the apse (by Toriti; *c.* 1294). Three saints; above them, the classical scroll.

200   Sta Maria Maggiore. Centre-piece of the mosaic festoon of the apsidal arch (by Toriti; *c.* 1294).

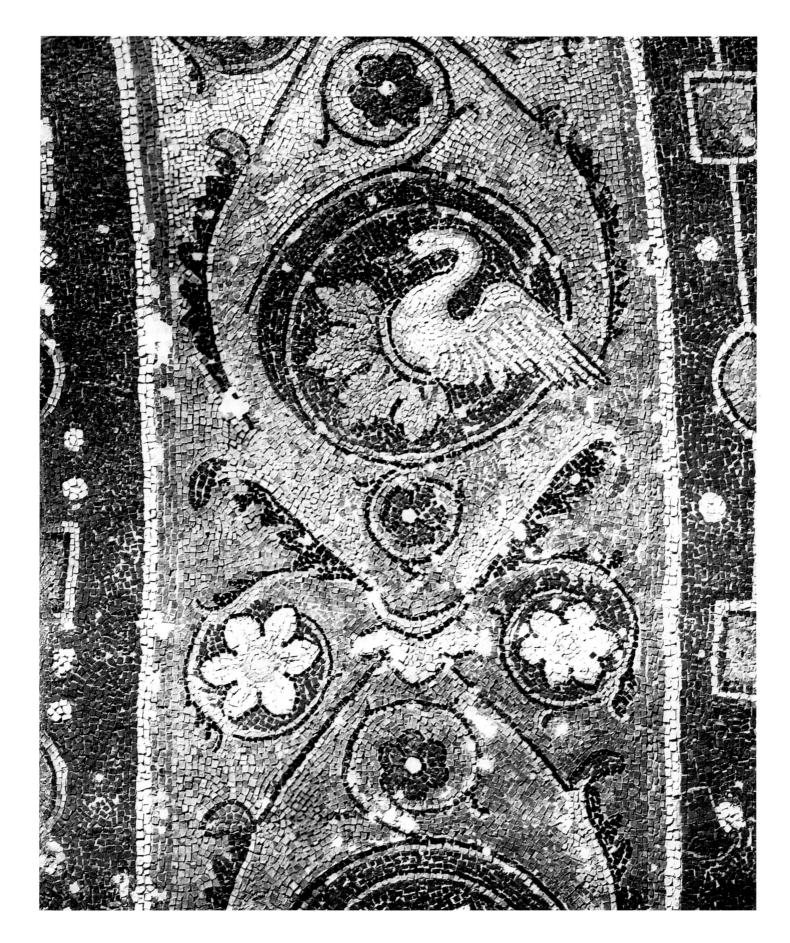

201   Sta Maria Maggiore. Pattern edging the outside of the apsidal arch (by Toriti; *c.* 1294).

204   Sta Maria Maggiore, the Life of the Virgin series (by Toriti; *c.* 1295–1305). The Nativity.

205 Church of the Martorana, Palermo. A Sicilian-Byzantine version of the Nativity (twelfth century, second half).

206 Sta Maria in Trastevere, the Life of the Virgin series (by Cavallini; c. 1295). The Nativity.

207   Sta Maria Maggiore, the Life of the Virgin series (by Toriti; *c.* 1295–1305). The presentation.

208   Scrovegni chapel, Padua.
The Presentation (painting by
Giotto; *c*. 1310).

209   Sta Maria in Trastevere,
the Life of the Virgin series
(by Cavallini; *c*. 1295). The Presentation.

212 Sta Maria in Trastevere, the Life of the Virgin series (by Cavallini; *c.* 1295). Detail from the Birth of the Virgin.

210 Sta Maria in Trastevere, the Life of the Virgin series (by Cavallini; *c.* 1295). St Joseph, from the Presentation (detail of Plate 209).

211 Sta Maria in Trastevere, the Life of the Virgin series (by Cavallini; *c.* 1295). The Virgin, from the Annunciation (detail of Plate 203).

213   Sta Maria in Trastevere, the Life of the Virgin series (by Cavallini; *c*. 1295). Detail from the Dormition of the Virgin. Apostles at the foot of the bier.

214   Sta Maria in Trastevere, the Life of the Virgin series (by Cavallini; *c*. 1295). Detail from the Dormition of the Virgin. Christ holds in his arms the soul of the Virgin, represented as a small child.

215 Sta Maria Maggiore, tomb of Bishop Gunsalves (*c.* 1298).

216   Sta Maria Maggiore, tomb of Bishop Gunsalves (*c.* 1298). Detail from Plate 215.

217   Sta Maria sopra Minerva, tomb of Bishop Duranti (*c.* 1304).

218   Sta Maria Maggiore, mosaics of the façade. The upper section (by Rusuti; perhaps *c*. 1305).

219   St Peter's. The seventeenth-century version of Giotto's *Navicella*, in a lunette within the porch. Detail from Plate 221. St Peter.

220   Sta Maria Maggiore, main mosaic of the apse (by Toriti; *c.* 1294). Detail from the lower band of decoration, showing the later insertion of the figure of the angler.

221 St Peter's. The seventeenth-century version of Giotto's *Navicella*, in a lunette within the porch.

222 The Vatican. Full-size cartoon of Giotto's *Navicella* made by Cosimo Bartoli in 1628, shortly before

the destruction of the mosaic.

223 Scrovegni chapel, Padua. The Funeral Procession of the Virgin (painting by a pupil of Giotto; 1310–20).

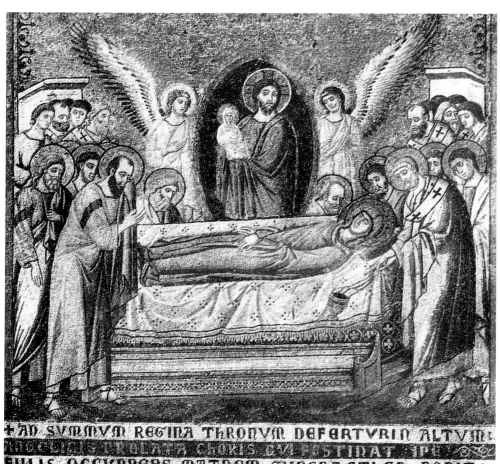

+AD SVMMVM REGINA THRONVM DEFERTVRIN ALTVM
HOC·... ·RLATA CHORIS CV FESTINAT ·IPE·
·FILIS OCCVRRENS·MATREM SVPERAETHER PONIT·

224 Sta Maria in Trastevere, the Life of the Virgin series (by Cavallini; c. 1295). The Dormition of the Virgin.

225 Church of the Martorana, Palermo. Sicilian–Byzantine mosaic representing the Dormition of the Virgin (twelfth century).

226 Sta Maria Maggiore, the Life of the Virgin series (by Toriti; *c.* 1295–1305). Part of the Dormition of the Virgin (this panel perhaps *c.* 1305).

227 Sta Maria Maggiore, mosaics of the façade (*c.* 1320). Part of the lower section, showing the vision of John the Patrician.

228 Sta Maria Maggiore, mosaics of the façade (*c.* 1320). Part of the lower section, showing the vision of Pope Liberius.

QV IOῊS PAῙ · IVIT · AῙ · PAPῙ LIBῙV PVISIOῙ QVῙ VIOGRAT

229 Sta Maria Maggiore, mosaics of the façade (*c.* 1320). Part of the lower section, showing John the Patrician visiting Pope Liberius.

230 Sta Maria in Trastevere, the Life of the Virgin series (by Cavallini; *c.* 1295). The Virgin (detail from the Donor panel).

231 Sta Maria in Trastevere, the Life of the Virgin series (by Cavallini; *c.* 1295). St Paul (detail from the Donor panel).

232   Sta Maria Maggiore, mosaics of the façade (*c.* 1320). Detail from Plate 228.

233 Sta Maria in Ara Celi. Lunette over the south door (school of Cavallini, probably *c.* 1300).

234 Sta Maria in Trastevere, the Life of the Virgin series (by Cavallini; *c.* 1295). The Donor panel.

235   S. Lorenzo fuori le Mura, mosaic of the triumphal arch (sixth century, last quarter).
St Peter. In the Byzantine manner.

236   Baptistry of St John Lateran, chapel of St Venantius. St Asterius: from the frieze outside the apse (seventh century, second quarter). In the Roman manner.

237   Original head, probably representing St Paul, from the mosaic (c. 800; copied in the *Tribune of Benedict XIV*) which decorated the Triclinium of the old Lateran palace. A retouched photograph. After Wilpert.

238   Fragment from the mosaic originally set up in the Triclinium of the Lateran palace (late eighth century), now in the Vatican Library.
The photograph has not been retouched.

239 Cathedral, Monreale, Sicily. Pentecost mosaic in the Sicilian-Byzantine style (c. 1180).

240 The Badia, Grottaferrata. Mosaic of the triumphal arch in the church (c. 1200). Apostles, on either side of an empty throne.

241 Cathedral, Salerno. St Matthew, from a lunette (*c*. 1195).

242 Sta Maria in Trastevere, mosaic of the façade. Part of the frieze. The figure on the left is part of the earliest work (*c*. 1190); the other three date from the middle of the thirteenth century.

243   The Badia, Grottaferrata. Mosaic
panel above the great door of the church,
representing a Deesis (Byzantine; eleventh
century, second half).

244   The Badia, Grottaferrata. Detail
from Plate 243.

194 The surface has deteriorated extensively in places —for example, across the lower part of the Virgin's face. The crowns, now removed, were a modern addition.

195 It will be seen that several figures—St John the Baptist, St Peter and St Paul—were repeated by Toriti with little variation in the main apsidal mosaic of Sta Maria Maggiore (Plate 197). Here the series of apostles between the windows completes this number. In the classical predecessor of this mosaic the Virgin was shown *orans*; her left hand still retains this position.

197 This mosaic, like the main apsidal mosaic of St John Lateran (Plate 195), had a classical predecessor, from which the superb scroll ornament and the decorative frieze along the lower border (Plates 62–66) were derived.

198 The kneeling figure is Iacopo Colonna.

199 The lower right-hand side, including the acanthus root, the river god and the ship, are modern.

201 The patches of white are plaster repairs, as they appeared before restoration carried out in the late 1920s.

202 The pose of the figure is comparatively rigid, and the treatment is austere. The result is magnificent, but still medieval.

203 Compared with Toriti's version (Plate 202), this by Cavallini is notable for its sense of rushing movement, its tenderness and its more articulate feeling for recession in the throne. It is a Renaissance work. The panel was perhaps set, as well as designed, by the master himself.

206 Here, as in the Annunciation (Plate 203), Cavallini has achieved a more graceful result and displayed a more delicate technique than Toriti in his version. The panel was perhaps set largely by assistants. The Taberna Meritoria below is an allusion to one of the legends of this church: that a spring of oil appeared on the site of Sta Maria Trastevere on the night of the Nativity.

207 This panel is one of the least effective of the series, in design as well as in detailed execution. (The mottled patches in the upper right-hand corner, and at the foot on the right, are repairs.) It is

very difficult to believe that it is, as it must be, very close in date to Cavallini's version of the Presentation (Plate 209).

208 Compare Giotto's painting with the version by Cavallini (Plate 209). Here the detail of the child flinging out his hand towards the Virgin is brilliantly effective, and the *aedicula* is architecturally more satisfying in the painting.

209 There seems to be a direct relationship between this panel and Giotto's version of the Presentation (Plate 208)—for example, in the treatment of the Prophetess' cloak. In this figure Cavallini's work is characteristically more classical in inspiration than Giotto's. The panel was set as well as designed by the master himself.

212 The nurse is feeling the heat of the water in the bath.

213 The leading figure, in the foreground, is St Paul.

215 The two saints specially honoured here, St Mathias and St Jerome, are also represented on small panels (now largely modern restorations) outside the apse, on the apsidal arch. The tomb was designed by one of the Cosmati family. The lower half of the mosaic has been largely restored.

216 This mosaic, and that of the tomb of Bishop Duranti (Plate 217), are specially important for providing comparatively exact dates of composition.

217 Like the tomb of Bishop Gunsalves in Sta Maria Maggiore (Plates 215–216), this was designed by one of the Cosmati.

218 This is the centre-piece of a large mosaic frieze of saints, which was damaged when the eighteenth-century façade was built on to it.

220 The figure of the angler, now unfortunately damaged, was perhaps inserted by way of an allusion to Giotto's *Navicella*, in which the angler was a famous feature. The white pointer shows where the original 'coastline' ran before the insertion was made.

221 For the layout of Giotto's mosaic, see Plate 222.

222 The marks are visible which show where the

cartoon was cut down to give it the arched form needed for the later version of the mosaic (Plate 221), when used as a model for that version. The details shown by the cartoon, from the upper registers of Giotto's original mosaic, to either side, were cut out from the cartoon and introduced at a lower level in the new version.

223 For the contrapuntal rhythms of the draperies and heads, compare Toriti's panel of the Dormition of the Virgin (Plate 226).

224 This panel was perhaps set mainly by assistants.

226 The rhythms are generally far more advanced than in Cavallini's version (Plate 224) and are comparable to those in the version by a pupil of Giotto shown in Plate 223. Also notable are the 'heavenly witnesses', as they are in Giotto's *Navicella* (see the cartoon by Cosimo Bartoli; Plate 222).

227–229 This part of the lower section of the façade mosaics in Sta Maria Maggiore is attributed by Vasari, probably without good reason, to Gaddo Gaddi. The interest in elaborate recession is notable. In Plate 229, the small figure on the left may be the artist.

232 The faces and hands are probably largely eighteenth-century work, made at the time when the porch was built on to the façade, and the mosaic was thus damaged.

234 In the lower left-hand corner is the monogram of the artist.

235 The surface has been cleaned, but not, apparently, reset.

236 This head has probably been almost entirely reset.

238 This fragment is evidently not by the same hand as the head shown in Plate 237.

NOTES ON THE PLATES. APPENDIX I

240 The draperies were perhaps designed by the artist who executed the mosaic shown in Plate 239, though the setting is almost certainly by a different hand.

241 Here is to be seen the fusion of Byzantine and western styles at its finest.

242 Note the relationship between the draperies round the ankles of the early figures—the two on the left—and the draperies in the triumphal arch mosaic, Grottaferrata (Plate 240). For a figure still later than the one on the right, compare Plate 146.

244 For the pattern of the halo, and the application of the colour in stripes of *tesserae*, compare the small apsidal altar-piece in the chapel of S. Zenone in Sta Prassede (Plate 126).

Appendix I

STA MARIA DI GROTTAFERRATA

THERE IS, UNFORTUNATELY, NO CERTAIN surviving example in Rome itself of the eleventh-century revival of the art of mosaic which is recorded in some of the medieval sources (see the discussion in E. Mâle, *Early Churches of Rome*, English ed., 1960, p. 139; also O. Demus, *Mosaics of Norman Sicily*, 1949, p. 207, with references on p. 239). Not far from Rome, however, there is an important mosaic which may be taken as evidence that the story of such a revival is no fiction. Grottaferrata is some dozen miles outside Rome, in the foothills of the Castelli. Early in the eleventh century the site, which had been inhabited in antiquity but was later deserted, was handed over to a community of Greek monks who had travelled up from southern Italy, under the leadership of St Nilus, to escape political disturbances which had made the life of the community impossible in the Basilicata. Nilus died before his followers were fully established at Grottaferrata. But the move proved to be permanent, and the community still exists at Grotta-ferrata, having carried out its services according to the Greek rite for an unbroken period of more than nine hundred years.

Under St Nilus' next successor but one, Bartholomew, the existing church (unfortunately to be greatly altered in the seventeenth century) was built. Details which remain from the old church include the elaborately carved door frame of the great door, with a mosaic in the tym-panum above (both the sculpture and the mosaic dating undoubtedly from the eleventh century), an eleventh-century font, and, on the triumphal arch, a mosaic evidently made in about the year 1200 (perhaps somewhat earlier) which will be briefly discussed later.

The rectangular mosaic panel above the great door represents a Deesis, and shows, in the centre, Christ enthroned, his right hand held up in blessing in the Latin manner, and in his left hand a book bearing a quotation in Greek from the fourth Gospel: 'I am the door; whosoever shall enter.' On Christ's right is the Virgin, *orans*, and on his left St John the Baptist, in the same position. On St John's right, placed between the Virgin and Christ's throne, stands a small figure; no doubt this is Bartholomew, under whose auspices, as Ecumenos, the church was completed. Though there have been some repairs, the mosaic has been well protected from the weather, and seems to be substantially in its original condition.

The plates show that this fine mosaic has, as might be expected, the technical characteristics that stamp the workmanship as Byzantine. For the flesh (faces and hands) the *tesserae* used are

243

relatively small. But what is most noticeable is the regularity of the work lines of the mosaic making it clear in which direction (horizontal, vertical or oblique) the craftsman was working at almost every point of the surface. There is, therefore, no doubt whatever that the craftsman was a Byzantine Greek. The fact that the blessing is given in the Latin manner suggests that in depicting this detail he was simply carrying out the instructions of his patron. Another possible indication of western influence is to be found in the forms of the drapery, especially in the double lines about the knee and the lower part of the leg in the figure of St John. These lines are closely paralleled in many of the Roman mosaics associated with Paschal (see Chapter Four), executed two hundred years earlier than this, but whether such lines were first used by Paschal's artists or not is by no means yet certain; those artists may themselves have derived them from eastern sources. It can, then, be confidently said that here, about a dozen miles from Rome, is a mosaic, executed by a Byzantine craftsman, which belongs to just that period when (we are told) Roman patrons were beginning to invite Byzantine craftsmen to Rome in order to revive the lost art of mosaic.

This mosaic embodies the strongest argument for the view that the small apsidal altar-piece in the chapel of S. Zenone dates from the eleventh century. There is an eleventh-century wall painting in the church of Sta Pudenziana (Wilpert, Plate 234) whose iconography is, in general, similar to that of the S. Zenone mosaic, and which suggests a revived interest in the sister saints St Praxed and St Pudenziana at that period. If the S. Zenone mosaic and the tympanum at Grotta-ferrata are compared, we at once notice that the form of the halo, with its edge of broken colour, is similar, and is not, I think, paralleled in any other mosaic of the Roman series. It may be objected that the rims of the S. Paolo haloes are also broken. But the pattern is quite different from those in the S. Zenone mosaic; and the fact that in S. Zenone there are several different patterns in the one mosaic does not, I think, invalidate the generalization. They conform to a type which (except in Grottaferrata) is not otherwise represented. Incidentally, one of the S. Paolo heads has, I think, a restored halo, giving no clue to the original form (Plate 20).

More important are the technical correspondences in the use of colour. Streaks of colour are applied in the form of lines, in thicknesses of one or two *tesserae*. This seems to be the technique to which Demus was alluding (op. cit., p. 383) in his reference to colour worked in 'short rows of one hue'. He associates this practice with the ninth and tenth centuries. The Grottaferrata mosaic, however, cannot be of such early date. It shows that this particular technical device, which has been noted above in Byzantine examples of the ninth century (see page 208) persisted, at least in provincial examples, till the eleventh. It seems possible, then, that the S. Zenone mosaic is the sole remaining Roman example of the eleventh-century revival of the art of mosaic which took place under Desiderius, and that the Grottaferrata tympanum, only just outside Rome, represents work of the same revival. The artists were not identical, but the same workshop seems to have been responsible.

Of great interest also is the later mosaic in Grottaferrata, on the triumphal arch. Its subject is most unusual. The twelve apostles sit on either side of the empty throne, with the Agnus Dei below. We would expect the scene represented to be an *hetimasia*—that is, a Preparation for the Last Judgment (compare the mosaic in S. Paolo fuori le Mura, discussed on page 297). But the apostles' heads are lit with flames, kindled from rays evidently intended to lead to a central figure above, and these flames are similar to those which are to be seen in representations of Pentecost. The fact that St Paul is not shown among the apostles lends support to the view that Pentecost is, indeed, the theme of the mosaic. (The figure at the left-hand end whose face reminds us of the traditional likeness of St Paul is, in fact, St Simon.) Above the mosaic there was a wall painting, the relics of which were revealed, and cleaned, earlier this century. As in the case of Sta Maria in Trastevere, as much was executed in mosaic in the twelfth century as money permitted; the design was then completed in fresco, the intention being, no doubt, to finish it in mosaic when financial resources should become available. From the Trinity in the centre of the painting above (Christ, on the knees of the Father, is represented as a grown, and apparently bearded, man) emanate the rays that light on the heads of the apostles below. On either side of the Trinity are throngs of angels, and on either side of these are Isaiah and David, who can be certainly identified by the inscriptions. The design, which was never in fact to be fully realized in mosaic, is perhaps unique in combining elements of a vision of the Trinity and worshipping angels with the traditional scheme for a Pentecost.

Stylistically, this mosaic yields two interesting points of comparison with the Roman series. Some of the portraits are very close to the tradition in which the S. Paolo artists (who, as has been noted, came from Venice) were working. The St Peter, for example, immediately on the right of the throne, or St Bartholomew, fourth from the centre on the other side, are strikingly similar, though they totally lack that curious quizzical expression which is to be seen in the S. Paolo mosaic; here the expression on the faces is grave. In fact, such portraits were the stock-in-trade of mosaicists working in the Byzantine tradition at this time, whether they worked in Greece, Sicily or Venice. These portraits are likely to have been made a generation or so earlier than those of S. Paolo—that is to say, in the later twelfth, rather than the early thirteenth, century. If, as I believe, the designer was one who worked on a representation of Pentecost at Monreale in Sicily (see Demus, op. cit., p. 453), this date would be established as certain. The highly individual forms of the drapery in the two mosaics seem to indicate that the designer was the same, even though the actual execution, in my view, is by different hands in the two examples. The influence of the great revival of the art of mosaic in Sicily, was, then, experienced very close to Rome— though, surprisingly, only to a minimal extent in the city itself.

The second interesting point of comparison with the Roman series lies in the close similarity of certain elements in the forms of the drapery (in particular the fold round the ankles, and some of the highlights and shadows) to work on the earliest figures in the mosaic of the façade of Sta Maria in Trastevere. If the effect of the Sicilian revival in twelfth-century Rome was small, it cannot, therefore, be entirely dismissed. The figures in Sta Maria in Trastevere have been described earlier in this book as western Romanesque in feeling, rather than Byzantine. The details just mentioned, however, show, once again, at how many points the two styles in fact closely approached each other; and, however western in style the figure of the Sta Maria Virgin may be, the draperies show unmistakable evidence of Sicilian influence.

There is a short but good account of the monastery, its history and architecture, by T. Minisci (*Santa Maria di Grottaferrata*, 2nd ed., 1966).

189

239

240, 242

Appendix II

THE 'MONOGRAMS' ON THE CLOAKS WORN BY FIGURES REPRESENTED IN THE MOSAICS

THERE IS NO LONGER ANY DOUBT about the origin of the ornaments, which may be described as monograms, which can be seen on the cloaks of some of the figures represented in the Roman mosaics. These monograms are a characteristic feature of the series, appearing in some of the earliest Christian mosaics and as late as the thirteenth century (for example, in the mosaic of Christ in the roundel of the Coronation of the Virgin in the church of Sta Maria Maggiore). This type of ornament, shown on the fold of the cloak, had its origin in Palestine. In its earliest form it was, apparently, purely decorative, the design itself being determined by the techniques of the weavers who devised it. At that time it was a strip of weaving in a different colour from that of the material as a whole; the strip is broken in a right-angled turn, and the two arms of the angle are produced in lines that grow from the ends of the strip and are flush with the edges.

These ornaments, known from their form (similar to the third letter of the Greek alphabet) as gammadia, were, in fact, used in Palestine at least as early as the first half of the second century AD. Textiles into which they are woven were found during the exploration (1960–61) of the Bar Kokhba caves, and in the account of the excavations the link with western mosaics is specifically mentioned (see Y. Yadin, *The Finds from the Bar Kokhba Period in the Cave of Letters*, 1963, pp. 223, 227–32, with references; plates 67 and 68; figs. 66, 74, 75 and 77). Their occurrence in fourth- and fifth-century mosaics both in northern Italy and in Rome may have been due in the first instance to the Syrian origin of the designs on which some of these mosaics were no doubt partly based. It seems more likely, however, that the use of the ornament was continued in the Roman tradition because it was felt to give, as it were, an authentic flavour. Such, it was supposed (perhaps rightly), were the clothes which the apostles and disciples actually wore.

While the gammadion in its early form is common in the early Ravenna mosaics (in the Orthodox and Arian baptistries; in the vault of the archiepiscopal chapel, 494–519; in some of the mosaics in the church of S. Apollinare Nuovo, and in the church of S. Vitale), it seems surprisingly rare outside Italy. In one example in Cyprus it is worn by an angel, as in the archiepiscopal chapel in Ravenna. But it does not seem to occur, either in this early form or in more developed forms, in Salonika, where we might expect to see it, perhaps partly because this region, to judge

Fig 9

24, XI, XII, 40
45, 46, 58,
XXVIII

78

from the mosaics, saw the coming into use of formal ecclesiatical vestments at an earlier date than in the west; also, in the Salonika mosaics saints are sometimes vested as ecclesiastics. Nor is it seen in the famous Transfiguration, believed to date from the sixth century, in the church of St Catherine on Mount Sinai. In this mosaic, the clothes are not vestments; in which case at that date, in Roman mosaics, one would expect to see gammadia on the cloaks. One wonders whether this is not one of several features in which many of the Ravenna mosaics are Italian, rather than Constantinopolitan, in character. But the possibility cannot be excluded (especially in view of the Cyprus example) that it is only chance which has preserved examples of the gammadion in the west and destroyed them in the east. We may fairly observe, however, that the monograms which descended from the gammadion did not become an integral part of the Byzantine tradition as they did of the Roman.

At first simply an ornament, the gammadion quickly became an initial, already occurring as such in the Arian baptistry in Ravenna, and perhaps also on one of the small apsidal mosaics in   78
Sta Costanza in Rome. That this letter was sometimes thought of as being the wearer's initial is evident, for instance, on the late eighth-century mosaic of the triumphal arch in SS. Nereo ed Achilleo in Rome, where the device on St Peter's cloak is the letter P (in its Latin form) and on John's, H (for IoHannes). But elsewhere it is either not an initial but a calligraphic ornament, or, where it is an initial, it often seems to have no relevance to the name of the wearer. In the mosaic in the chapel of S. Aquilino in Milan the monogram appears in what has been held to be the original form on Christ's mantle, but there are variations. One of these is the I, which was perhaps afterwards taken to stand for IHCOYC (meaning not necessarily that the wearer is Christ—as he is, however, in SS. Cosma e Damiano—but sometimes, perhaps, that he is, so to speak, Christ's man).

Occasionally a fairly early form of the monogram is used in a comparatively late mosaic; this may be evidence of an early original. For instance, some of the apostles between the windows in the apse of the church of St John Lateran wear the ornament, its design being of an early type. Dating from the nineteenth century in their present form, these apostles were presumably closely modelled on Toriti's thirteenth-century version. But that may itself have been based on a far earlier original, and the occurrence of this early pattern is one piece of evidence to suggest that such an original, presumably of the fifth century, existed.

In the ninth-century mosaic of S. Marco, Christ's mantle is decorated with small patches, or   XXIII; cf. 124
bars, apparently intended to represent pieces of embroidery. These do not seem to have been derived directly from the gammadion, but perhaps were an independent feature of Byzantine   89-91
dress, like the large rectangular patches, or *tablia*, also presumably of rich embroidery, let into the   94, 95
edges of the cloaks worn by court officials. Such *tablia* occur in the 'procession' mosaics of S. Vitale, Ravenna, showing Justinian, Theodora, and courtiers; an example in Rome, executed a hundred years earlier than those in S. Vitale, is the mosaic showing the young Moses at the court of Pharaoh's daughter in the nave series in Sta Maria Maggiore. It was perhaps from some   X
such source as the mosaic of S. Marco that decoration (taking the form, apparently, of embroidery patches) passes into certain French Romanesque manuscripts; it is to be seen, for example, in the Ascension design in the Limoges Sacramentary of *c.* 1100 (Paris, Bibliothèque Nationale, Lat. 9438; illustrated in the catalogue of the 1954 exhibition: *Manuscrits à Peintures du VIIe au XIIe siècle*, 1954.) For the subject of these *segmenta* of embroidery, see C. Cecchelli, 'Il Costume' (pts 12–16 of *I arte minori e il costume*, in the series 'Vita di Roma nel Medio Evo'), n.d., p. 817. See ibid., p. 1076, for an account of the *tablion*.

BIBLIOGRAPHY

This bibliography does not attempt to be comprehensive, and includes only those books and articles that I know are important for my own approach; thus there are no entries concerning the architecture or archaeology of the churches, nor the general artistic history of the long period covered. The lists give, however, the main references, within the larger works, to individual mosaics, under the headings of individual churches. G. Matthiae, in *Le chiese di Roma dal IV al X secolo*, gives a valuable general bibliography. Works referred to in the 'General' section of the bibliography will be subsequently referred to by the surname of the author only.

J. CIAMPINI, *Vetera monumenta; in quibus praecipue musiva opera sacrarum profanarumque aedium . . . dissertationibus iconibusque illustrantur*, Rome 1690.

O. DEMUS, *The Mosaics of Norman Sicily*, London 1950.

E. MÂLE, *Early Churches of Rome*, Eng. trans. (1960) of the French ed., *Rome et ses vieilles églises*, Paris 1950.

G. MATTHEW, *Byzantine Aesthetics*, London 1963.

G. MATTHIAE, *Le chiese di Roma dal IV al X secolo*, vol. 1 of Roma Cristiana, Rome 1962. In the bibliographical notes given in the next section for individual churches, the references to passages relating to mosaics in this volume of *Le chiese di Roma* are set out in detail. They are not given for vol. 2 since there the focus of interest has shifted. Matthiae is perhaps the greatest modern authority on the Roman series of mosaics as a whole.

C. R. MOREY, *Lost Mosaics and Frescoes of Rome of the Middle Period*, Princeton 1915.

H. P. L'ORANGE AND P. J. NORDHAGEN, *Mosaik von der Antike bis zum Mittelalter*, German ed., trans. from Norwegian, Munich 1960.

G. B. DE ROSSI, *Musaici cristiani e saggi di pavimenti delle chiese di Roma anteriori al secolo XV*, Rome 1873–99. Each page of text has a French version below the Italian. As there is no consecutive pagination throughout this book, references are given to the heading of the section, then, when necessary, to the foliation as printed within that section.

G. VASARI, *Lives of the Painters*. References are to the edition (in four volumes) in the Everyman Series (London 1963), a translation, edited by W. Gaunt, of the second edition (Florence 1568).

A. VENTURI, *Musaici cristiani di Roma*, Rome 1925.

S. WAETZOLDT, 'Die Kopien des 17 Jahrhunderts nach Mosaiken und Wandmalereien in Rom', *Römische Forschungen*, vol. VIII (*Misc. Biblioth. Herzianae*), Vienna 1964.

J. WILPERT, *Die römischen Mosaiken und Malereien der kirchlichen Bauten vom IV bis XIII Jahrhundert*, 4 vols, Freiburg 1916.

INDIVIDUAL CHURCHES

Sta Agnese fuori le Mura

MATTHIAE, p. 209.

DE ROSSI, 'Mosaico dell' abside di S. Agnese fuori le Mura'.

Sta Cecilia in Trastevere

MÂLE, pp. 91–93.

MATTHIAE, pp. 273–275.

DE ROSSI, 'Abside ed architrave del portico di S. Cecilia in Trastevere'.

S. Clemente

DE ROSSI, 'Abside della basilica di S. Clemente'.

E. SCACCIA SCARAFONI, 'Il mosaico absidale di S. Clemente in Roma', *Boll. d'Arte*, XXIX, II, 1935, Series III, Section I, pp. 44–68.

WILPERT, pp. 516–523.

SS. Cosma e Damiano

MATTHIAE, pp. 147–148, p. 273, p. 277.

G. MATTHIAE, *SS. Cosma e Damiano e S. Teodoro*, Rome 1948.

L'ORANGE AND NORDHAGEN, p. 57.

DE ROSSI, 'Abside dei SS. Cosma e Damiano'.

WILPERT, pp. 1070–1073.

Sta Costanza

F. W. DEICHMANN, *rühchristliche Kirchen in Rom*, Basle 1948, pp. 26–27.

MATTHIAE, pp. 133–137.

DE ROSSI, 'Musaici del mausoleo appellata di S. Costanza'.

W. N. SCHUMACHER, 'Dominus legem dat', *Römische Quartalschrift*, 54, 1959, pp. 1–39.

W. N. SCHUMACHER, 'Eine römische Apsiskomposition', ibid., pp. 137–202.

H. STERN, 'Les Mosaiques de l'église de Sainte Constance à Rome', *Dumbarton Oaks Papers*, XII, 1958, pp. 157–218.

WILPERT, pp. 272–321.

S. Crisogono

P. TOESCA, *Pietro Cavallini*, Milan 1959, p. 15.

DE ROSSI, 'Musaici in S. Maria d'Araceli ed in S. Crisogono'.

Sta Francesca Romana (Sta Maria Nuova)

MÂLE, pp. 139–140.

MOREY, pp. 17–24.

DE ROSSI, 'Musaico di Sta Maria Nuova'.

St John Lateran

The basilica

C. CECCHELLI, 'A proposito del mosaico dell' abside Lateranense', *Miscell. Biblioth. Herzianae*, 1961, pp. 13 et seq. This opens with a full bibliography.

G. J. Hoogewerff, 'Il mosaico absidiale di S. Giovanni in Laterano ed altri mosaici romani', *Atti della Pont. Accad. Romana di Archeol. Rendiconti*, Series III, vol. XXVII, 1951–54, pp. 297–326.

De Rossi, 'Musaico dell'abside di S. Giovanni in Laterano'.

J. Wilpert, 'La decorazione Constantiniana della basilica Lateranense', *Riv. di Archeol. Crist.*, VI, 1929, pp. 53–150. This supersedes the section in Wilpert's original work published in 1916.

The baptistry

Anon., 'Restauro dell' abside della cappella di S. Venanzio', *Atti della Pont. Accad. Romana di Archeol. Rendiconti*, Series III, vols XXIII–XXIV, 1947–49, pp. 402–405, with sketch on p. 401 (on the most recent restorations in the chapel of St Venantius).

Ciampini, pp. 238–242, with engravings: one facing p. 240 and showing the vault of the chapel of St John the Evangelist; one facing p. 241 and showing the vault of the chapel of St John the Baptist, since destroyed.

Matthiae, pp. 138, 145, 211.

De Rossi, 'Abside della cappella delle SS. Rufina e Seconda nel battistero Lateranense', 'Volta dell' oratorio di S. Giovanni Evangelista nel battistero Lateranense', 'Musaico dell'oratorio di S. Venanzio'.

Wilpert, pp. 251–256, 731–735, 735–742.

S. Lorenzo fuori le Mura

P. Baldass, 'The Mosaic of the Triumphal Arch of S. Lorenzo fuori le Mura', *Gaz. des Beaux Arts*, vol. 49, 1957, pp. 1–18.

Matthiae, pp. 205–206.

A. Muñoz, *La basilica di S. Lorenzo fuori le Mura*, Rome 1944.

De Rossi, 'Musaico dell'arco della basilica di S. Lorenzo nell'Agro Verano'.

S. Marco

Mâle, pp. 93–94.

Matthiae, p. 277.

De Rossi, 'Musaico dell'abside della basilica di S. Marco'.

Sta Maria in Ara Celi

De Rossi, 'Musaici in S. Maria d'Araceli ed in S. Crisogono'.

Sta Maria Domnica (della Navicella)

Mâle, pp. 86–87.

Matthiae, p. 274.

De Rossi, 'Abside di S. Maria in Domnica'.

A. Terenzio, 'Chiesa di Sta Maria Domnica, Restauro dei mosaici', *Boll. d'Arte*, XXIX, 1935, Series III, Section II, pp. 199–200.

Sta Maria Maggiore

No references are here given to the strictly archaeological controversy which took place on the evidence of the facts disclosed by the restoration begun in 1927: for details, see the work by Cecchelli (himself one of the protagonists) cited here.

M. Alpatoff-Moskau, 'Die Entstehung des Mosaiks von Iacobus Torriti in Sta Maria Maggiore in Rom', *Römisches Jahrb. für Kunstwiss.*, 1924–25, pp. 1–19.

G. Astorri, 'Nuove Osservazioni sulla tecnica dei mosaici romani della basilica di Sta Maria Maggiore', *Riv. di Archeol. Crist.*, XI, 1934, pp. 51–72.

C. Bertelli, 'Un antico restauro nei mosaici di Sta Maria Maggiore', *Paragone*, March 1955, pp. 40–42.

A. W. BRYANCK, 'Das Problem der Mosaiken von Sta Maria Maggiore', *Festschrift Hans Hahnloser*, 1961, pp. 21–26.

C. CECCHELLI, *I mosaici della basilica di S. Maria Maggiore*, Turin 1956.

CIAMPINI, pp. 195–224 (with engravings showing the state of the mosaics of the triumphal arch and nave in the late seventeenth century).

P. KUNZLE, 'Per una visione organica dei mosaici antichi di Sta Maria Maggiore', *Atti della Post. Accad. Romana di Archeol. Rendiconti*, 34, 1961–62, pp. 153–190.

MÂLE, p. 62 (nave), pp. 62–66 (triumphal arch).

MATTHIAE, pp. 139–142 (nave); pp. 139, 142–144 (triumphal arch).

DE ROSSI, 'Musaico dell'arco trionfale e delle parieti laterali di Sta Maria Maggiore', 'Facciata di Sta Maria Maggiore', 'Musaico dell' abside di Sta Maria Maggiore', 'Sepolcri di Guglielmo Duranti e di Gonsalvo Card. di Albano in S. Maria sopra Minerva ed in Sta Maria Maggiore'.

M. L. THÉREL, 'Une Image de la Sibylle sur l'arc triomphal de Sta Maria Maggiore', *Cahiers Archéol.*, 12, 1962, pp. 153–171.

WILPERT, pp. 412–473 (nave), pp. 473–493 (triumphal arch), pp. 506–511 (later mosaics, including the series on the Life of the Virgin).

Sta Maria sopra Minerva

DE ROSSI, 'Sepolcri di Guglielmo Duranti e di Gonsalvo Card. di Albano in S. Maria sopra Minerva ed in Sta Maria Maggiore'.

Sta Maria in Trastevere

C. CECCHELLI, *Sta Maria in Trastevere*. Rome, n.d.

MÂLE, pp. 140–145 (main apsidal mosaic), pp. 145–147 (façade).

A. PRANDI, 'Pietro Cavallini a Sta Maria in Trastevere', *Riv. dell' Istit. Naz. d'Archeol. e dell'Arte*, I, 1952, pp. 282–297 (the series on the Life of the Virgin, illustrated with photographs taken at the time when the material used for protection against war damage was dismantled).

DE ROSSI, 'Musaico dell'abside di Sta Maria in Trastevere', 'Facciata di Sta Maria in Trastevere', 'Zona inferiore dell' abside di Sta Maria in Trastevere'.

P. TOESCA, *Pietro Cavallini*, Milan 1959, pp. 8–12.

SS. Nereo ed Achilleo

MATTHIAE, p. 271.

DE ROSSI, 'Musaico dell'arco della basilica urbana dei SS. Nereo ed Achilleo'. On fol. I (verso) the drawing, discovered by de Rossi, of the original mosaic of the apse is reproduced, whence our Fig. 4.

S. Paolo fuori le Mura

CIAMPINI, pp. 228–233. Facing p. 230 is an engraving of the mosaic of the triumphal arch as it was in the late seventeenth century.

MATTHIAE, p. 144 (triumphal arch).

DE ROSSI, 'Musaico dell'arco di Placidia nella basilica di S. Paolo sulla via Ostiense', 'Musaico dell'abside della basilica di S. Paolo fuori le Mura', 'Facciata di S. Paolo fuori le Mura' (the mosaic as reconstructed in the church).

W. N. SCHUMACHER, 'Eine römische Apsiskomposition', *Römische Quartalschrift*, 54, 1959, pp. 137–202.

S. WAEKOLD, 'Zur Ikonographie des Triumphenbogens Mosaik von S. Paolo', *Misc. Biblioth. Herzianae*, 1961, p. 19.

WILPERT, pp. 159–554 (apse), pp. 554–558 (triumphal arch).

St Peter's (the old basilica)

The oldest mosaic below the *confessione*

B. M. A. GHETTI and others, *Esplorazioni sotto la confessione di S. Pietro*, 2 vols, Rome 1940–49.

Various antique fragments

F. J. MATHER, 'An Unidentified Mosaic Head from Old St Peter's', *Studien zur Kunst des Ostens* (*Festschrift für J. Strzygowski*), Vienna 1923, pp. 17–18, Plate III, 1.

L'ORANGE AND NORDHAGEN, Plates 50 and 51.

G. B. DE TOTH, *Cenni storici della basilica Vaticana*, 1953, p. 18. De Toth regards the fragment discussed in the two publications referred to above as dating from the Renaissance period.

WILPERT, pp. 359–367 (includes a discussion of the original mosaic of the apse and its reconstruction by Innocent III).

Fragments from the oratory of John VII

MATTHIAE, pp. 216–218.

P. J. NORDHAGEN, *The Mosaics of John VII*, Acta Instituti Romani Norvegiae, vol. 2, 1965, pp. 121–166. The most important technical study of any of the mosaics discussed in this book.

DE ROSSI, 'Musaici dell'oratorio edificato del Papa Giovanni VII nella basilica Vaticana'.

G. B. DE TOTH, op. cit., Plates 16, 17, 19, 20.

WILPERT, pp. 388–400.

The mosaic of the *confessione* of St Peter

DE ROSSI, 'Musaico nella nicchia della confessione sotto l'altare maggiore della basilica Vaticana'. De Rossi reproduces a sketch made early in the seventeenth century, showing that since that date there has been drastic remodelling.

The Otto II mosaic

MATTHIAE, p. 280.

DE ROSSI, 'Musaico nelle Grotte Vaticane appellato del sepolcro di Ottone II imperatore'.

W. PAESLER, 'Giottos Navicella und ihr spätantikes Vorbild', *Römisches Jahrb. für Kunstgesch.*, 5, 1941, pp. 49–162 (includes a discussion of the original position of the Otto II mosaic).

G. B. DE TOTH, op. cit., Plate 44.

S. Pietro in Vincoli

H. S. CHÉRAMY, *Saint Sebastien hors les Murs*, Paris 1925 (for the date of the plague which may settle the date of the mosaic).

MATTHIAE, pp. 220–221.

G. MATTHIAE, *S. Pietro in Vincoli*, Rome 1960.

DE ROSSI, 'Musaico sull'altare di S. Sebastiano in S. Pietro in Vincoli'.

Sta Prassede

B. M. A. GHETTI, *S. Pietro*, Rome 1961. See also the note on Montini's guide to Sta Pudenziana, cited below.

MÂLE, pp. 87–91.

MATTHIAE, pp. 273–276.

DE ROSSI, 'Arco ed abside della basilica di S. Pietro', 'Musaico dell'arco di S. Pietro', 'Musaico dell'oratorio di S. Zenone in S. Pietro'.

WILPERT, p. 1068 (triumphal arch), p. 1070 (apse).

Sta Pudenziana

MATTHIAE, pp. 137–138.

G. MATTHIAE, 'Restauro—il mosaico romano di Sta Pudenziana', *Boll. d'Arte*, XXXI, 1938, Series III, pp. 418–425.

MONTINI, *Sta Pudenziana*, Rome 1960. Montini includes a reproduction of an eleventh-century painting in this church, clearly associated with the small apsidal mosaic in the chapel of S. Zenone in Sta Prassede, though which derives from which is not clear. This painting is also reproduced by Wilpert (Plate 234).

DE ROSSI, 'Musaico dell'abside di Sta Pudenziana'.

Sta Sabina

CIAMPINI, pp. 186–195.

MATTHIAE, pp. 139, 276.

DE ROSSI, 'Musaico della parete interna sopra la porta ed archi della nave maggiore di Sta Sabina sull'Aventino'. De Rossi includes an account of the *opus sectile* decorations of the nave.

S. Stefano Rotondo

MATTHIAE, pp. 210–211.

DE ROSSI, 'Abside della chiesa di S. Stefano Rotondo'.

WILPERT, p. 1074.

S. Teodoro

MATTHIAE, p. 205.

G. MATTHIAE, *SS. Cosma e Damiano e S. Teodoro*, Rome 1948

DE ROSSI, 'Musaico dell'abside di S. Teodoro'.

WILPERT, p. 1074.

S. Tommaso in Formis

DE ROSSI, 'Porta del convento dell'ordine della redenzione degli schiavi a S. Tommaso in Formis sul Celio'.

Chapel of Sancta Sanctorum

DE ROSSI, 'Musaico della cappella del Sancta Sanctorum nel Laterano'.

WILPERT, pp. 175–180.

OTHER MOSAICS

Giotto's *Navicella*

W. KÖRTE, 'Die Navicella des Giotto', *Festschrift Wilhelm Pinder*, 1938, pp. 223–263.

W. PAESLER, 'Giottos Navicella und ihr spätantikes vorbild', *Römisches Jahrb. für Kunstgesch.*, 5, 1941, pp. 49–162.

A. VENTURI, 'La data dell'attivita romana di Giotto', *L'Arte*, 1918, pp. 229–235.

L. VENTURI, 'La Navicella di Giotto', *L'Arte*, 1922, pp. 49–69.

The *Tribune of Benedict XIV*

MATTHIAE, pp. 271–273.

WILPERT, pp. 155–162.

LIST OF COLOUR PLATES

INDEXES

References to plates are given after the text references. Colour plates are indicated by Roman numerals, monochrome plates by italicized arabic numerals

GENERAL

THEMES AND SUBJECTS

This index only includes mentions in the text, and illustrations. For a list of Old Testament subjects in Sta Maria Maggiore—incidents from the stories of the Patriarchs, of Moses, and of Joshua—see pp. 85–89

CHURCHES AND OTHER BUILDINGS
CONTAINING CHRISTIAN MOSAICS